Take Another Little
Piece of My Heart

Also by Pamela Des Barres

I'm with the Band

TAKE ANOTHER LITTLE PIECE OF MY HEART

A GROUPIE GROWS UP

Pamela Des Barres

William Morrow and Company, Inc.,

NEW YORK

It is the policy of William Morrow and Company, Inc., and its imprints and affiliates, recognizing the importance of preserving what has been written, to print the books we publish on acid-free paper, and we exert our best efforts to that end.

Library of Congress Cataloging-in-Publication Data

Des Barres, Pamela.
    Take another little piece of my heart : a groupie grows up /
Pamela Des Barres.
        p.   cm.
    ISBN 0-688-09149-0
    1. Des Barres, Pamela.   2. Groupies—United States—Biography.
I. Title.
ML429.D47A3   1992
781.66'092—dc20
    [B]   92-19882
                                                              CIP
                                                              MN

Printed in the United States of America

First Edition

1 2 3 4 5 6 7 8 9 10

BOOK DESIGN BY GLEN M. EDELSTEIN

This book is dedicated to my adored and adoring Mother—

Margaret Ruth Hayes Miller

Love your life out
JACK KEROUAC, 1958

Take Another Little
Piece of My Heart

P-P-P-Prologue

must be one of the most lighthearted people on the planet. I feel like I've lived fifteen lifetimes, and I still weigh only 112 pounds! Oh, I've been through a lot of unbelievable shit, but at least all the thrills and chills, rock-and-roll heart-bruising, subconscious self-abuse, and co-co-codependence have led directly here, and I am one happy chick. Would you believe I still wake up every day and say, "Yay!!!"

When I was a flamboyant, wacky, peace-and-love, rock-and-roll teenager, I wanted to fit it ALL in because I assumed that when I hit my forties, it would be a downhill slide to sitcom heaven. I thought I would be spending a lot of time doing normal-formal things like mending, baking, cheering on my son in the big game, taking my daughter to baton practice, kissing my husband's ass, reading romance novels while the dough rose, and shedding a simple tear. That's why I tried to cram every day chock-full of amazing stuff, so I could iron shirts, pack lunches, watch *Roseanne,* and be content to reflect on the Stuff That American Dreams Are Made Of. I lived my early years so hard and fast, I just figured by this time I would be ready to relax and take it easy. I am delighted to announce that this is *not* the case.

CHAPTER ONE

I

I am the world's most famous groupie. Isn't that something? I keep going over the incidents that created this phenomenal fact, only to have a bunch of question marks floating over my head. It's true I wrote a book about my life as a young girl when I hung out in raging New Hollywood—"freaking out" onstage with local bands, creaming my lace undies over the brand-new long-haired boys littering the streets. I also chronicled my relationships with a bunch of different guys, most of whom were musicians, but I never expected to be introduced on the *Today* show as "Queen of the Groupies." Wow. What a twisted and unique legacy. I never know whether to defend myself or take a bow. Should I have my own TV show or move to some remote island and gnaw on mangoes all day long? Did I live it up just to have to live it down?

When I met the Byrds on the Sunset Strip and knocked on that backstage door, there was no word for what I was doing, but what was WRONG WITH IT? Who was I hurting? I *had* to find my place in and around the music I loved so much. Nothing—not even the panicky fear of foolish failure—was going to stop me. In the nineties there is a little more room in the industry for rock-crazed women, although there are still nowhere *near* enough A & R females, if you ask me. But back then there was NO room, and I *needed* to be near the inspiration. And guess what? I was a welcome visitor and probably an inspiration myself. As I wandered around backstage throughout those madmadmad years, all I really wanted was to locate Mr. Right. Mr. Forever. Someone I could devote myself to. And he had to play the devil's music.

Actually, I'm really proud of my thrilling heritage. I've always considered myself to be a freewheeling feminist, a lover of men and a champion of chicks. In "Like a Rolling Stone" Bob Dylan prodded and provoked, "You shouldn't let other people get your kicks for you," and my life-style was validated. Thanks, Bob. I have always been determined to get my own glorious, heartaching kicks. Despite the hard-core fact that we all make big, fat mistakes, all of us have moments in life when time stands still for a few illuminating, mesmerizing split seconds and we are brilliantly grateful to be in our bodies, on the planet, ALIVE right now!! The reason for being comes into focus, everything shimmers with clarity, and The Hills Are Alive With The Sound Of Music. Know what I mean?

When I was Jimmy Page's doll-face of the moment, I got real chummy with the rest of the band, and one night before Led Zeppelin swept majestically onto the stage, one by one they slipped their big, hunky turquoise bracelets on my arm for safekeeping. I stood by the side of the stage touching the trendy, treasured Indian silver, watching my friends make rock-and-roll history, feeling honored and blessed. Gotta whole lotta love. I knew I would have my hands all over the exquisite, coveted Jimmy after the show, and I was awash with luminous gratitude. Of course, I was only twenty years old at the time. Ha! After Jimmy's day off, which we spent holed up in my tiny pink bedroom, under Grandma's handmade quilt, listening to *Led Zeppelin II* until I had it totally memorized, Peter Grant, their infamous, mountainous manager, called to tell us we were all going to Vegas that night to see Elvis. It was way over overwhelming. I sat in between Robert Plant and Jimmy Page in the front row while the leather-clad King scorched the room with his gigantic voice, flaunting his royalty in grand, steaming style. (It was before he got gaudy with those big, sequined tents and lost his mind to/in the rigors of prescription madness.) Even though Jimmy declined an audience with His Majesty—why, I'll never know—and I lost the opportunity to converse with the King, it was still one of the most shimmering nights in my history.

There was also the lovely night I walked right onstage with the Doors. The day before the show I had discovered Jim Morrison digging around in his fridge, wearing leather pants so low you could see his crack, living right down the hill from one of my best friends in Laurel Canyon! I had been hanging out in the danger zone, inhaling a lethal substance called "Trimar," which I have since found out was an intense liquid version of PCP. In fact, my freak flag is constantly at half-mast, mourning the brain cells that bit the dust in those lazy, hazy heydays. Come back, come back, coome baaa-aaaack. But way back in the Summer of Love sunshine, I did the neighborly thing and went down to introduce myself to the Lizard King. Being in the most cockeyed condition imaginable, I promptly did a full back bend in the middle of his living room and found myself gazing up at his redheaded girlfriend/soon-to-be-wife, who asked me impolitely to leave. As I offered her a hanky full of Trimar, which she declined with menace, Jim hissed from behind me, "Get it on!" and moments after I headed back up the hundred rock stairs, he was tapping on the door, wanting to try a spot of the ill-advised liquid. Hours passed as we lolled and rolled around under the chemical spell, laughing our pixilated asses off. I don't remember when he went back home, but I slept almost comatose until the Doors soundcheck at the Hullabaloo the following afternoon. As I stumbled down the stairs on my way to the club, I almost tripped on the many broken Doors demos, which I figured the redhead had hurled down as Jim climbed up. Or was it the other way around? Either way, she must have been entirely unamused. Poor Pam Morrison! Can you imagine the shit she had to put up with through the years?

Dolled up to beat the band in my handmade stripy bell-bottoms, and armed with a quart jar of Trimar, I propped myself casually by the backstage door. Jim slunk up to me, snarling, pulled me to a ladder leading to a musty storage area full of props and fixtures, where we reclined on my tatty muskrat jacket like it was a plush four-poster love den. Inhaling, kissing, slobbering, moaning, rubbing, stroking, touching, damp, wet, hot, almost passing straight out from sheer passion, until the strains of "Light My Fire" filtered into our tripping heads. Uh-oh. Was this soundcheck? How long had we been writhing around in nirvana? His exquisite face disappeared, and I was flat on my back, oozing steam, a dripping lace hanky in each hand. I made my way slowly down the ladder and followed the music, dragging the muskrat, hankies, and half-full quart jar right onto the stage where Jim was clutching the microphone like he had just clutched me. I stood there rock-stock-still, gaping at the audience that stared at me like I was an apparition until a nice roadie came to my rescue, escorting me to the wings.

II

There have also been times when I felt really out of my element, when the people in the room loomed out of reach, floating sky-high while I remained with my spike heels Crazy Glued to the floor. I was so wrapped up in trying to maintain my cool in certain startling situations that the glowing reality escaped me until much later. All because I was afraid to let go of my tormented, twitching ego long enough to notice that every one of us is going through the exact same thing. Everybody is a part of everything anyway. I think Donovan said that. (An incredibly long time ago when he wore flowing white robes.)

Like the time I was sitting around in a pent-up hotel room with the Rolling Stones after that poor soul had been knifed to death in front of the band at Altamont. I was concentrating on my composure instead of attempting to console Mick Jagger. He had invited me back to the hotel after the show which had been full of historically bad vibes from assorted Hell's Angels and too many too-high people. I hadn't heard about the killing until I had Mick on the phone and he told me to "come right over." I sat in that dismal, quaking room with the entire band, plus Gram Parsons and Michelle Phillips, while the Stones tried to figure out how the hideous thing could have happened. I was only twenty years old but wished so hard that I could slip a drop of insight into the conversation. I sat mute, counting the seconds as they slowly slid by. Each one of them hurt. I ached to offer condolence and actually did put together a humble sentence of sympathy, but it wasn't enough. Mick said he was thinking of quitting rock and roll. I didn't protest even though my thighs cramped at the thought. I looked over at Michelle Phillips curled into a big chair. The corroded old line, "A woman's place is in the home" popped to mind. MY mom's place was in the home. I could even picture her in her seersucker pedal pushers, pulling weeds in our chain-link—encased backyard, so what was *I* doing with the world's raunchiest rock-and-roll band as they discussed murder and mayhem?

How about the time my new photographer friend called to ask if I would like to be in a small film he was directing for this new trio from England, the Jimi Hendrix Experience? I danced in one of the very first rock videos, "Foxy Lady," wriggling around in skimpy blue velvet to the nihilistic sound oozing from this wild man's guitar. From my vantage point behind the stage I watched the eyeball on his hand-painted jacket contort and wink, but when he wanted my phone number, I just couldn't bring myself to give it to him. "Pam, dear, there's someone on the phone for you. It's Jimi Hendrix." "Thanks, Mom." I tried to melt into the psychedelic walls when I wasn't perched on top of the plaster Greek column go-go-ing hard and fast. . . . "Here I come baby, I'm comin' to GETCHA". . . . How did *I* get there? Me, Pam Miller from Reseda, California? I had obviously *wanted* to be in these exalted places, in fact I worked extra hard at being in the grooviest place at the grooviest time, only to go cross-eyed with angst when the dream came true. But I have to give myself credit, because even though I palpitated from head to toe during these excruciatingly magnificent moments, at least I *got* myself there. Determination overpowered my heebie-jeebies every time, praise the Lord.

I was *so* intimidated when I finally met John Lennon, but since I was functioning pretty well within my top-flight insecurity, the famous and infamous never knew how hard my guts trembled. He had been on a rampage around L.A. for a few weeks, and word of his *loco,* angry escapades was out all over town. He had just been tossed out of the Troubador for heckling some poor comedian and wearing a Kotex on his head. What kind of statement was he trying to make, I wonder? Not only women bleed? I met my ex-love Keith Moon at the Record Plant, where he was visiting a Nilsson-Starr-Lennon session. It was a rough night for me anyway: I had to tell the loony-tune Mr. Moon that I had fallen in love with Michael Des Barres and could no longer wipe his wacky brow at the crash of dawn. When Keith introduced me to the intelligent Beatle, I saw a gleaming warning signal flash across his wildly famous face and waited for the tornado. He stared at me with daggers, repeating my name over and over and over again until all the letters turned into rancid alphabet soup. How do you respond to that kind of onslaught? Gee, it's nice to meet you too?

It slowly got better as I became accustomed to hanging out with the hierarchy. Being the governess for Moon and Dweezil and living at the Zappa household really helped me to graduate from novice to know-it-all. I came to appreciate those incandescent moments even more because I was a true participant instead of a stressed-out observer. All the aspiring rock gods, especially the boys from England, couldn't wait to meet Mr. Z., so the house was always full of velvet trousers and British accents. I no longer had to peer through imaginary binoculars into the land of aahs. Forever-memories were created every day. The hills were on fire with the sound of music.

III

I never wanted to grow up, I figured, Why should I? Growing up represented giving up, becoming a faceless everywoman with boring superficial responsibilities. By staying young at heart, I would never have to think about "taking charge" of my life. I could meander through the daisy patch, hand-in-hand with a gorgeous, messy, free-spirited rock dude that I could worship-adore and do things for. But now at age forty-three, I ask myself, Why did I always feel like these precious jerks were doing *me* a favor? I kept counting my lucky stars while I ironed shirts, made copious cups of tea, and pandered to their every whim. And I can't really blame them for my Miss Conduct! What about the concept that *behind* every great man stands a woman? Which macho dog came up with that gem? I bought into that idea totally and went around making sure my man walked several paces in front of me, so if he happened to drop something, I could pick it up and he just might feel a gallant sense of obligation to me. In the early heart of the nineties that sounds pretty fucking twisted, I know, but at the time it just felt natural. Many years would pass before I realized I was giving myself the itsy bitsy end of the stick. I've come a long way since then, baby, and it hasn't been a piece of cake.

I eventually found my own personal free-spirited rock dude, my darling Michael Des Barres, and was married for a truly long time. And I certainly thought it was going to last forever, believe me. I watched my precious mom hold her marriage together against all odds and studied her example without even trying. I also got to witness Gail Zappa tending, mending, and fending for Frank twenty-four hours a day—taking umpteen tips from the high priestess of rock wives. I have always been a devoted slave to my men but never considered it a fiasco until I was struck by 3-D lightning not too long ago. I was in therapy with my Jungian analyst, complaining about my errant ex and his reckless sexual adventures that had hijacked our marriage, when I was struck dumb by the realization that *I* had been half the problem! I had become a classic codependent way before some now-filthy-rich soul had coined the term. Of course I have always been ahead of my time. Ha! The word *codependent*, like any other label, pissed me off at first, but I had to face facts, dolls. If the term fits, slide into it like a skin-tight cat suit. I now prefer "cocreator" because it's always a fifty-fifty deal. By catering to Michael, doing everything for him, kissing his royal ass, and attempting to alter him *for his own sake,* I had helped to create a man who had no choice but to rebel. I thought if I ripped out my heart every once in a while and offered him another piece, he would feel totally loved—totally beholden. I stood in front of him screaming, "Take it! Take another little piece of my heart, now baby. You know you've got it if it makes YOU feel good."

So many women my age are either adoring, diminished do-gooders, slavishly devoted to the men and children in their lives, putting themselves at the very end of the list, and rotting with boiling resentment or hard-bitten gals determined to wear the slacks and hold the reins. Their lips become slits of fierce, hard-won independence, and it's not very cute. I've always avoided the grown-up middle ground, but for the last couple of years I've been on a big search for this elusive pathway: take care of my man by taking care of myself. The goal sounds simple enough, but I've had to wade through reams of conditioning and blind rebellion, trying not to lose sight of the joyous, exciting day-to-day gift of life. I'm working on being independent—on trusting and respecting my wacky self—but not to get so serious that I get wrinkles on my forehead and trample on the things that thrill and delight me. It's definitely an adventure, and I'll always expect illuminating, mesmerizing moments to come along and clog up my day.

And thank God they do. I had a heart-stopping split second not too very long ago. Bob Dylan was playing the Greek Theatre, one of my fave venues in L.A., and I had backstage passes. What else is new? There are very few concerts I go to anymore without some sort of badge or sticker. Call me a snot, but I've been doing this shit for so long, I deserve an award, much less some sort of stupid inner-sanctum sticker. I have to say, though, that a pass for Bob Dylan thrilled and delighted me. Oh yes. I went rolling back in time, when I spent hours and ages in my rock-and-roll room in Reseda, listening to Bob break and enter. He busted into my confused-teen bouffant with an atomic wand and made me question *every single thing* in the universe. I wanted to yell "Chaaaaarge!!" and tackle all the hypocrisy and bullshit on the planet *all by myself!* So, twenty-five years later, when I pushed that backstage door open and Bob spread out his arms and said, "Pamela!! There you are! I just finished reading your book, cover to cover, and you're a really good writer," not only did time stand still for me, but I felt like popping open with pride. When I get inspired, I feel it right down into my fingertips, my pumping arteries, marrow, flushed cheeks, tear ducts, clitoris. I felt truly excited and awe inspired that night. People were all around, buzzing, humming like bees, congratulating Bob on his mighty performance. Hearty congratulations for the mysterious man with too many answers. He held a tumbler full of some bourbon-colored booze; grizzled, frizzy, black leather vest; smiling, mumbling thank-yous, shaking hands. His guitars in the corner, gleaming, his girlfriend

Carole and her dressy friends melding into the team of onlookers. Jack Nicholson, Anjelica Huston, Harry Dean Stanton, David Crosby. I had had my sparkling moment. Another backstage scene in which I revolved around the star player like a fringe planet around the sun. But it's okay. I'm one of those people who adore. It feels so good to be able to *adore* someone, doesn't it? That brief moment seemed the same as those sparkling drops in the ancient days of groupie yore, but this time I was getting back some of the outrageous output of adoration, appreciation energy. One of my main heroes appreciated my work. What a fucking thrill.

Yet another killer drop in the bucket of life took place at a dinner party held by my main doll-girl, Patti D'Arbanville, where the elusive Mr. Dylan put in an unexpected appearance. I arrived late, and he was the first person to greet me. "Pam, I missed you on *Oprah,*" he called out, and I stopped dead in my tracks. Now, I don't let just anybody call me Pam, except for my aunties, who just refuse to admit I grew out of "Pam" when I bought my first package of tampons at Thrifty drugstore, but I just couldn't correct Bob Dylan.

Pam, I missed you on *Oprah.*

IV

I hope that life will continue to thrill me until I cease to be. If I ever feel myself sliding into that woe-is-me shit, it doesn't take much to jolt me back out of the pit. I rush off to a Salvation Army thrift store and poke through a bunch of old crap in hopes of finding an overlooked treasure. Some fabulous old brocaded jacket with peace-sign pendant attached, maybe. It's always a possibility. I can cruise the bookstores for a signed Kerouac or the latest in codependence literature to keep myself from falling under some sexy snake charmer's spell, or I can grab my kid and go down to Little Tokyo and rent some unruly Japanese animation that Nick can translate for me while we sip cans of that amazing sweet, creamy "milky-tea." While I'm at it, I can also purchase some of those screwy, contorted, nameless Oriental vegetables with roots coming out of both ends and figure out how to eat them. I can pull out some Gram Parsons records and melt into yesterday's thick promises, or listen to an outrageous new band trying to knock back some walls. That usually straightens me right out. I can also whip up a cool dish for my boyfriend that tastes better than a billion-dollar meal served on the roof of some fancy revolving restaurant, or take a few deep breaths, spin inward, merge with the cosmos, and see that radiant silver cord that hooks us all together. The possibilities for avoiding that pity pit are endless.

I truly believe every one of us has a story to tell. We all rage and weep, laugh and mourn, have a lot of sex or not enough, fall in and out of love. We work hard, struggle, beg, plead, and play, and it's all very important. We're the stuff that dreams and nightmares are made of. It's all in the telling, dolls, and I'm going to tell you about the last fifteen years of my life, most of which were spent with the man I thought I would be with forever. But that fuddy-duddy fossilized cliché "Life is full of surprises" is one of those big, fat inescapable truths. It can work for you, or it can creep up and kick you in the ass. I think the trick is to have eyes in the back of your head. Expect the worst. Expect the best. Expect a fucking miracle. It's always Anything Can Happen Day.

CHAPTER TWO

I

When *I'm with the Band* came out, my husband of twelve and a half years, Michael, and I were on the verge of separating. I had such mixed-up, sad, and final feelings. I had accomplished so much by writing reams of cathartic madness, clearing away so many pent-up questions that still lurked in my heart like lonely apparitions. Writing about my loony, beloved past was like cleansing my soul with a heart-shaped metal scrub brush. Painful, bittersweet good-byes. I could finally let go of the magical Fab Four and Paul McCartney's dreamy thighs, Jimmy Page's ebony, velvet curls, Gram Parson's haunting anguished sob, Mick Jagger's haughty, prancing majesty, the wild and free utopian love-ins, the Sunset Strip, shredding crushed velvet and rotting silk flowers, my rose-colored, Mr. Tambourine Man sunglasses, hazy, stoned-out moments with people long gone: Keith Moon, John Bonham, Gram, Brandon De Wilde, Jim Morrison, Miss Christine . . . and now I had to let go of my forever-darling, Michael.

My book party in L.A. was held at an itsy underground club in Venice called the Pink. Originally it had been a lesbian bar, hence the colorful name. Risqué chic from top to bottom. All my friends were there, the pinkest champagne was festively flowing, and I had finally accomplished something of my own that made me proud. My KISS pal, Gene Simmons, was looking at me with his businessman eyes, dollar-sign pupils. Justine Bateman arrived on a shiny Harley D., scanning for Leif Garrett. My ex-lost love Donnie Johnson sent a bouquet from Miami that was almost embarrassing, taking up an entire corner of the crowded, bzzzz-ing room. Congratulations, Sweetheart. There was a gooey cake with plastic Beatle dolls on top, forever in mid-song, representing Chapter One. Girlfriends from high school said, "So you made something out of that loony life of yours, after all." Bravo. Or is it brava?

I had been to a zillion psychics; they had all told me I was a "late bloomer" and my success would come "later in life." That's something you're not too thrilled to hear when you're barely eighteen, but that sweet day at the Pink, it seemed that "later in life" had finally arrived. My book was stacked up all over the mini-cavern, the scent of hundreds of roses making me feel giddy and tipsy. Loud sixties memory-music had everybody shouting out instead of just speaking up. The day had come. It was finally my turn to curtsy, and Michael's turn to bow out gracefully. Ouch.

I was wearing a white, dragging-the-ground, frothy ripped-up lace number, high spiked diamanté heels, and red, red lips; looking madly elegant but feeling like an emotional moron. Veering from wacko gleeful to overwhelmingly melancholy, I felt like I was walking a shredded, golden tightrope. Holding hands with friends, kissing cheeks. Happy/sad. Michael made a poignant, inspired toast with sparkling apple cider about love and regrets, his dark, dark eyes shining with unshed tears. Champagne glasses were held high as he praised my budding talent to the giant skies, cracking up everybody with spot-on one-liners. I was beginning a rock novel called *Blush,* and with his glass in the air, Michael closed his disarming, charming Pamela pitch by saying, "Her first book made you shiver. Her new one will make you—blush." Applause, applause. Even when his life was collapsing around him, he could send people reeling with his wit and hysterical charm. Laugh, laugh—I thought I would die. All his clothes were still in the closet, tapes in the tape deck, photos on the walls, Opium colognes and body lotions lining the cupboards, his index finger still jammed tight into my solar plexus, but I missed him already.

II

I grew up believing that true love lasts forever. It's still an ideal that I aspire to, even though I've been squashed flat and hung out to dry in the ice-cold, harsh-assed, whipping wind of reality. It's such an age-old story of betrayal and pain that I hardly know how to tell it. Michael and I have been apart four years now, and it's true that our old and trusted pal Mr. Time has healed the open, oozing wound. But nothing will ever take away those days, weeks, and months when suffering, angst, and terror were the rules of the game. It can't be any other way when your life flies apart like the biggest bully in the world has stamped your flawlessly concocted dollhouse to smithereens.

And an amazing little dollhouse of dreams it was. I never would have believed for a split second that the California earthquake might come along behind the naughty bully and make sure it was well and truly crushed flat. Michael and I had worked up a pretty lively life scenario for ourselves. Never had any idea what was around the corner of any God-given moment—who might walk through our door and stay awhile, what borderline-renown personality would call and invite us to some sort of spectacular event. Our dinner parties and yard sales were attended by the coolest of the cool. Madonna dug into my heart-shaped carrot cake before it was cut, Billy Idol wore Michael's old boots down the street. Life was a tempting dessert full of surprises. Our little boy had a gigantic IQ and a heart-stopping smile. It was assumed all around that Michael and I were the Perfect Couple—a match made where it counts. Surrounding our tantalizing yet cozy-wozy love next was the unwieldy, gold-spattered world of show biz and all its come-hither, half-assed promises. But I'm leaping ahead of myself here, so let's go back, let's go waaay back—to the days before the Sex Pistols, when David Bowie was still androgynous, when John Lennon was still very much alive. When Pamela Des Barres was still Pamela Miller from Reseda, California, looking real hard for love.

III

Michael and I met on a movie set in Manhattan. My ex-passion and old friend Keith Moon didn't show up to play the part of the debauched, mongrel rock star, so the director of *Arizonaslim,* Chuck Wein, had to comb the gutters and agencies of New York City, seeking an impossible overnight replacement for the reckless, feckless drummer of the Who. He came up with the lead singer of a glam band called Silverhead, and I was ever so curious to see who I was going to adore on screen. I arrived at the location, an upscale pad in the West Village, in costume. It was three below zero and I was decked out in turquoise Betsey Johnson knitted short-shorts—

Miss Casual, together, star-of-the-movie. In my mind's third eye I can still recall the exact instant I set eyes on Michael Philip Des Barres.

It was his twenty-sixth birthday, which in retrospect is pretty propitious. The birthday boy was scroonched up on the couch alongside one of the bit players, a flitty-eyed girl with a shag-do who was attempting to engage him in conversation. He came out of the void as I made my noisy entrance, and stared at my chill-bumped ass with crazy blue-black eyes. Encouraging, to say the least. The degenerate rock star and I had quite a few scenes together that day, so I yanked out my script in hopes of some rehearsal. Wearing silver lamé cut down to the belly button, a fake, tatty leopard coat, ladies' white patent flats and with a chiseled face full of yesterday's makeup, Michael watched me walk toward him with a lion's den grin full of chipped British teeth. (What's wrong with the dentists over there, anyway?) He obviously lived an audacious and irresponsible life; just the kind of person who has always been intriguing to me, much to my dear mother's dismay.

Michael and I hunkered down to rehearse and wound up snorting piles of coke together. I had tried to stop taking all drugs a couple of times before and almost overcame the urge entirely after going on a two-week papaya fast. I felt so whistle clean and gunk-free; like all my insides were just born. I floated around in a natural sprouted-wheat celestial state for a few days afterward, determined to stay pure. In the early days of zoning out on pot and psychedelics, I considered it some kind of inner soul search, but now I knew better, and besides feeling my liver shudder, I knew that Jesus, Buddha, and Paramahansa Yogananda were shaking their heads in shame and sorrow for the goofy chick who kept slipping off the path. So Michael and I did our scenes together—high as kites—the first of which involved lounging in the back of a limo, discussing Elvis Presley, one of our many, as it turned out, mutual heroes. Since a portion of my heart belonged to an unavailable Southern hunk back home, I wasn't instantly smitten with Michael, so was able to be myself, and he was mesmerized. He told me he loved my all-girl band, the GTO's (Girls Together Outrageously), and had harbored a secret desire to meet me after seeing my picture in *Melody Maker*. Was that the one where I stretched out across the conference table?

Michael and I worked hard all day on the low-budget disaster, and by night-crash I was a twitching wretch, wringing my hands in coked-out despair. Debonair Michael, obviously a drug pro, dug up a couple of Valiums from the flitty-eyed extra, graciously placed them in my sweaty palm, and disappeared into the mad night. I was surprised he hadn't attempted to woo my ass, but of course it made him all the more provocative.

I slept like sixteen tons and met up with him the next evening where we were filming the backstage scene with his glitter band Silverhead. I perched on his lap, because it was in the script—ha ha—and he casually stroked my thigh while wailing with a gigantic, raspy voice, rehearsing the raunchy set. KISS was the opening act, and I could hear the *thump-thump* of Peter Criss's bass drum through my sling-backs, while Chuck filmed the whole scene. Something was certainly going on inside my lacy undergarments as I wriggled on his scrawny lap, why deny it? He came back to the Beekman Tower with me and tossed my costume across the room in a brazen heap, plowing into me with his lips until I screeched him to a halt. How much can you take? We couldn't do the full deed because Michael had caught some unmentionable infection in Japan and was chivalrous enough not to plant it inside me. A true gentleman. I suppose that's why he hadn't tried to win me over on the first night. "It's just as well," I burbled to myself. "Do I really need this rumpled, stoned-out smart-ass in my life? He's a rock guy who lives across the ocean, and I've had enough of that shit." We went shopping the next day, and he spent an entire week's per diem on little trinkets for me, red velvet pumps for himself, and a fancy, romantic dinner at the famous Luchow's, where we drank fine wine from chilled crystal goblets. White-haired violinists came to our table, playing Strauss waltzes while Michael and I drilled lust holes into each other and ate great buttery lumps of rich food. I think I stuffed down an entire duck crammed full of bing cherries. Poor little quacker.

As the antique music waltzed around us, Michael told me he came from a long, long line of blue-blooded French aristocrats; he was titled and would one day be the Marquis Des Barres. At present he was but a mere Count. He grabbed hold of my hand and announced that I would make a ravishing countess. "I think we shall be married one day," he said matter-of-factly, right in my eyes. And here I thought I was just having a little fun.

It was no laughing matter, even though there was a lot of laughter involved. Michael pursued me, got in the way of my Southern romance, and trampled it right down on his way to my front door. My mom's eyebrows were raised; she hoped it wasn't serious. Silverhead came to Los Angeles and took the underage groupie crowd by storm, but even though the baby bumpers made themselves mightily available, I was the one hanging onto the lead singer's tatty leopard coat. We made intrinsic love in his crumpled bed at the Hyatt House, musky, tangy bonding all night long. Michael ripped up the Whisky a Go Go in a last attempt at original raunch. The band put out two racy records that not enough people bought. Silverhead should have made it massive, but when they got back to England they busted up instead.

Michael made me fall in love with him. He insisted. He demanded no less than instant total commitment, which I was absolutely ready for. Long distance I found out that he was already married, but even though I almost fainted with stunned grief, it was too late for either one of us to back off. We moaned and loved into the crackling phone wires, pledged foreverness, played with ourselves until it hurt. As soon as he could dig up the required loot, he would leave behind the first wife, his record company, his parents; give up his entire former existence and come straight to me.

IV

When that day of all days finally arrived, I waited anxiously at LAX, wearing a skimpy, defiant ensemble, watching all the normal folks saunter out of the plane, my yammering heart gift-wrapped, ripe, and ready to be handed over to the final man in my life. Take it!!! Michael arrived forever with his hair dryer in a paper bag and a five-dollar bill wadded up in one of his patent-leather baby-doll shoes. Staggering out last, he was so far behind the others that I had started to shake and shiver like a bad-tempered snowman was standing behind me, sliding his icy finger down my feverish spine. In those long few seconds my mind churned. Had he missed the plane? Bumped into his wife? Changed his mind? Passed out on someone's floor in London? Then we saw each other, our eyes rapt with relief, desire, adoration, fear. We grabbed on and held tight, locked together at last in a keyless knot. We stopped for a drink at the first bar we bumped into, and he cast his full fate to the Santa Ana winds, spending all the money he had in the world on a couple of cocktails. We murmured to each other in the darkened airport bar, swearing eternal and profound true love, full of sweet-eyed, honey-dripping, sticky-faced tears, and promises, promises. Big Important Promises. He tossed the hair dryer into the trash on the way to the car because I pointed out that it had a European plug and wouldn't have worked

in our little Hollywood love lair. He was a man without a country
or a hair dryer, and even though his hands were empty, they were
all over me. This man had surpassed many hard-core, sweaty, and
serious odds to get to me, had left a wacky, mortified wife, a set of
loony, mismatched, busted-up parents, a glitter-glam career, and a
super-trendy record company. I was bound and determined to show
him my unceasing, undying affection and appreciation, starting right
now! Put yourself in my hands, honey bun. Leave it *all* up to me.
You know you've got it if it makes you feel good.

We got into my little Volkswagen and drove, all touchy-feely, to
my Hollywood fairy-tale pad on Maryland Drive—a do-it-yourself
thirties charmer over somebody's garage, hidden by leafy apricot
trees—the perfect passion haven for pent-up lovers. The walls
were full of Mickey Mouse, Snow White, Elvis and James Dean,
along with a devilish shot of Robert Plant, which Michael promptly
removed and replaced with a shot of himself, grinning devilishly,
both hands on his cock. We settled down in front of the black-
and-white TV and watched happy, ancient half hours, rolled around
in the sheets, screaming with nasty glee, shutting out the entire
big, bad world. I made American cheese sandwiches on white
Weber's bread, long before they had fake whole wheat, turned
Michael onto Dr. Pepper, and the combo became our constant meal
of choice.

Housekeeping came second to racy frolicking, and a delicious
onion dip I made a few days earlier had started to odor up our
little amore area, but we couldn't seem to locate the offending
bowl of goop. After sniffing around, Michael finally discovered it
on top of the fridge, but as I grabbed it to toss down the cluttered
sink, I noticed the dip was moving! Infested with wriggling white
maggots, the onion dip was alive!! Hurling it to the ground below,
I shrieked so loud and made such a silly-billy racket that Michael
was rolling on the floor with glee. Nothing is more gross than a
bowl full of maggots. Absolutely nothing. Michael had missed the
gruesome sight, so I imitated the writhing bowl with my face and
fingers, and I thought he would pass out from laughing. He made
me imitate the seething onion dip many, many times. Just the
other day he said, "Let's see what those maggots looked like,
Pam-pam."

In 1974 I was consumed with love, I was alight with it, drugged,
dewy, and damp with it. This was what I had waited for since the
first time I saw Snow White open her eyes and gaze adoringly at Mr.

Charming. Michael firmly held my hand in his own, like it had always been there. "You are the woman for me," he stated in his delicious British accent, and I blithely overlooked the fact that my prince who came several times daily had a lethal attraction to the dark side, while I liked to live smack dab in the sunlight. He was a combination of exotic, aristocratic, angular royalty and debauched, street-rat, riotous self-indulgence. He used big, scary words, knocking them off carelessly while I scribbled them down to look up in my Webster's, which I kept sequestered under the bed right next to my almost forgotten diary. Since finding my One and Only, I didn't need to rant and moan as copiously. My old diaries lined the bookshelves like yesterday's desperate hours.

October 10, 1974—It's amazo how one's life totally *changes when love flies in the window and there's another person next to you all the time. You just give up your old trips, except for family ties and career, but sometimes I find I'm letting them both slip, along with everything else!*

One cheery, blasé afternoon, as I wandered back from our local Ralph's market, ready to stick a couple Stouffer's in the oven, I could hear unusual crashing noises inside the pad and dashed up the stairs to find Michael, naked and enraged, throwing my porcelain doodads against the wall. Surrounding him were all my diaries, one of which was open to a page I assumed he had taken particular offense with. He glared at me, and I retaliated with a phony grin-shrug. "Oh well, perhaps someday??" Michael spat the words at me. "SOMEday, eh?" *What* had he read in my diary, and why? "Why are you looking at my diaries?" I dared to peep. "WHAT do you mean, 'Oh well, perhaps someday,' Pamela, darling?" He picked up the offending book, shoved it in my red face, pointed to the incriminating passage, and I remembered a couple months earlier, meeting Jeff Bridges at my friend Bud Cort's party and thinking he was sexy stuff. He had checked me out all evening, and I had written of my blasphemous hopeful response. Oh well, perhaps someday. But I didn't mean it! I hadn't meant anything by it. It was *meaningless!* I humbled myself before my darling, so afraid of losing him to the ghost of Lloyd Bridges's youngest son. The tempest swirled around me, but Michael finally calmed down as I ate the last bite of crow and licked the plate clean. At least there were no maggots around and he hadn't destroyed the diaries. The next day I took all the little black books and tucked them safely in Mom's garage. I had gotten an eerie early glimpse of Michael's temper potential, and even though the typhoon tizzy abated, it was a long, long time before we could enjoy a Jeff Bridges movie together.

I was engaged to marry a married man, but things could have been worse. He promised to expedite a transatlantic divorce just as soon as he could afford it, and I floated on thin air. One lusty evening while Michael soaked in the tub after a bewitching romp in the hay, I was poking around for a couple of dollars and found a photo of the first Mrs. Des Barres in his wallet and lost my entire mind. Isn't jealousy like a fucking disease? I studied her pale face and red curls like they held the answers to *every* question ever asked by anybody in the entire meta-galaxy. I started to burn. The searing heat started in my toes and moved rapidly, rabidly through my shaky thighs, up my spine, into my cheeks, and burst into a bonfire trapped raging inside my skull. Why did he carry this picture of her around? Did he miss this bitch? She looked like she needed rescuing, so plaintive and delicate, wearing a pretty flowered dress. I can still see that damn photograph in full and living color. Calming myself, deep breaths, counting to ten . . . "Look what I found, honey," trying for blasé so-what, sounding more like a petulant bleat. He, of course, was incredibly casual, "Oh. I thought I threw that away," he said, yawning. Very convincing. So what could I say? I gnawed on it for a while, my brain membranes eating themselves, then crumpled the blasted photo, tossed it in the trash, and climbed into the tub to have a small discussion about his shredded wedlock. He said they had really broken up before he met me. But hadn't they been married only three weeks before that fateful day we got together on the Manhattan movie set? Yes, but it was one of those last-ditch attempts *on her part,* to save the crumbling relationship. They had to have lots of three- and four-way sex-ins, obliterating themselves on any available substance to drown out their waning passion. They fought all the time, broke things over each other's heads, and threatened to kill each other more than once. They met at drama school when he was only eighteen, and seven years later they were still wallowing around in yesterday's teen dreams. It was over. Over. OVER. I scrubbed his back with a loofah; he told me he loved me. He said that I was the one he had waited for all his life. It was destiny, fate, kismet that brought us together. Part of the divine plan. Of *course* he had forgotten all about that antique picture in his wallet. Absolutely. We were just two jealous fools in love.

V

While Michael and his big-shot manager decided what to do with his magnificent set of lungs and blatant star power, I resumed my acting career and got myself a new agent, a hefty chunk of a gal called Freda Granite. Her miniature office was stuck way out in the Valley, and she specialized in kids. Rodney Allen Rippy, the happy black child who cutely hyped Jack-In-the-Box burgers was her super claim to fame. The second interview she sent me out on was for a new character on the soap *Search for Tomorrow,* Amy Kaslo, a post-hippie chick pre-med student, a warm and funny girl who was secretly in love with her best friend's fiancé. And I got it! My mom and dad were oh-so-proud of me and couldn't wait to tune me in daily. All those acting classes and two-bit plays were finally going to pay off.

But what a tortured, mixed blessing it turned out to be. I would have to relocate to New York and leave Michael languishing in the city of angels, way too soon—I had just gotten him back! The dear boy had no money and I couldn't afford two pads, so we had to let go of the Dr. Pepper palace on Maryland Drive. Through a friend of Chuck Wein's, I had already found an apartment in the West Village, on the corner of Seventh and Bleecker above a French bakery. I was going to be roommates with a cute little airline stewardess appropriately named Debbie. The plan was for Michael to move in with his new manager, who happened to be the biggest coke dealer on earth. Oops.

This mighty man was putting together a supergroup after having seen Michael perform a solo at the Hollywood Revival and Trash Dance, where many shrieking females ripped his pants half off. His nuts were actually in the spotlight momentarily because, as usual, he had no use for underwear. I happened to be right on stage with him because my ex-group, the GTO's, re-formed for the big night to sing "Mr. Sandman" totally off-key but spilling over with soul. Mercy and Cynderella had gone missing, so Sparkie and I had rounded up some last-minute replacements, and we sounded pretty good. Just as the curtain rose, there was a crash, boom, wallop, and here they came— Mercy, heading for the microphone, wearing a lopsided rainbow afro, and Cynderella tilting in all the wrong directions—rarin' and ready to belt it out. What could I do? They were the true Girls Together Outrageously and belonged onstage. After a screeching rendition of "Sandman," we were ready to back up Michael on his Elvis medley. You never caught a rabbit, you ain't no friend of mine. The doowops were out of sync, but I was up on stage again—only this time my love-man was out front. Seeing the sweaty, swooning faces of the fans as they grabbed for Michael's crotch made me more gaga than ever. Mine *mine* MINE!!! Iggy Pop, Ray Manzarek of the Doors, and the New York Dolls were also on the bill, and the night sort of made history as the final, phantasmagoric glitter event. Despite the hallucinatory hyped-up name tag, it was all a bit sad and tawdry. How could I, at age twenty-five, be part of a revival already? Michael hadn't even hit his rock stride. And Iggy Pop was in his prime, wasn't he? I doubt if he even remembers the event, he was so far gone. Younger kids who thought they had missed something were hanging onto the coattails of the sixties, trying to go back in time, as Ray Manzarek and his spooky Doors organ attempted to jolt them back to the splendour of '67. Jim Morrison had been dead a mere four years.

I was ready to call it a day, but *Creem* magazine wrote the whole thing up glowingly: "Representing the first generation of the whole thing were the GTO's, reunited for the show, filling things out with a dash of nostalgia. They were, of course, charming. They, and especially Miss Pamela, have never really stopped performing, the only difference this time being the fact that they were up on a stage. They sang 'Mr. Sandman,' and then, in best Sandra Dee–Bobby Darin tradition, they were joined by Michael Des Barres, one of the period's hottest British imports and Miss Pamela's husband-to-be." A tired-looking teenager wearing an old fur coat over her mini-skirt approached me as I lovingly mopped Michael down after his set. Eyeing the scene she got a sour look on her face. "Haven't you given up yet, *Miss* Pamela? That's real funny. You're about as much of a 'miss' as my fucking *mother*." Michael took a swipe at her and just missed. I ignored her—she should have kissed my pioneering groupie butt.

The Trash Dance was a symbolic flash-crash ending for me, even as Michael's future manager yelled hot-air promises in my ear while Michael disarmed and glad-handed record-business types, trying to keep his balls tucked into his tattered trousers. My husband-to-be had been a glitter-glam innovator back in Britain, and it was only a matter of time before America gave him his due, and I would always stand by him. Give him two arms to cling to—and something warm to come to—when nights are cold and lonely. But secretly I felt like giving the whole dilapidated, shoddy rock scene a big, juicy raspberry. Engaged to a hot British import, on my way to gigantic TV

stardom in New York City, they could all just kiss my tight trail-
blazing ass *adios*.

I had proven to the street dogs that I had gotten my rock-and-roll
man, and we went out once in awhile so I could smear it in, but I
had lost interest in being part of a fading scene. You couldn't trust
the new L.A. groupies, who were desperate, discouraged, groveling
ego seekers. The love of music had become secondary to preening
in *Star* magazine, standing next to Anybody In A Band. It was scary
out there. It was fictitious and haunted. The magic dust on the Sunset
Strip had turned into sticky wads of filthy goop that stuck to the
bottom of my platforms. I worried about Michael diving into those
shark-infested, murky waters, but singing and posing were the things
he did best. Those pre-Pistols, post-Zeppelin days were a vast musical
wasteland for me; so little originality was allowed to leak through
those towering big-business giants who made the music industry what
it is today. In the middle seventies rock and roll was in a state of
flux, changing from intimate love and guts to arena power and pack-
aging. And now, in 1991, one measly singer can get a billion-dollar
advance. Backstage doors are wrapped with barbed wire equipped
to electrocute. It's frightening.

V

The cocaine manager with the false grin bought Michael and me
tickets to London so we could have a seductive little holiday before
I started my soap, and we stayed up in his mom's attic, a cozy, rosy
mush-den of delights. I cooked his meals, rubbed his back, brought
him *Melody Maker,* hung on his every witty, loving word. We made
love to the red hissing of an aging electric heater, and one night after
a blissful handing-over of throbbing body parts, I sniffed a scorch in
the air. Was it me? No, the red nightie my mom had worn on her
wedding night had caught on the heater during our pumped-up frenzy
and was being eaten by mini-flames. Michael wrestled the singed
rayon from my sweaty body and stomped on it with his bare feet.
So brave! The treasured nightie-heirloom was partially blackened,
but I decided to save it forever anyway.

I had been trepidatious about meeting Michael's bohemian, jazz-
loving mother, having spoken to her on the phone several times
about her treasured only son. She had despised the first wife, Wendy.
Would I measure up? Irene Gladys Des Barres, with the dark flashing
eyes, seemed at first to be the doting, adoring British mom. She

invited me into her home, made toast in the morning and cocoa at night, and spoke constantly about the inestimable value of her only child, Michael, and how good she thought I was going to be for him. I was starting to get comfortable on the fat, feather-stuffed sofa when Michael reminded me to <u>watch out.</u> He had warned me to expect anything because his mom was a true eccentric, having been a burlesque queen who hung out with jazz musicians and smoked hash joints as far back as he could remember. But I wasn't prepared for the overnight transformation. One morning after a perfectly charming evening with her watching telly, she woke up silent and scary, giving me hollow, accusing looks, snickering under her breath, and rolling her eyes at everything I said. I had put the bread into the bread bin the night before, and she was outraged. "Doesn't she know the bread will *die* if it's locked up like that?" she hissed at Michael. No toast slathered with sweet butter and currant jam for me. Michael shook his head woefully and told me not to take it seriously. Any idea I had about becoming chummy with my future mother-in-law vanished into the chilly London air, and when we left town, she wasn't even around to say good-bye. It was deep-down eerie, and I thought about the little boy Michael had been, having to put up with that schizo lunacy and those twisted, haunting, dark blue eyes, so much like his own. Michael had told me that his parents had sex only once, and he was the product of that bent and futile union. He would have lots of tragic, buried stuff to weed out one day, and it scared me, but I knew I could handle it. I could probably even *fix* it. Yes, indeed.

And where *was* his father? Irene gave us an old phone number for the one and only Marquis Philip Des Barres, squanderer of family fortunes, and after calling around town to find the old geezer, we planned to meet him at a pub in Oxford Circus for a friendly drink and chat. He was already sequestered in a booth when we arrived, holding hands with a round-faced, underage blond girl, whispering in her ear while she giggled gleefully. Wearing an elegant but shoddy black suit, ascot askew, his face lined, his bald head gleaming, he could have been the girl's great-grandfather except for the fact that he gazed at her small chest lasciviously and gave us a naughty wink when we sat down. He acted as if he had seen his son just last week instead of many years before. The old fellow still held himself like royalty—obviously used to being the total center of attention—and when he insisted on paying the bill, pulled a handful of Tuinals and Seconals out of his pocket with the wrinkled wad of pounds. The pills rolled all over the seat, and he gathered them up, laughing wickedly, and popped one into his mouth seemingly without a spot of remorse. His upright, rebellious pride was ragged but entirely intact. What an unholy heritage I was about to inherit.

I had of course realized Michael's penchant for the seamy side of life—and now I knew for sure that it ran in the family—but being the optimistic overlooker that I am, I always tried to see my own true love in the kindest, blindest of light. I had certainly taken my share of mind-altering chemicals, wanting to dig around inside myself, trying to find Really Big Answers, hoping to see God. I had sometimes even *enjoyed* the muggy escape from scary, shocking reality, so I truly understood the need to search for the EXIT sign once in a while.

But Michael seemed to be on his own private search-and-destroy mission. Drugs of enlightenment and inner discovery had been replaced by hard, mean, addictive powders and downer death pills, and Michael seemed seriously devoted to them. He loved to get higher than anyone else in the room, pass out, and start all over the next day. How could I move to New York and leave him in L.A. with his habit? It was worse than sharing him with another woman. He might even wake up dead someday, my panicky heart kept repeating. Dead someday. Dead someday. He ingested any drug that anyone gave him, cocaine being his "drug of choice." He drank out of any bottle until it was empty, but since he didn't think he had a problem, his sharp, smart mouth shut me right up when I started blathering on and on. Woody Allen didn't take drugs, and he was a creative soul; Frank Zappa had never even smoked a joint. Who else? Who else? I searched far and wide for shining examples but was hard-pressed to find any others. Michael's heroes were all high-as-kite fuck-ups, so deciding all I could do was be a luminous example of squeaky-clean sanity, I swore off all obliterative substances, hoping, praying he would follow suit.

To my delight, Michael got bombed only twice the whole time we were in England, which gave me unwarranted hope that he would continue on this immaculate pathway in Los Angeles while I forged a new career on national television. Oh God, please keep him clean and straight. After much gazing, clutching, and more weepy promises at Heathrow Airport, he slammed back to the manager-dealer's bachelor den, and I poured prayers into my journal on the plane to Manhattan.

November 14—Away from my darling Michael, but his smile fills my mind. The last ten days have been glorious, I didn't know there were any more things we could do with our bodies. Blazing hot. He's never looked or felt better to me. God, I hope he takes care of himself—he needs me around— I hope he's strong. God keep him, don't let him wig out. I trust his soul and hope to go through L-I-F-E with him.

VI

On top of being worried spitless about Michael, I was a wretched bag of nerves on my big-deal soap job. I started studying with the wildly acclaimed William Hickey at the Berghof Studio, and even though he was constantly sipping on some mysterious clear liquid, he thought I was a stupendous actress. I made sure he never caught *Search for Tomorrow.* All my fellow soap actors were encouraging and helpful, but my confidence quotient was pathetic. I could hardly even smile, because I felt like I would crack down the center and expose the sorry smidgen of talent I really had. I carried around a little blurb about my character, Amy Kaslo, and read it over and over between takes, hoping to capture her deep-down essence.

"AMY KASLO—A new friend of Liza Walton. Amy could have been a camp counselor but is now a full-scholarship medical student at Henderson Medical School. She is a warm, funny, slightly ethnic girl as open and full of sparks as the furnace her father fed at a steel mill in Pennsylvania. She comes from working-class people whose feet are firmly planted on the ground, and her parents are just a little suspicious of a girl who sets her sights as high as their daughter has. Going after a medical degree is a little crazy, and if that's what she wants, she is going to have to do it on her own. They can't help feeling that aiming too high makes it easier to fall."

I could certainly relate to that, but "slightly ethnic"? I'm about as white-bread and homogenized as it gets. I don't know about Amy Kaslo, but Pamela Ann Miller had always aimed too high, only to find that when she got there she was petrified. All of a sudden my hundreds of acting classes dribbled down the drain as I paced around my dressing room trying to learn lines that had been changed over and over again. "Come in, Liza! Gee, why didn't Bruce come with you? Come to think of it, I didn't see him in the student lounge. I wonder if anything happened to him? Do you think he's all right?"

There was a lot of "business" my first day of filming. The full-of-sparks Amy was having a housewarming party and had to drain the spaghetti through a tennis racket. Real cute. Real impossible. The guy playing my bespectacled boyfriend Grover was almost as nervous as I was, so we rehearsed our lines until they were meaningless drivel and somehow got through the stray spaghetti strands, grueling shouts of "action" and the clapboard slamming down in our faces. The shuddering shy guy bringing Grover to life was John Heard, and he's on the big screen all the time now, so I suppose he figured out a way to deal with his willies. I never did. Oh, I had days when I felt like I didn't embarrass myself, and even thought I was pretty good once in awhile, but for the most part, I was filled with dread when somebody yelled "quiet on the set."

I felt like throwing up with actor-jitters, but that wasn't the only problem. My character was supposed to be smart, hip, and sparkly, but I found myself spewing plot lines half the time, explaining away everybody else's unseemly actions, and mooning mopily around over my best friend's nerdy fiancé nonstop. They brought Michael Nouri in to play my gorgeous rebel brother and my best friend Liza promptly fell for him, but I still didn't get to grab Brucie boy; I consoled him instead. Awwww, you'll be okay, Bruce. She wasn't good enough for you anyway. I wanted to do something naughty and evil-spirited like the bad girl on the show, played by Morgan Fairchild; instead, I was cutesie-poo Amy—Amy a lump of pre-fab putty, tossed around in the hands of the soap writers like a boring, sniveling jerk with a bouffant. Why did the hairdresser have to tease me out so wide and use half a can of hairspray? Amy Kaslo started out to be a freaky hippie chick, didn't she?

I wanted to rush back to Hollywood and riot on the Sunset Strip, frolic in a ripped-up lace tablecloth at one more love-in, and pounce on Michael with *Father Knows Best* mewling in the background. I wanted to bonk the heels of my normal nurse shoes together and whisper, "There's no place like home, there's no place like home . . ." and find myself at the Country Canyon Store drinking Dr Pepper in the sunlight. Instead I was under harsh fake lights, shaking in front of a soulless lens, wearing a severe white medical smock dyed gray for the cameras. What was I doing in such stiff, unhip circumstances?

Michael was out on the streets in Hollywood the day of the Amy Kaslo debut and was wildly trying to locate a TV to watch his girlfriend play-act. He wandered around asking passersby if he could please watch their TV for a half an hour and lucked out just in time when a very large black lady and her daughter invited him in to view their tiny black-and-white set. After settling down in their bungalow off Fountain and Argyle, he had to fend off their seductive, double advances while poor, old Amy attempted to strain spaghetti through that accursed tennis racket. He told me this nutty story on the phone that night, where I was curled up in my loft bed, needing him so bad. He was rehearsing with his new band daily and getting real high at night, and because he knew how hysterically opposed to obliteration I was, he started lying to me. I gobbled it up, pretending his constant sniffle was not self-induced. Yes, honey, I know. You can't seem to get rid of that nagging cold. Take lots of vitamin C. Drink vast quantities of liquid. Get a lot of sleep. Mmm-mm, yes angelman, I love you, too.

Everybody was getting stoned, weren't they? It was no big deal, right? Michael could handle it, couldn't he? Had I known about Alcoholics Anonymous at this point, I would have had some much-needed assistance, but AA was still a backwoods, naked-swaying-lightbulb concept, not even a consideration. Instead, I found a cosmic healer-teacher-saint called Hilda, who provided holy relief from my inner battering ram with her weekly meditation meetings. I could lose track of my panic-stricken, skittish brain, spiral freewheeling into the celestial void and close up the honky-tonks for a little while. It was my first real, true experience of leaving it *all* behind without a guilty hangover. Hilda told us about a holy lady called Amal, long gone from this planet, who would answer prayers if you asked three times in a row. I slept in a T-shirt with her face on the front and begged and pleaded with her three times three times three times daily for Michael to see the light, shed his desire for drugs and alcohol, and humble his precious, sleazy self before the Lord of his choice.

VII

Two long months later I got to go home for Christmas and rekindle my unwieldy romance. I was nauseated with anxiety, faint with anticipation, but five minutes in each other's eyes and it was like I never left at all. Instead of crashing at the manager's raucous pad, we stayed with our friend, Ben Edmonds, the *Creem* magazine editor who had gotten me an airline ticket home when I was stuck in Toolieville, Georgia, with Silverhead a few months before. I had actually traded him one of Mick Jagger's garments from *Performance* that he had given me when we were carousing. I think Ben had a contest with it: Why I Want to Swaddle Myself in Mick Jagger's Velvet Dress in Fifty Words or Less. Michael and I borrowed a mattress from my dear old roommate, Michele Myer, and lazed around in Ben's spare room, doing it so many times I was raw. He bought me an engagement ring on Hollywood Boulevard for $32.50 complete with itsy diamond chip, slipped it on my finger in front of my parents' heavily laden Christmas tree, and I was set for life.

> **January 3**—*Michele is real upset, she thinks I devote too much time to Des Barres. We went to Disneyland on N.Y. Eve and brought '75 in with Mick and Min! So great! His new supergroup is coming together, so that's what he'll be working on when I split. Ah, sweet worry, will you split, too? We've talked about the drug thing and he says he'll be cool. God, Amal, watch over him. I've had several nasty, paranoid dreams about it, though he's only been blasted a couple times.*

To say I was writhing around in my beloved's bone marrow wouldn't be an exaggeration.

I talked Michael into spending New Year's Eve at my home away from home, The Happiest Place on Earth—Disneyland. As a kid, I had dashed home from school daily to chortle along with Jimmy Dodd and the Meeska-Mooska-Mouseketeers, and Mickey Mouse came to represent all that was innocent and good—no dark side whatsoever. My parents took me to Disneyland for my birthday the year it opened, 1955, and I became one with Fantasyland, soaking the carefree Dumbo-Peter Pan-Snow White innocence into the soles of my black patent shoes, pink lace socks. I *needed* to share the park with Michael; he *had* to realize the importance of Mickey Mouse and his slaphappy cronies in the grand scheme of things and what they meant to me. When Mickey kissed Minnie at the top of the Fantasyland castle at the stroke of midnight, Michael kissed me. He probably would have liked to have been rollicking, dead-drunk, raving at a madclub, escaping reality, but he was holding on to me while two small people in costume planted one on each other's fake noses. But was I escaping reality? Uh-uh. I was pushing the fucking mouse down his throat, but Michael loved me enough not to wring its neck. Yo ho, yo ho, a pirate's life for me.

After closing down Disneyland, we spent two days in Ensenada, Mexico, with Daddy and his best friend, Ruben, eating cucumbers on sticks sprinkled liberally with chile pepper, riding horses bareback on the beach, buying big silver crosses and loud embroidered vests, taking a much-needed siesta under the smiling orange sun. Ruben and his wife threw a barbecue in our honor, and his many robust children, all dressed up in their frilly best, served us various chunks of blackened seafood drenched in lime juice. Michael drank many beers with my dad, and they shared a warped, semi-bonding experience; two hugely different worlds colliding with peculiar panache. "I go gold-mining too, O.C.," I heard Michael say, tilting back the cowboy hat he had worn in my dad's honor. "I dig for gold in the record business. Ha. Ha?" The long-haired, rake-thin, bejeweled and jangled English pop prince and O. C. Miller—Clark Gable look-alike, coal miner from Avery County, North Carolina—each sniffing the other from head to toe while casually discussing the current events of 1975. "No matter what they say about Watergate, Mike, Nixon did us some good." I wish I had taken a picture.

We didn't realize Michael would need his passport to get back across the border, so when the squinting, macho, mustachioed gendarme leaned his big face into Daddy's Caddy and asked if we were all American, I piped up proudly, "My fiancé is British!" O.C. gave me the evil eye and, sure enough, the square-shouldered squinter asked for Michael's papers. "We didn't think he would need them," I squeaked. Michael was silent, and I knew he was way past pissed. After a lot of hassling, pleading, and cajoling, which didn't work, the high-powered border patrol kept Michael in Dos Equis land overnight. We dropped him off at a supposedly safe, crummy motel right by the border. All he had with him was a copy of Vincent Bugliosi's *Helter Skelter* and a beat-up gold leather jacket.

I had to go to the scary coke manager's pad to pick up Michael's passport and got to see the fancy little hole Michael called home while I emoted in Manhattan. He had my picture hanging over the couch he crashed on, and I got a rapturous little tingle while Mr. Dealer chuckled in the background with his cocaine residue, fishy grin, and jittery hands. I tried to deny it to myself, but he and Michael shared a common, albeit depraved, drug bond that I had excluded myself from by trying to set a Goody-Two-Shoes example. I attempted to smile back at him after the passport was procured, but my grin muscles were paralyzed.

I tried to sleep at my parents' house for a couple of hours before I set out on the trek back to Mexico but was so distressed about my man trapped in his nighttime Tijuana net, I couldn't even keep my eyes closed. Worried weak, I flew through the bright blue morning in Daddy's metal-flaked copper-colored Caddy (painted in Mexico, of course; Earl Scheib was nowhere in sight) with Michael's important passport in the pocket of my jeans and was so relieved to see my man waiting for me outside the border dump. Once ensconced within the frozen-aired comfort of the Fleetwood, he cuddled into me and cracked me up with his tale of woe in TJ. He said it had been a Helter-Skelter frightmare, with Anthony Quinn look-alikes looming in the shadows, loitering outside his flimsy door all night long. "I kept expecting Charlie, disguised as Viva Zapata to knock the door down and offer me some acid," Michael moaned at me. He could be amusing in the most dire circumstances. He had shoved the only piece of furniture besides a charming, squeaky cot—a three-legged table—against the door because there was no lock. Since all his neighbors resided in cardboard boxes, he realized he should have been grateful for the shelter, but his terror was compounded by reading about wack-eyed Tex Watson and Charlie's zombie kill-girls. Sitting on the floor by the window, next to the misfit table, he read the hideous revelations by the only available light; a lone bulb out in the hallway, surrounded by drunken, dusty moths. A fabulous topper to his first south-of-the-border vacation.

A few days later I got on yet another plane bound for New York, while Michael stood by gallantly. I bit my tongue hard so I wouldn't beg and plead with him one more time to stay away from the devil drug cocaine and the liver eater alcohol. When I was settled in for the five-hour flight, I plunged into my purse, trying to locate a roll of Tums for my lonesome, aching tummy, and came across a little note Michael had hidden inside. "My Darling Pamela, please don't worry your beautiful head about my bad habits. I want to be a success more than I want boils. I love you more than ever, and your love and concern for me are too strong for the negativity one can get caught up in. Sweetheart, I adore you and I won't hurt you." Michael's skin was flawless and fortunately he was splendidly vain, so I was always telling him he would break out with big, red gonks if he ingested too much evil poison (one of my ploys to keep him straight). In his inimitable fashion, he was reassuring me he would take care of himself, and I prayed to the saints, holy lady Amal three times, Mother Mary and her beloved son Jesus that he would.

CHAPTER THREE

January 24—*Michael's birthday and our first anniversary! I'm so in love it's desperate. I hope we can stick it out during all these separations. Sometimes I get a sick feeling in my tummy. Fear? Anxiety? Realizations? I have got to try to understand the boy. It worries me so, and it's bad for me to worry. It's just as bad for my soul as what he's doing is for his soul. God bless me. God bless him, God bless us. Karma, karma, it's all karmic; past lives reuniting us to completion. Oh help.*

Speaking of past lives, Led Zeppelin sizzled into town and my dear, old friend Robert Plant sent a limousine to Bleecker Street so I could enjoy their show at Nassau Coliseum in style. They splintered the place as usual and afterwards took me to a dastardly bash, way out of town at a creepy old guy's house in the sticks. There was no lighting, no refreshments, no ambiance, and very few party-goers in attendance, and I was confused until it dawned on me that the grotesque old fellow was a notorious, drug-scum-dealing dog. Rod Stewart was there in one of the dingy, darkened rooms, Mick Jagger was hovering. Keith Richards loomed around in the gloom like a stormcloud warning. I sat on Robert's lap, trying to make small talk with Jimmy Page's momentary doll, while these rock giants paid respectful, dutiful homage to this bald troll.

Mr. Page had undergone several transformations since he tossed his naughty whips into the trash for my blushing benefit so long ago. I still had chaotic, tangled feelings about my ex–shame-flame. The gooey soft spot I had for him remained but was slowly eroding. It scared me to think that he had never been who he seemed to be. What was lurking under those ebony ringlets and cherubic petal face? His beauty was even fading. Going, going . . . He told a girlfriend of mine that the idea of blood mixed with semen excited him. She didn't spend the night. Poor old Bonzo was always stoned-out drunk morose. He even slugged my friend Michele Myer in the jaw for absolutely no reason and got himself kicked out of the Rainbow Bar and Grill, his Hollywood home away from home. It was sad, sad, sad. When Zeppelin went on the road, it was as if they had been given permission to pillage, rampage, cut loose, and poke holes into millions of eardrums with that unprecedented, massive chunk of top-heavy metal. But when I tried to picture them at home in front of a glowing fire, sipping a nice cup of tea with their wives, the image was hard to conjure up. Robert was still majestic, John Paul Jones, silently enigmatic, but their glory days were crunching, blaring, grinding gradually to a halt.

Even though I had just danced with the demonic Led Zeppelin darlings and decided to stay away from rock madness, I dolled up my skinny self a few days later and went to an Alice Cooper show at Madison Square Garden to revel with my old friends in their success. Alice, the prototype for several copycat ghoul rockers, had opened for the GTO's at the Shrine back in '68, and seven years later he was being called a legend already. Pretty extreme. It shows you how rocky the rock world had become. We were having a grand old time backstage after the show, and I was feeling vivacious and sparkly when Bebe Buell strutted by, took in the scene and exclaimed, "Miss Pamela! You look so *good*! I hope *I* look as good as *you* do when I get to be *your* age!!" I was twenty-six and she was twenty-three. There was a stunned hush and Neal Smith, Alice's tall, blond drummer admonished her tacky rudeness, which she, of course, pretended to know nothing about. "Did I *say* something? What did I *say*?" Her eyes were glittering fraud. Bebe had been Jimmy Page's concubine after appearing as a *Playboy* Playmate, and I considered her to be one of the new breed of groupies who created a nasty disturbance just to be noticed. I thought it was sad that you couldn't trust the new groupie girls. There was no camaraderie, no girlfriend affection: It was every bitch for herself. Bebe later lived with Todd Rundgren and had several notorious flings with people like Elvis Costello and Stiv Bators. We get along fine today. Why not? You have to let go of old crap, or it will become a layer of slimy scum blocking your vision.

II

My most major ex, Don Johnson, and the girl who pulverized my heart harder than anyone else ever had came to stay with me for a couple of weeks on Bleecker Street, and luckily my United roommate was up in the friendly skies somewhere. They slept in her bed, just outside my loft room, and every night I had to put a pillow over my head because their thrilling goings-on made me miss Michael so-ooooo much. Melanie Griffith was still only seventeen years old, but— thank God—had ceased to be a nubile thorn in my side. She was in New York doing publicity for her early spate of films, in which she played the innocent, Lolita-like danger-angel, torturing the likes of Gene Hackman and Paul Newman with those long legs and turned-up nose full of freckles. She and I shopped up the Village, and every time I oohed over something, she ran in and bought it for me. The only way I found to smoosh her generous nature was to keep quiet, but she must have seen the covetous shimmer in my eyes when I spotted some dangly heart earrings. As I took out the groceries to prepare the evening wad of vegetables, I found the heart-shaped sparklers nestled in the broccoli florets.

May 6—Feeling very warm and content, having just come back from the Russian Tea Room with Melanie, also a hoity-toit club where she's a member. We talked our buns off and danced and had a great time. I feel very sisterly toward her—almost motherly. She and Don are having problems, and I hope they'll make it. It's amazing how things turn out. Life is such a learning experience, I feel so opened up and twinkling, even though we found an actual rat in the living room today. D.J. came to the rescue.

Donnie chased the rodent around, swinging a curtain rod while Melanie and I stood on various pieces of furniture, squealing like we were in a nincompoop cartoon. We begged him not to flatten the frightened creature, and he finally coaxed it into a brown paper bag and hurled it out the window, back onto the scummy streets of Manhattan from whence it came.

Hard as it was to be strict with the Johnsons around, due to their lust for life and everything in it, I started a severe health regimen, which severely limited my evening fun options. Who wants to go out to dinner and watch someone starve? I even had to give up the Pink Teacup, the cool, old soul food joint directly next door to the bakery under my pad. The greasy odor of fried chicken livers and scrambled eggs with onions wafted through my window while I crunched granola, wheat germ, and lecithin with raw milk. I dropped alcohol, gave up caffeine, used pure maple syrup instead of sugar in my herb tea (the only thing that has stuck, except now I use it in my coffee), and took all the fat out of my extremely boring diet. I had stopped red meat three years earlier with Donnie at the first Hollywood health food restaurant, Help, and now added dairy products to the growing list of no-nos. The big jolt of excitement came when once a week I went down to Christopher Street to cheat heavy with a cone of goat milk ice cream. Whoopee. I lost many, many pounds and paid a solemn nutritionist a hefty hunk of my soap salary to deprive me of the yummy things in life. At least I was skinny and looked good. It didn't seem to make much difference. On top of Bebe Buell's wide-eyed backstage comment, I got one more gigantic rusty nail slammed into my jumbled self-esteem. One rainy afternoon, after my two measly lines had been severed from the student lounge scene, I was fired from *Search for Tomorrow.*

The soft-eyed producer, Bernie Sofronski, who is now married to Susan (Partridge) Dey, could hardly look at me as he explained how I had been replaced by a big, clean-looking blond girl who understood the character better than I did. He said my heart wasn't in it and I didn't trust my own talent. Truer words had never been spoken. They had actually been holding auditions for the new Amy right in my face, and I hadn't noticed. "Does the rest of the cast know?" my ego bawled at him when reality sunk in. Yes, Bernie said, they had even participated in the auditions. "I told them they couldn't tell you," he wimped at me, looking down at a pile of dumb, corny *Search* scripts. I was mortified. Sobbing silently, I wished I could sink through the floor and wind up on Mr. Toad's Wild Ride in Fantasyland. In the middle of John Wayne's star on Hollywood Boulevard. On the dance floor at the Whisky a Go Go, whirling my brains out. Anywhere but this puny, stuffy office on 57th Street in New York City.

When I came out of the office, my costars—Morgan, Michael, and John—were standing sheepishly in the hallway, waiting it out. I felt like I was burning at the stake while they hugged me, making me feel better and much worse all at once. The actor's ego is the most fragile thing on the planet, and they understood all too well how dejected, rejected, and deflated I felt. They took me back to the Russian Tea Room, where I trampled on my health regimen with three White Russians and two black ones. While my acting mates patted on me, I tried to eat a gushing, buttery chicken Kiev, but my unsuspecting tummy retaliated, and the tempting morsel was whisked away. "This is probably the best thing that ever happened to you," Michael Nouri stated encouragingly. "Who needs an idiotic soap opera? You'll get back to Hollywood and star in a Scorsese movie." And hogs will dance in heaven, right, pal? I called my weirdo acting coach Bill Hickey, and he assured me I was too good for the show anyway, and with my squashed ego semi-assuaged, I packed up all my stuff, grabbed Debbie and a guy from acting class, Joe Hardin, to help with the driving, got a spanking-new, drive-away Cadillac and headed west. Don and Melanie helped load up the car and stood at the window above the French bakery, waving as I started the three-thousand-mile trek back to my darling Michael.

III

After a four-day, whirlwind drivathon, with only one major stop to swoon over the glory of the Grand Canyon, I got back just in time. Michael had been getting used to living the bachelor life, thriving on it, basking in it, and I felt like a cowgirl, inept with a lasso as I tried to corral him back into my devoted, adoring heart.

June 1, 1975—*It was real weird the first couple of days home, uncomfortable even. He's just so used to being on his own—I felt like an intruder, but I'm working on it. I see no signs of drugs, but a few mumblings here and there tell me he's been indulging during my absence. He's kind of into himself and withdrawn—even from me. We found a pad today, a pink and green old Hollywood bungalow right above Franklin Avenue on El Cerrito Place. It's so lovely, lots of bamboo, plants, and sunshine, lots of cooking in my big yellow kitchen.*

The other side of the perfection surfaced in the diary a few weeks later:

July 28—*I really wish at times that I was with a normal-formal guy and didn't have to worry about competing with music and drugs. I don't mean to sound negative, because everything is coming along beautifully. Michael's new band, Detective, has just signed to Swan Song. I always knew we had a link with Peter Grant and the lads, for better or for worse. But even if it's looking real good now, I know that Led Zeppelin are a hazard in my life.*

Detective—the new HEAVY, cranking band Michael put together—signed on to Zeppelin's exciting label Swan Song and started
tons of rehearsals for the first record. The band consisted of Michael
singing lead; the tall, lanky pouf-haired Michael Monarch, ex-Step-
penwolf, on lead guitar; Jon Hyde, a true redheaded health freak
with pale, white porcelainlike skin, on drums; Tony Kaye, the elegant
ex-keyboardist from Yes, on piano; and a soul-brother bass player,
Bobby Pickett.

The Zeppelin liaison was a mixed blessing in disguise. I was in
Hades-torment, knowing their wretched excess would tempt my fiancé into his usual oblivion, but being signed onto the new label
Zep had conjured up with Atlantic Records was extremely presti-
gious as well as frighteningly hip. I would have to grin and bite it.

Detective had to work a lot with the VP of Swan Song, a young
loooong-haired, brainiac hipster, Danny Goldberg, who turned out
to be a true long-lasting friend and an instant ally for me. Once a
full junkie, Danny had reformed, gotten sober, and was attending
the same spiritual Hilda meetings in New York where I had found
such helpful solace. I now had one more hip straight person to add
to that short list that included Frank Zappa and Woody Allen. "Danny
doesn't get high and he's cool," I announced with semi-regularity,
but even though Michael adored Danny, he kept on going right down
that familiar path of disrepute.

One evening Jimmy Page called to say he would like to come by
and meet the whole lineup, and while Michael rounded up the mad-
men, I made impromptu hors d'oeuvres to pass around while they
brainstormed about Detective's future in the limelight. Jimmy was
in one of his humble, gallant moods and asked the band to open for
Zeppelin on their next U.S. tour. He went so far as to announce his
intention to produce the Detective record himself! Many cocktails
were consumed and toasts made, laughter and euphoria abounded.
Jimmy still called me "Miss P." and kept giving me warm, memory-
laden glances, which made me feel good. It has always been important
for me to remain friends with my ex-loves. Why slather so much
time, attention, and energy on someone only to have them disappear
into the void with bad feelings?

Zeppelin had moved into Malibu Colony planning to rehearse for
their tour in Los Angeles and, as usual, the town was buzzing. A big
meeting was set up for Detective to sign the Swan Song contracts,
but at the last minute it appeared the contracts had been slightly
rearranged by Zeppelin's bizarre lawyer Steve Weiss. The champagne

got warm while my Michael and Michael Monarch had the contracts surreptitiously checked out across town. I sat on the humongous lap of Peter Grant, cajoling, cavorting, and attempting to keep his mind off the fact that the two Michaels were exceedingly late for the major moment. Even Danny Goldberg started getting grim. I was the sole entertainment while time ticked, t-i-c-k-e-d slowly by. Steve Weiss kept drunkenly checking his Rolex, and I was wearing see-through thin when the Michaels finally burst into the room with pens poised. Michael told me later that he would have signed the back of Peter Grant's bald head to get his green card. "If somebody asks what musical direction Detective is taking," Michael said ruefully, "I'll tell them our only direction is straight to the bank. This is green-card rock and roll at its finest." When it was all over, I was so relieved I almost sobbed when I could alight from the lap of the world's most gargantuan and influential rock-and-roll manager.

Michele Myer booked the Starwood, the lowdown club of the decade, and Detective decided to put on a show for their enigmatic, soon-to-be-legendary bosses. The guest list was ours, because dear old Mack truck Shelly was in charge, so the place was teeming with rock puppies ready to ravage. I took turns petting Michael backstage and casually lounging in the front corner booth with Jimmy Page, Peter Grant, and road manager Richard Cole, trying to hide my jitters with lots of ha-has and anecdotes about the good ol' days back in '69. Jimmy didn't have much to say and kept slipping off into a little nap. Hmm. All the hipsters downstairs kept peering up at the booth that housed the holy, but a soiled version of Mr. Clean stood guard in front of the red velvet rope, so there was no chance of intruding worshipers. I once saw Richard Cole kick a fan's teeth right out of his head at the Rainbow Bar and Grill for approaching Robert Plant from behind. The bicuspids and molars flew through the squalid air, but the person removed from the premises was the worshiping intruder, and I am not kidding.

There was some trouble with the soundboard at the Starwood that night, and Peter alternated between nudging Sleeping Beauty and checking his gigantic gold watch, which resembled a small grandfather clock. I happened to be backstage when that most wondrous and protective of all roadies, Mr. Cole, came to warn the band not to ask Jimmy to jam because he was "very sleepy" tonight. Uh-huh. Okay, Richard, no problem. I sat between Jimmy nodding and Peter nudging, watching my darling husband attempt to be heard, trapped within the screeching wall of noise. Take out your Detective badge, honey, and arrest those fuckers! After a few numbers, Jimmy nodded his approval and staggered on to smaller and worse things, with Peter assisting his mega-mega-megastar past the velvet rope and into the Hollywood night.

Even if Michael felt like he was selling out for various shades of green, excitement was still high, but a few weeks later Robert's five-year-old boy Karak died of some mysterious intestinal disorder before Robert could even get to him, which threw the whole Zeppelin camp into a nightmare of despair. Shortly after Robert returned to England, he drove his car into a ditch and had to have his leg rebuilt. Eerie whispers about their much-blabbed-about-but-never-proven pact with the devil started to surface again, while the other three members holed up in the exclusive Colony in separate seaside homes. One night after Michael talked to Jimmy on the phone, I asked how old J.P. was holding up, and the Des Barres wit shimmered through the seemingly hopeless situation, "I'm sure someone's on either side of him, taking care of that," he snickered forlornly. Shaking his head, he stared out into space where question marks bobbed up and down. "He just asked me not to give John Paul Jones his phone number."

Detective rehearsals completed, the band chomping to get into the studio, the old rock-and-roll waiting game continued. Jimmy became unreachable, and Peter Grant kept putting Michael off, telling him Jimmy was "preparing" for the project. We had gotten gloriously chummy with Danny Goldberg, but even he was kept in the dark. As the days went on and on, Michael exuded a gloom that descended over the bamboo, plants, and sunshine that left me weak in the thighs. Detective needed Jimmy Page to produce the record because of the high-impact jolt of publicity that would attend the proceedings, besides the fact that Jimmy "understood" the music, having been pretty much the originator of the heaviest of all metal. How could I help my darling fill his empty waiting days? I tittered around him, full of ideas, attempting to make him happy about being alive even though he was trapped in rock-and-roll limbo. I overcompensated with a smiley-smile until my face cracked, empathized and sympathized until I became invisible.

He was up all night, passed out 'til noon, and after plotting all kinds of hopeful, hypeful clichés, aching to rouse him from that blue, blue mood where thunder cracked and it stormed all the time, I tiptoed into the bedroom with a stunning plate of eggs. "Oh, God," he moaned, seeing me there like Tinker Bell in an apron. "It's not worth it, honey, it's just not worth it." He rolled over and faced the wall. Insomnia was eating his brain stem. Platitudes poured forth from me like sickly sweet sap from a Vermont maple: "Everything will be okay, sweetheart!" "It all happens for a reason!" "Something better will come along!" "Have faith, Michael, trust in your higher self!" "Let's go to Disneyland, and everything will be just fine!" He peered out from his mourning place, wanting to yank out my tongue, but suffering had worn him down. He snapped like a vicious turtle instead, so I suffered the slings and arrows of his outrageous misfortune, bobbing and weaving, hoping to escape from his fancy English boarding school, finely honed verbal onslaught. Pamela Miller, human dartboard. "You'll never come close to understanding what goes on in my mad head," he told me, and it hurt to be left out of his turmoil, but I understood that he had to take it out on someone, and I knew that he loved me, so I kept on doting, catering, and smothering him with cupid's bazookas until the storm was over. His pain was louder than mine, so it always took precedence—but I knew love would prevail, and I could deal with anything as long as I had my heart safely entwined in his.

More than two months passed before Michael was finally summoned to Malibu by Peter Grant. We allowed ourselves to get edgily excited, hoping the ambiguous Mr. Page was ready to produce the Detective record. Michael had arrived home one morning at 3 A.M., having stayed too long at some drug geek's house in Laurel Canyon, bombed and complaining that he needed one more song for the album. I had been so relieved to see him but pissed off at the same time, so scrawled out a song called "Recognition" in about ten minutes, just to prove it could be done. Michael loved the lyrics and had them in his pocket when he leapt confidently into the Zeppelin limo.

As I paced around praying the meeting was going well, day turned to night and night to day again. It was the first of uncountable nights I would spend alone while my husband was out rampaging through town. The phone sat mute. He didn't even call. Was he celebrating without me? Snorting reams of coke? Swallowing handfuls of various multicolored capsules? Swigging Jack straight out of the bottle? The fear inside me was alive. I could see his liver disintegrating, his heart stopping, *ka-bump, ka——bump, ka—* The sun was fully up when he staggered in, and in one instant I knew all was not right with the world. His eyes spun black in their deep sockets, he twitched, he sniffled, he looked crazed-high, but I was afraid to confront him because the wacked-out look on his face broadcasted bad news. Before he crashed out for the next day and a half, he told me how a forlorn Peter sat him down, pointed to Jimmy, who was nodding out in a corner, and told him Pagey wasn't able to produce the record because of his heroin problem. Poor Jimmy, poor Peter, poor Michael. Poor ME!!! When Michael came out of his self-induced stupor twenty hours later, I lured him back to the world with Nutty Orange Marmalade Chicken and a fabulously healthy salad topped with toasted sunflower seeds and golden raisins. He washed it down with half a dozen bottles of Chablis.

IV

With Mr. Page backing out of the picture for heart-cracking personal reasons, Danny finally found a replacement to produce the Detective project. Since the new producer's first name was also Jimmy, when the album came out everybody thought it was Mr. Pagey being cagey, and Michael let them think what they wanted.

Detective's sound was big and bold, thunderous and blatant. Michael wrote the lyrics, guitarist Michael Monarch wrote the screaming licks that strained to be melodies. The deafening volume hurt your ears real good, but Michael's arteries popped halfway out of his throat, smarting to be heard. He woed to me that he felt like a heavy metal puppet in a hellhound lip-sync parade. The greedy bastards. It's a holy roller miracle he doesn't have to wear double hearing aids like Pete Townshend.

Detective was on the final edge of megaton metal and had a raucous, loyal following; local gigs were packed full of raving metal dogs and spandex-clad girls with ratted, dyed black hair who gazed up at Michael wantonly, tongues lolling. Half-disrobed tarty babes hit on him as if I were invisible— "What are you doing later, Michael? Want to get together?" He acted as if he had never seen the teased beauties before, brushing them aside like annoying wasps. I was always with my man, hanging on tight, my eyes blazing at those naughty girls with lingering glances. I even elbowed one of the most brazen right in her billowing mammaries, but as far as I could tell, Michael didn't even notice these rampant females, and I believed he was devoted to me, body and soul, so when Detective played San Francisco, that loopy city where everybody seemed anesthetized, I stayed home to paint the kitchen pink.

A few days later I went out to get the mail, and there was a letter addressed to Michael that the record company had kindly forwarded to El Cerrito Place. I examined the obvious girly handwriting with big, fat, loopy vowels, and before I could even hand it over to Michael he grabbed it and dashed down the back stairs. My heart screamed. I stood there, stuck in the kitchen, staring at the dirty dishes until he reappeared, musing out loud, "Isn't that odd, the envelope was empty." Mr. Innocence shrugged, and I pushed the rising rancor deep down inside and tamped it flat. I studied his face for a fib and couldn't admit I saw one.

We were a unit. Joined at the hip. Hand in glove. Two hearts beating as one, forevermore. I was sewn into his flesh like a brand-new body part, a human IV giving him a fresh, new, squeaky-clean lease on life. My entire well-being was reliant on the look in his eyes.

I had finally started to face the only time bomb that stood between us: his addiction, which of course had a long, warped stem leading back to his alien childhood. But what could I do about it? Begging and pleading only drove him out of the house, so I tried to hold my nagging tongue while he told me disconcerting tales of boy-woe like he was reciting the alphabet. One Christmas he had been left alone in a crummy hotel room the entire day, and when his parents finally returned, his mom bitterly cut apart her gift to Philip, a carton of cigarettes, with a pair of tiny nail scissors and threw the little pieces in his face, cursing him long and hard. Seven-year-old Michael got nothing. It was rare that his parents were together, and a lot of nights the young Michael slept next to Irene while she frolicked with black jazz musicians, the smell of hash filling the small flat as he tried in vain to fall asleep. On El Cerrito Place he still had insane bouts with the relentless monster insomnia, which I tried to tackle with massage, herbs, spiritual advice, and a lot of pleading to Jesus for some blessed zzz's for my man.

V

Despite my over-devotion to Michael, I stayed close with my parents, being their adored only child, and watching my daddy fall prisoner to his failing lungs was a poison dart in my already lacerated side. Due to a constant, lung-chewing cough diagnosed as black lung from slaving in the Kentucky coal mines, Daddy had to quit his job. He still drank eight or ten beers a day and played poker with his cronies but was otherwise a frustrated, bottled-up he-man with no-where to flaunt his fading energy. He kept coming up with different projects that filled the house, the first of which was a poster of a lovely lake and mountain scene that took up an entire wall. He got dressed in his finest bell-bottomed leisure suit and made Mom take stacks of Polaroids of him with his fishing rod in the backyard until they got the right size photo so he could glue himself onto the massive mural. Whenever anybody came to visit, he would make them study the wall scene until they spotted him sitting on a log, holding his fishing rod over the lake. He roared with laughter every single time, like it was the most clever idea ever dreamed up. Eventually he got a gigantic replica kit of his navy ship that was blown in half during a battle in World War II and spent a couple of years painstakingly putting it together, even though his hands were being wickedly assaulted by arthritis. It was a grand day when he finally attached it to the wall-lake where it floated for a dozen years without being bombed.

The first Detective record sold enough copies that Swan Song requested another. This one would be produced by a brilliant but stoned-out young British producer, Andy Johns. Why did everyone who worked with Michael have to be so drug oriented? In between taking care of my increasingly bombed fiancé and trying to help out my parents, I decided to be brave and slog back into the acting world. I had already ditched Freda Granite, signing with a family agency called Barskin, and the first job I went out for I snagged; the part of a hippie girl called Apple on a local soap. In 1977 hippies existed only on faraway farfetched farms, but I was playing one right here in Hollywood! I wore long shapeless dresses and acted up a blizzard with a Charles Manson—type guy who wore a pasted-on beard. He was trying to get a tender, nubile Genie Francis to join his mind-controlling commune, and Lady Apple was caught in the middle. Luke eventually came to Laura's rescue, and all was well at *General Hospital*. They seemed to love my work and hinted about a regular spot on the soap, but it never manifested. I did a day's shoot on a lifelike half-hour show called *Emergency!*, where I got to languish in a freezing cold hot tub in a skimpy bathing suit, screaming, yelling, and hollering to save my goose-bumped skin. I forget why I couldn't just climb out of the tub, but I think it had something to do with a stunt dog and a chewed-up live wire.

My bizzy-dizzy schedule got crazier because our lard-ass landlord liked the way we fixed up our beautiful bungalow and wanted to move in himself, so I had to tromp all over Hollywood, looking for an appropriate pad in our up-and-down, hand-to-mouth price range. I found a renovated, revised, slick apartment off Fountain Avenue, and after a big yard sale in which we sold all of our cool bamboo, antique lamps, and forties collectibles, Michael and I moved in with a bunch of new modern crap, thinking we would be a couple of contemporary, up-to-the-minute urbanites. Leaving all taste behind, we shopped for massive, tweedy "playpen" couches, Lucite-and-glass end tables, those god-awful chrome lamps that bend all over the place, and large, arty, modern prints in silver and gold frames. I don't know what got into me.

Our moderne pad became a second home to Danny Goldberg, who had gotten fed up with the unprofessional and chaotic Zeppelin regime and left his difficult position as Swan Song VP. The three of us got ascloseasthis, and on those long nights when Michael got lost Danny became a spiritual partner, consoling me, praying with me, and holding my hand. He had recently started managing a cosmo-girl-singer called Mirabai who trilled nirvanic, chanting melodies for Hilda at those rally-type spiritual meetings in New York. She had just surged out on her own in hopes of spreading the message to the masses but wound up in the arms of Michael's newest wunderkind producer, Andy Johns, having scary sex and reeling around on large quantities of various illegal substances. It was as if she was trying to do all kinds of really gross earthly things to make up for the lost time she had spent on the heavenly plane. She and I had become sisterlike, so when she tossed Danny and me to the winds like worn-out holy mantras, our hearts splintered together, and we had many mutual commiseration sessions.

I continued taking classes to perfect my art. I scrubbed disgusting floors and removed globs of germy gum in exchange for private lessons with some nobody slob who couldn't seem to see my brilliance. The pompous, smelly underdog coach had me stifled in the pit of Pinter and wimping around in *The Seagull* until the sweaty afternoon when I finally threw down my stubby broom and stalked out, my heart as dry as a sun-bleached bone. He told me I would *never* make it as a true ACTRESS. Just like he never made it as a true ACTOR. Ha ha ha. Sob sob sob. I wept openly in the hard daylight on the corner of Spaulding and Sunset until some nice old lady hobbled by and tried to comfort me. I got into my VW and drove back home to the playpen couches and god-awful lamps that bend all over the place.

VI

Oh, my Hero in Heaven, was housekeeping my destiny? Could a normal-formal nine-to-five existence lie ahead? Despite the fact I had my stoned-out rock-and-roll man and a burgeoning acting career, I started a bad slide into semi-normalcy. I wanted to be a creative force, let my talent pour forth, but I was living half of Michael's life for him, which left only half for me. Since the wild boy never learned to drive in England, I did all the driving in L.A., taking him to meetings, rehearsals, gigs. I took care of our checking account and paid the bills. I cleaned the house, bought the food and cooked it— even lamb chops with mint sauce, though I didn't believe in eating babies and hadn't had a bite of meat in five years. (When I was a little girl, I always asked my mom if what was on my plate was a baby or a grown-up. But now I was a devoted wife-to-be, so I blessed the little baa-baas and plopped them in the pan.) I was in love and felt no resentments whatsoever. It just seemed natural—my obligation as a female to do, *do,* DO it all for my man.

It was strange and impossible for the women of my generation to figure out our place within the confines of a romantic relationship. My mom gave up any creative aspirations she had to take care of my daddy because she believed she had no other choice. (She did work before they were married, however.) It was the way of the world, the American Way. In the sixties the feminist movement shoved choice down our delicate throats, and a girl with any brains at all was forced to ponder the many frightening new potential options. I had scary visions of defiant, liberated women marching en masse down the street, while I watched my sweet mom pressing Daddy's Budweiser work shirts, little drops of sweat forming on her furrowed brow. To give her credit, as soon as polyester hit the market, Margaret Ruth Hayes Miller threw away the ironing board in a liberating act of protest, which forced Daddy to get into leisure suits in a big way.

I just kept doing what I thought was expected of me. My much desired role of good little wifey included waving good-bye on nights when Michael went out to rip up the town. With the TV spewing, I lay in bed affirming that his addiction would cease, but it was desperation affirmation, out of control, adverse hope in vain. Not calm, cool, and collected prayer but an emotional, jagged fear of his habit and my own cold-sweat response. Staying home was a form of masochism because I knew he would take a ton of drugs when I wasn't around, but subconsciously I couldn't bear to see him squash and squelch himself due to my peering, peeking oppressive presence. Very kinky, indeed. Most peculiar, mama.

I wrote sporadically in my journal, attempting to sort it all out:

April 8—*Michael is asleep next to me, having spent until noon with Rod Stewart. We went out to a Todd Rundgren party, and I see why I don't miss going out. Yuck! Everyone except Todd around was snorting coke . . . SO fashionable, not my idea of a good time. I came home by myself.*

April 15—*Just finished painting my nails, all alone. Michael is out seeing Iggy Pop. Went to see Dolly Parton at the Roxy last night and met David Bowie. So what. I still can't get into being out and about. Very odd considering that's just about all I used to do. I'm more comfortable with my cats. I'm an old woman, I guess.*

June 4—*New York. Do I have reason to worry or what? I think I'm being paranoid, and then I get here to see Detective play and it's just as crazed as I imagined. I really asked for this one—I pleaded with the Gods for a pop star, and here I am, knee-deep at almost thirty. Everyone is so stoned, and the scene is as small as a pinhead, but I have to realize it's Michael's career. He loves the nightlife and clubs, always seeks a reaction, thriving on feedback. God, he's as insecure as I am.*

I spent so many nights alone in our unrumpled bed that I came to expect lots of long, sad, stretched-out days while Michael recovered from his mystery dawn-busters. I started writing sobby songs about the sorrows of solitude. In fact I called one of the Tammy Wynette tear-drippers "Sleeping Alone":

She wakes up every hour
And looks at the clock by the bed
She reaches out and touches
The pillow where her man lays his head

He's been out all night
And the sun has been shining since the dawn
Thank God the night is over
'Cause nothing's worse than sleeping alone

The sun usually starts shining at dawn, doesn't it?

CHAPTER FOUR

I

At least Michael's revels were bringing in some money—
enough so we could make a pilgrimage/vacation to Las
Vegas to see the treasured, obese King at the Inter-
national Hilton. We checked into a grand, tacky suite
with a bed the size of Nebraska, ate high on the turkey,
lost twenty dollars playing blackjack—it was Splurge
City! There were concessions all over the lobby overflowing with
gaudy Elvis trinkets: cheap, highly flammable scarves, big, fake rings,
TCB necklaces, color shots of the sweaty King spreading his white
sequined tent wide like tarnished angel's wings. The nasty, smirk-
lipped bad boy with black penciled eyebrows had been swallowed
up in rolls of blubber and acres of polyester, but we loved him still.
We love you, Elvis, oh yes we do, we couldn't love anyone as much
as you.

The book by his Judas bodyguards had just hit the stands, and
Michael and I lay in our mammoth bed, staring at the ceiling, knowing
Elvis was twenty floors above us doing unmentionable things. We
could just picture him up there, contemplating his vast array of
"medication," deciding which combo of pills would do the trick tonight. Did he really inject himself in the groin with Dilaudid? We
decked out hard, cruised through the cacophonous gambling din,
and handed our tickets to the smug, smarmy seating dude, who
promptly sat us in the back row. Wait a minute! Unfair! Michael
leaned over to me and whispered, "Maybe I should give him a
twenty?" We were sickeningly naive about Vegas slim-slam protocol,

I suppose. "Do you think it might help?" I whispered back. It did. The creep moved us halfway down, giving us an oily smirk. As we sat through a macho, rotten-mouthed comedian, Michael leaned toward me again. "If I had given him twenty more, we'd be in the orchestra pit!" The lights dimmed and rose—Elvis in front of us! A lot of Elvis in front of us. But the voice had never been better. Enthralled speechless, we grabbed each other's hands, ecstatic. We were right in the middle of one of our forevermoments, and we knew it. Elvis rubbed off layers of sweat, tossed the sopping scarves to beehived middle-agers, but even though I reached, I wasn't close enough to rejoice in the King's secretions. As he left the stage to don yet another sparkling tent, Michael laughed, "If I had given that bum a fifty, we'd be swinging on Elvis's TCB pendant!"

When we arrived back home from the neon desert, sated and dizzy with King-itis, I found potential good news in the mailbox. One of the acting photos I sent out landed on the desk of a corny ex-TV actor, and he wanted me to call him right away! He seemed to take a serious shine to me after our first hour-long meeting at the house of his famous girlfriend, and I had cloud-capped Hollywood hopes.

In his high-pitched, squealy voice, he told me I "had something," he was going to "discover" me, and give me a "coming-out" party on a fancy yacht, but alas, he turned out to be a pig with a capital *P.* I had had a few run-ins with power-mad, horny would-be movie moguls, but this one took the fucking cake. He took me to an intimate dinner with one of his once-upon-a-time-star pals, had professional shots done for me by an old-timey photog who raved about my presence in front of the camera and sat with me for hours promising to make me famous. My already weak self-esteem had been flattened by the nobody slob acting coach, so my naive and humbled ego was assuaged by these flattering tidbits.

One lovely afternoon the actor and I were brainstorming about my important career when his girlfriend's teen movie idol son walked through the room and spotted me. I had met him a couple of times, so I said hello and he gave me a very curious look, complete with warning signal, like "What the fuck are *you* doing here? *Watch out.*" My blundering heart turned over and sure enough, that very day after asking what I was going to do for him in return for his generous promotional favors, the actor gave me the single most putrid line ever uttered by someone with a penis: "A man has needs." He wanted sex. He wanted head. He wanted a hand job in return for making me a star.

I saw the party yacht sailing off into the sunset as I stumbled out of the clean-cut Beverly Hills house with white shutters like on *The Partridge Family*. I had even asked the eager has-been, "But what about your girlfriend?," and he shook his head and said again, "She's out of town right now and, honey, *a man has needs.*" I didn't have enough balls (fallopian tubes?) to tell him what I thought that day, but I would certainly love to bump into him right now. Yes, indeed. I wish I could divulge the name of the cheesy Hollywood throwback, but he's the type who would probably sue me for telling the truth.

II

Needless to say this typical, pathetic Hollywood incident made me question just about everything I was doing and what it all meant. Michael was enraged and wanted to have one of his menacing roadies do some serious harm to the actor's needy male area, which didn't happen but made me feel loved. I took stock of myself every once in a while, and since I was pushing thirty and still found myself in these questionable situations, it was time for a serious review:

The statistics are as follows—I'm five feet three and a half inches tall, but I always write five feet four inches on my acting résumés, which I send out constantly despite my insecurity problems. I fluctuate between 110 and 117 pounds. I'm 114 right now, which is a bit too heavy, so I go to the Beverly Hills Health Club for toning up the tummy. I have bluish eyes—not extremely blue so that people comment on them very often—they are also pretty small and nearsighted, and I have a turned-up nose that I got from my mom and a full, pretty mouth that I got from Daddy. It all fits well together, but I've always had a lousy complexion, small tits as well, which agonized me in teen years. I live with a stunning, talented, beautiful, and crazy man, whom I met three and a half years ago, and we plan on getting married this year. We live right in the heart of Hollywood in a totally gay building. He sings rock and roll, and I call myself an actress. I'm a lazy person most of the time, and I have silly, negative thoughts even though I'm aware how destructive they can be. I'm also sickeningly naive. My career has flopped out, so at times my confidence aches, but I get up and do it anyway. I get migraine headaches for an unknown reason, but my health is fine otherwise. I haven't eaten meat in over five years. I'm in the most professional acting workshop so far, and I pray they don't throw me out after I do my first scene on Tuesday. (See! My confidence is in agony!) I write songs—so far the only ones recorded have been on Detective's albums.

I read one or two books a week and relish it and someday want to write the story of my nutty life. I worry about Michael because he drinks so much and gets so manic and self-destructive—but I also know he's following the dots and I have no control.

I was wallowing in confusion and needed a spot of spirituality to jolt me out of the constant inner nattering that clogged up my head. So I got up real early one Sunday morning and drove our new '73 Toyota, bought with Michael's Detective money, up into the glorious hills of Ojai to hear Krishnamurti speak the solemn truth to a hushed pack of soul searchers. I listened so hard that my eardrums throbbed, still only grasping part of his profound life-altering message. He sat up on the platform, an eighty-year-old white-haired Indian man wearing some pretty classy duds—no orange robes for him, no cloud of camouflaging incense—and reminded us that "the speaker is only up on this platform for practical purposes," just so he could be seen and heard. He didn't consider himself above anybody. We were all one. Hmm. When he said, "The thinker *is* the thought," did he mean, we *are* what we think? Or we create the world around us and what happens to us by thinking certain thoughts? "The observer *is* the observed," he said. Did that mean we *are* what we see? We create what we see? Or we see what we *are* if we look real hard? I was a sincere seeker under the oak trees and wanted to transform myself instantaneously.

My heart was full of cosmic hope when Michael said he would go with me to see Krishnamurti the following weekend. I just knew that with his awesome brain power he would grasp the message totally and take the first joyous step on his spiritual path. We sat cross-legged in the beautiful oak grove together, blissing out, and after Krishnamurti's talk, consumed lots of brown rice and broccoli with other hungry, humble seekers in perfect tranquility. We bought tapes of the lectures and some deep inspirational books: *You Are the World, Think on These Things.*

The next night Michael went out to see Bad Company at the Forum and didn't come home for two days. I dried my puffy eyes and wrote another song about the pain of loving an escape artist.

He takes you to the edge
But he leaves you standing there
How can you follow a shadow
Through the exit door to nowhere?

I felt alone, I felt betrayed. I was so concerned about the rotting of Michael's liver, I never thought too much about other women, even though there was this one horrible, scrawny public-relations bitch who hung around, condescending to me like I was just another airy-fairy, girly-girl. She had short, manlike hair, paper-thin slit-lips, and—scariest to me—piles of cocaine. In my lowest white-powder nightmares I pictured Michael teetering, dancing gleefully in the darkness, with jibbering ghouls all around him, leading him to his final resting place, three sheets to the wind.

III

Screw the slit-lipped PR dog!! Glory of ultimate glories, I was finally going to get married! Michael's transatlantic divorce came through, and we started making wedding plans. My parents were relieved and ecstatic. Even though they had been supportive and loving, it had been hard for them to accept that their daughter was living openly in sin.

My daddy was on oxygen most of the time, and his weight kept climbing up and plunging down due to the monstrous selection of pills he had to drop all day long. My mom even had to set the alarm in the dead of night to slip him a couple of capsules. But despite his gnawing discomfort, he wanted to give me away on the big day. He rented a deluxe cream-colored tux with flared trousers and invited his best pal Ruben in from Mexico.

Nobody had the dough to toss a sock-'em-rock-'em wingding, so I asked my friend Catherine if we could do the deed in the glorious green of her Laurel Canyon backyard. As soon as she said yes, Mom started making her special teriyaki chicken wings for two-hundred freaks. My parents also bought the champagne and a vast array of fresh flowers that my dear friend Michele Myer picked up downtown at 4 A.M. Punch bowls, chairs, tables, and an actual bower to stand under during the ceremony were rented. Catherine recommended a Unitarian preacher that we hired for fifty bucks, and I rewrote the marriage dialogue to suit a modern couple. I kept "love and honor" but deleted the word "obey"—and no *man* and wife for us! The nerve! After looking at some artless new gowns, I came to my senses and found my wedding dress for six dollars at the Aardvark on Melrose Avenue, a little girl's antique communion frock from the twenties that I embellished with peach and ivory satin ribbons and tiny velvet flowers. I made my own veil, spending many hours winding ivory ribbons round and round the headpiece for a (Romeo and) Juliet effect, "The Wedding March" running round and round my love-soaked head. Here comes the bride, all dressed in white, here comes the groom. Here comes the groom. *Here comes the groom!* After the necessary nuptials, my darling groom would get his precious green card and wouldn't even have to take a ballpoint to Peter Grant's shiny pate.

I'm getting married in the morning, ding-dong the bells are going to chime! The Moment was set for 1 P.M. and everybody had arrived all dressed up and were already stuffing their faces full of chicken wings and tricolor health dip, downing the potent punch I had concocted. Peach-colored crepe paper fluttered in the breeze, aunties and uncles decked out in polyester mingled with Misses Mercy and Sparkie in full-throttle GTO regalia, Zappa children were everywhere, cameras were poised, Tony Kaye sat by the record player, waiting to start "The Wedding March," the odd-duck, rail-thin minister wandered around under the bower studying the new script, even the lowbrow public-relations girl had the nerve to show up, looking uncannily like Scrooge McDuck in her ill-fitting white suit. An astounding bouquet of white roses arrived with a sweet telegram from Percy, Pagey, Bonzo, and John Paul Jones, and everyone was impressed. Several members of local poufy-haired rock bands admired the bride-to-be, who was smiling wide on the outside.

But where was the groom? Bobby Pickett, the bass player who had thrown Michael's bachelor party the night before, was there already, looking slightly chagrined. I looked pointedly at him, but he just shrugged with wide, questioning eyes. My daddy was resting in a fold-up chair, taking a few quick whiffs of oxygen for his short walk down the aisle. Mom, of course, was looking at me, her face full of loving mom-concern because she read me just like a book and never missed a page, to quote my old friend Gram Parsons.

I was coming to the conclusion that Michael's feet had frozen solid, when here he came up the steps, looking sheepish in the fancy ivory suit he bought from our chic hairdresser, Peter Vizer. No sleep had come between Michael and his revelry; bloodshot bourbon eyes betrayed his last all-night bender as a single man, but I was too relieved to let it bust the major moment. Before he could even adjust to Catherine's decked-out backyard and all the dolled-up wedding guests, Michael Philip Des Barres was standing in front of the zany preacher and saying "I do." Daddy had walked me proudly down the imaginary aisle while a scratchy, ancient rendition of "The Wedding

March" trumpeted from Catherine's bedroom window and I stood next to my unwieldy Prince Charming, trying to catch up with my love-scorched heart, which was beating a thousand miles a minute. Michael's hand trembled, and his eyes teared up as he slipped the gold band onto my finger, where it remained for over a decade.

The treasured ring is now in a soft, quiet place in my antique jewelry box. I thought sure it would be all that was left of me after my ashes were scattered to the four winds, but as I said, life is full of surprises. Expect the best, expect the worst. And *always* expect a blankety-blank miracle.

We were supposed to leave for Palm Springs directly after the ceremony, but my darling husband could hardly see straight, so we went home and opened our presents. Mario, the Whisky a Go Go manager, had put fifty bucks in our wedding card, and we wound up with three blenders, two toaster ovens, lot of objets d'art (ha!) and seven hundred-dollar Tiffany coins from Sharon Arden, who is now Mrs. Ozzy Osbourne. At the time she worked for her father, Don Arden, an ominous rock manager who even scared Peter Grant out of his size-fifteen shoes. My mom got us a whole case of maple syrup for our coffee and tea, which was my favorite gift.

We stayed at our fave little joint in Palm Springs, the Pepper Tree Inn, where we basked in the steaming hot tub and the realization that the two of us were now One. I had zero doubt that I had found my life partner—through thick and thin, in sickness and in health, etc., etc., so help me, God. As we walked down the on-fire, palm-treed sidewalks, Michael stopped bermuda-shorted strangers to show them my wedding band. "I'd like you to meet Mrs. Pamela Des Barres," he said proudly to gray-haired couples. If I admired some touristy trinket in a store window, I found it later under my pillow. Late in the hundred-degree night, after a lazy day smearing Bain de Soleil on each other, we wondered aloud about our future Des Barres offspring. "I need a boy," Michael said wistfully, cradling me in the spoon position, "to carry on my mad family name." Life was sweet.

Detective got a gig in Hawaii playing at the site of some famous volcano, and we had another honeymoon under the big, round ball of sun. Michael and I had an exquisite time roaming through the blatantly colorful, fragrant flowers and watching gorgeous postcard-perfect Hawaiian men dive a hundred feet straight down into the turquoise waterfalls. We drank gigantic scooped-out pineapple shells full of dangerous rum and posed in front of tacky tiki gods until we used up a dozen rolls of film. The rest of the band went out in search of mayhem every night, but Michael stayed in the hotel with me. The wife. We lounged around and ate a lot of papayas and fancy fruit pancakes with tropical syrup, watched TV, cooed, cuddled, and got real nasty late at night. One balmy morning as we ate fluffy mango waffles on the terrace, Michael reached for my hand. I guess I was gleaming. "I'm never going to forget how you look right now, baby, so beautiful, so happy with your big Hawaiian breakfast." My only moment of mortification came when the sound went out during the Detective show and Michael mimed drinking, smoking, snorting, and shooting to keep the crowd amused. Ha ha ha.

IV

The brief, sweet escape behind me, I went back to pounding the sticky Hollyweird pavement, seeking fame. Masochism, anyone?

The word was out that the amazing guy who had pulled off *Rocky* was going to direct a movie about wrestling and a love interest was needed. Could that be me? My agent finagled an audition, milking my soap credentials for way more than they were worth, and after finally deciding on a short, sexy black dress, I drove to Universal Studios to meet Sylvester Stallone.

Waiting in those Hollywood offices when your heart is a yammering hopefest, an unknown nobody aching to be *somebody,* is enough to liquify your insides. The secretaries treat you like parakeet poop, and you have to handle it with devil-don't-give-a-shit nonchalance. I picked up *Variety* and gave it a practiced once-over, waiting to be announced. The double door opened, and I made my entrance. Gonna fly now.

I took in the scene: Stallone behind a massive desk, picture window behind him with a view of the lot, a couple slick-looking guys lounging around, drinking coffee, soft, muted lighting, thick beige carpeting . . . "It's you!!" he shouted. I looked behind me to see if anyone else had come into the room. "The Real Don Steeler!!" he raved. "I've wanted to meet you for years!!" I actually pointed at myself, just like in the movies. "Me?"

It was true, I had danced on *The Real Don Steele Show,* wiggling around in a flashy go-go ensemble while different bands lip-synced to their Top Forty tunes. I had to hang all over host Don Steele and tell him how handsome he was before the cameras rolled, but I never dreamed a future superstar might be watching. Somebody who could make me a star myself!! Sly (ha!) and I had a fine chat, then I read cold from the script he handed me, just the way I learned in Charles Conrad's acting class. When I got home, Michael told me I had a screen test the following Monday. I couldn't breathe. The movie was called *Paradise Alley,* and the part I was up for was Stallone's love interest, a hooker with a heart of twenty-four-carat you-know-what.

I studied the lines until I was shouting them out in my sleep. I went to Frederick's of Hollywood and bought a lacy negligee for my screen test with Stallone that was going to take place *in bed*!! I had Peter Vizer streak my hair with shimmering golden highlights that would gleam just right, had a pearlized pink pedicure, since I was going to be barefooted, and bought a bottle of fruity white wine to calm my sizzling nerves. I felt like sparks were shooting off me. Ping! They gave me a trailer on the Universal lot with my name on the door, and I drank three glasses of fruity confidence while I waited my turn. Six girls were testing, and I was third on the list. Time was given a sleeping pill. It seemed like hours crawled by, and I tried not to get too tipsy as I paced shreds into the mini–motor home carpeting. I looked in the mirror and found fault with my entire being, powdering and repowdering my nose to matte perfection. The second girl, Joyce Ingalls, had been "testing" for over an hour and it worried me.

When I finally got under the covers in front of a bunch of bored guys behind cameras and Stallone climbed in with me, I was ready. I remembered all the lines and did a really good, choked-up reading, almost coming to tears as the scene closed. My final line was "The clock's runnin'" because I had decided to charge him for the time in bed with me. I loved the big lug, but he didn't love me, so he could just pay for my services. So there. As I got dressed in the trailer, I was so full of hope that my heart seemed pumped with helium. I sang Dave Clark Five songs at the top of my lungs all the way home. Glad all over, yes I am—glad all over, baby, I'm glad all over, so glad you're mi—i-i—i-ine.

I waited by the phone for a whole week for the call to glory, but it never came. Joyce Ingalls got the part, had a fling with Stallone, and was later almost severed from the film when the fling came to an abrupt halt. It was one of the times that Sascha almost left him, right before his fling with Susan Anton. It's amazing how we know these silly facts about famous people, isn't it?

The Real Don Steeler did get a small role in *Paradise Alley;* as Vonnie, the naughty girlfriend of the bad guy played by Kevin Conway. I was delirious about snagging this morsel of work. Maybe I might actually infiltrate the tawdry sanctity of show business! Even though I knew the roses had zero scent, I wanted to bury my nose in two dozen long-stemmed red ones and breathe deep.

January 8, 1978, has started off with a bang! I worked all week on Paradise Alley *for Sylvester Stallone, and I was good! He put his enormous arms around me after my big scene with Armand Assante and said, "That was great—you ran the full gamut of emotions." I know when he sees the dailies he'll use me again in one of his upcoming movies. I had only one line, and he gave me three more. He likes me and thinks I'm talented and so does everyone there. He is so sweet and nice and self-confident and gorgeous, even though I think he has personal problems of a grand nature. (Stature? Kevin says he's only five feet nine inches and wears lifts all the time.) The gossip is that he gets major crushes on starlets and then crushes their hearts. Oh well, it doesn't affect me. It really makes me feel like a different person to be* working! *It puts other things (like my relationship) in perspective. Look out, I predict big-time stardom for Armand Assante.*

I came away from *Paradise Alley* with some serious high-apple-pie-in-the-sky-hopes. The little taste had whet my star-bitten taste buds, and I wanted more more *more!* The following week I had a crumb tossed at me in the form of a local car wax commercial. Wearing yet another pair of tight-ass shorts and a halter top I scrubbed and rubbed on the hood of a dull dirty car, straining to get those darn spots off! Here comes my next-door neighbor, Broderick Crawford, the fifties TV star from *Highway Patrol,* one of my very favorite half hours, holding a fabulously bright bottle of some sort of Turtle Wax, ready to do the neighborly thing and help me out. After expressing amazement in several different ways over the glory of the product, I was cut loose. I hung around to watch Brod's closeups, reminiscing about my childhood when he had represented all that was strong and lawful. He leered at me and reeked of gin at eleven in the morning, but kiddy memories die hard and I wanted to have my picture taken with him. He took the opportunity to press against me without anybody noticing, but I understood. I gave the photo to my dad and he was impressed. He had my mom put it in a frame. I guess he thought his daughter was finally going places.

Feeling high about my car wax experience, I went trotting into my commercial agency to see if the big babe, Sonia, would start sending me out on a lot more interviews. I wasn't getting my share! Instead of the glowing reception I expected, all I got was a tongue-lashing from the elite waxlike Sonia about the way I had been dressing for these normal soap-suds interviews. She told me I had to go on a search for boring Midwestern-acceptable, straitlaced outfits. I suppose she realized my closet wasn't brimming with shirtwaists and acceptable shoes. I remember exactly what I had on for this punifying, finger-pointing experience—a short hot-pink ensemble full of lavender flowers and Frederick's of Hollywood sling-backs. It reminded me of the time I got expelled from Cleveland High for "looking absurd," one of my very favorite, top-five high school memories. My humbling blush matched my painted red toes, and I promised to head straight for Sears.

V

Michael went to San Francisco to see the Sex Pistols and came back knowing down deep that Detective was a dinosaur that had to be stuffed, mounted, and put to rest. He was only going through the motions anyway, since the band's second album had gone nowhere slow. He told me the Sex Pistols were about to stomp all over the leaden music industry with their gigantic punk boots, chop off the excess, and kick it to death for bad measure. It was only a matter of time before the pistol-punk shot would be heard 'round the world.

Michael was in serious trouble with his drug and alcohol problems, spending more and more time out in the wilderness, but what good did it do to dye my brains black and envision a funeral? Despite his nightmare life away from me (I squeezed my temples impossible to keep from seeing the whole thing in sordid, florid Technicolor), I kept up the fantasy front of married perfection, trying *so hard* not to think about his "other life" and the possibility that it might involve "other women." Since I took care of the money, I knew he wasn't spending a whole lot on cocaine—how was he getting it? Things disappeared from the house, a pair of diamond studs he got from Sharon Arden, a leather jacket. "I guess I lost them somehow, honey." Uh-huh.

Several months before, I had stopped whining and begging with him, because I finally realized it never did a smidge of good, and my most recent form of retribution was taught me by my sweet mom— the punishing Silent Treatment. Back in Reseda the Dodgers game would blare; Vin Scully all excited about Wally Moon's homer; the Swiss steak sizzling on the grill, the pop, crack, and sizz way too loud, like the dumb hunk of beef was cooking inside my head. My big, powerful daddy was bent low by the silence emanating from my five feet-three-inch mom. Silence directed right at him. Somehow when I did the same to Michael it wasn't as intense. When I withheld my love it was still apparent, like I had rubbed that pheromone sparkling gold-dust lotion all over my body, mistaking it for Vaseline Intensive Care.

But one sad dusk after Michael had gone missing for thirty-two hours following a record company cocktail bash I was burning with accusations. I had the shades drawn, wallowing around in the bleak certainty that another grotesque encounter was on the horizon. Or maybe he had OD'd somewhere? Been in a horrible accident? Waiting for his appearance after he had been missing in action was insufferable, unendurable. I couldn't read, eat, hang out with friends, or watch TV. I just got madder and sadder until my entire being was a red-hot brick. By the time he stumbled through the door with his eyes stuck together and his mouth lined with old, destroyed chewing gum, I actually had a fever.

This time he was even more disheveled and vacant-eyed than usual. He had blood running down his neck and ragged rips in his clothes. "I just got hit by a car." He recited in a monotone drone, "A car just hit me." In supreme silence I cleaned the gash on his chin, bandaged it up, and got him out of his wrecked clothes. He was a zombie, his eyes a bomb site, and even though I sat him down in a chair and could look straight at him, Michael Des Barres, my honey husband, was definitely AWOL. I slapped him in the face to wake him up. He just sat there. I slapped him again. He didn't move. I slapped him really, really hard, tears gushing, a sound coming out of me that I didn't know I could make. He stared straight ahead, one lone tear dripping down his chiseled, reddening cheek. Oh, Michael, I love you! I hate you! Where are you? Where have you been? I could just see him out in the wild, untamed, filthy night, squirming in the underbelly of transgression. Why are you doing this to me? To yourself? Don't you know you are my whole life? Please, *please* let me make you sane, content, at peace with your anguished soul!

I got him to bed, and he was out like a black light for the next twenty hours while I blubbered to every guru who was ever born. I still had no idea I was dealing with a disease. I saw Michael as a man who was ruining his life, ruining my life, tromping on our happiness—drinking it, snorting it, dropping it with selfish, cavalier abandon.

I fully expected another one of those peeling, gold-plated silences to follow this miserable, wrenching altercation. I slept on the furthest edge of the bed, a mile away from his blasphemed body, my heart in two separate bloody pieces, and had been up for two or three hours when he emerged from his black-cloud coma. Usually I ignored his attempts at conversation, the observations and pleasantries he made through squinted eyes. I knew his head felt like a squashed cantaloupe, and the knowledge that he felt god-awful gave me a fictitious, holier-than-thou upper hand. It was the only time I could look down on him, smugly ensconced within my pure, unravaged temple. I went to the market, cooked his meals, did his laundry, drove him places, but I temporarily withheld adoration; my only power. But something was different this time. "I'm a fucking cocaine addict," he announced thickly, with truth clearly in the room with us. "I'm an alcoholic and a goddamned drug addict, baby." He sort of staggered down onto his knees in supplication to me—and I went to him without hesitation, holding his head against my tummy. Our tears streamed. This was a revelation. Would he finally be delivered? Could the miracle be close at hand?

CHAPTER FIVE

I

When Michael went back out on the road with Detective he promised to *try* to stay away from the evils that hotel rooms bring: butt lickers who carry razor blades and mirrors around in hopes of hanging out with the band, tempting females with full bottles of Jack Daniels, seventeen joints, and a bong shoved in their spandex waistbands. The night of the Big Confession we made up in front of the mirror, doggie-style, and six weeks later, as I perused the calendar, I realized I hadn't bled since. Hmm. The birth control we practiced was the old-fashioned rhythm method. It had always worked so well that I figured the tilted uterus inherited from my mom had given Michael's tap-dancing sperm the bum's rush, sending them wriggling off in all the wrong directions. But making up that night had been ooh-la-la. I could swear I saw the soul flutter into my middle and lodge itself there; a smidgen of smiling light within the frenzied, pent-up thrusting. I instantly recalled witnessing that Tinkerbell flicker of radiance in the mirror. Wow. Double, triple, quadruple WOW.

I sat there in a stupor fiddling with my tits. Were they a tiny bit bigger than usual? Were they sore? Wowie zowie. The next day I went to dear, old Dr. Aaron and peed into a cup. He had been my doctor my whole life and was there the morning I was born, although he didn't quite make it to the actual birth. Mom popped me out all by herself six weeks early while waiting for someone to give her a saddle block. Since she never got her painkilling drugs, I was born unaddled, wide awake, and squalling. She said I flew out so hard and fast that she was scared I would slide off the table and dangle by my umbilical cord.

So I went home and waited to find out if the rabbit had died, trying to imagine how the impregnated pee could exterminate the floppy-eared mammal. I knew they had stopped murdering hares in the name of motherhood eons earlier, but it still depressed me to ponder it. Back in '78 a pregnancy test took longer than it does now, so I had to get through an entire weekend with tornado visions of bonnets and booties, bottles and bassinets whirling round and round in my dizzy dreams.

I wanted to skewer Michael with the possibility of Daddom in person, so I was skittish the Sunday evening he came home from entertaining jaded America, and he was, as usual, exhausted. After unpacking his ravaged wardrobe, making him a nice cup of tea, running a bath, and pulling back the covers so he could climb into our queen-size cuddle-den, I told him we were expecting an important call in the morning. He looked confused and asked hopefully if I had gotten a callback on a movie or commercial. I was touched; he was always real supportive of career endeavors and also very good at commiserating when things fell through. "No," I said, stirred-up giddy and apprehensive at the same time. "Doctor Aaron is going to call." Dot dot dot. "My period is late." Dot dot dot. "Wow," he said softly. My sentiments exactly. He then put his arms around me reassuringly and squeezed me real sweet and hard. "We would have to look for a bigger place, wouldn't we?" he said, and it was like he sang me a lullabye.

Michael slept and I didn't, but when the phone rang at nine the next morning, he raised up groggily to get the big news. It was the doctor who rescued me from sliding off the stainless steel table twenty-nine years earlier, and he told me exuberantly, "Congratulations, Pamela, the rabbit died."

II

My parents were ecstatic about the upcoming bundle of joy, especially Daddy, who decided it gave him the perfect reason to stick around the planet a while longer. He just *knew* I was having a boy. Right after the big news was announced, however, he took a scary turn for the worse and wound up hacking and choking at St. Joseph's in Glendale, the very same hospital where his only daughter drew her first breath. The doctor told Daddy he didn't think he would live to see his grandchild, and Daddy laughed in his face until the hoot turned into a grinding, coughing hack, and the doctor said, "See what I mean, Oren?" I like to think the doctor was using reverse psychology, because Daddy came home two weeks later swigging a six-pack, playing poker, counting the days until he could teach his grandson the finer things in life—like how to build a rotary engine and the *only* way to clear a stopped-up bathroom drain. I'm sure five-card stud was not out of the question, either.

For Michael and me the joy of our blessed event was profound yet certainly more complicated. Until then, motherhood had never entered my mind. Being an only child, the rare time I spent with small people had been up at the Zappa household when I held kitchen-court as the zany nanny, making cinnamon toast, dancing half-naked around the table with Keith Moon. Somehow it hadn't seemed like real life; it was all so dazzling and there were always shooting stars in my eyes. I had never really thought of Moon and Dweezil as children anyway, since Frank and Gail treated them as equals from day one. The munchkins even called their parents Frank and Gail. They still do. Did I want my kid to call me Pamela or Mommy? My own impending motherhood seemed so overwhelming at times that I had to sit down and put my head between my knees, until I got too round to bend over, that is.

I never got morning sickness but had to gnaw on saltines and swig seltzer every afternoon for the first few weeks. This was before trendy, flavored sparkling water came into being. No kiwi-passion-fruit, no raspberry-vanilla bean. It was the dark ages fourteen years ago when Perrier was still bubbling under the ground somewhere outside Paris. I preferred plain seltzer to Nestea but was very willing to quaff down many glasses of the brown stuff to grab the national commercial Sonia sent me up for.

The audition was held in a boring office full of listless execs who had already interviewed twenty-eight other perky-eyed girls by the time I arrived. I had to fiddle around, pretending I was oh-so-hot and bothered at a barbecue full of my husband's important business associates. This stressed-out wifey needed to take the Nestea plunge! That would cool her right off! I must have been frazzled exactly right, because I got a callback and had to fall backwards into a gigantic, glistening pool, holding a nice, tall glass of cool, refreshing Nestea. I was a little late after hunting around to find the type of bathing suit that didn't reveal my looming mound of baby, and had to start falling backwards in the slapping water before making nice to any of the grim-faced Nestea people. I fell a dozen times, keeping a satisfied, grateful grin on my face. By the tenth trip into the chlorinated depths, I felt like I was having a psychedelic experience and wondered dizzily if the baby was having a good trip. I drove home with my ears popping, my water-logged brain sloshing mindlessly, and the phone was ringing as I walked in the door. I got the job!

I left for New Mexico two days later, envisioning all the satin booties and frilly bassinets the Nestea loot would buy the Des Barres family. I was so excited that somewhere over the Grand Canyon I made the mistake of telling the clothing person that I was pregnant, and she flipped. The whole team of commercial geeks went into a flurry of confusion, and at the last second I had to have Dr. Zeidner (my new gyno who brought Dweezil into the world) send a telegram saying I was in good enough health to fall backwards into a pool several times holding a nice, tall glass of their thirst-quenching product.

By the time of the shoot I was so practiced at the plunge that I perfected it in only three tries. Nobody cared about me in my puffy pink dress anyway, focusing totally on the Nestea and how the sun glinted on the sparkling tumbler, how the ice cubes tinkled just so, the travels of the water driplets down the sides of the glass, and exactly how much of the brown liquid slid down my throat before the plunge took place. I drank so much tea to get the gulps perfected that when I climbed onto the plane headed home I was tea-logged and numb, having to head for the pee pot every twenty minutes. But it was worth it: Not only would the commercial bring us a wad of needed cash, but I would make enough for my Screen Actor's Guild insurance to cover all my maternity bills, except for the hospital phone calls.

III

Still, our finances were dodgy, and our apartment was too small. I had started looking around for picket-fence-Father-Knows-Best–type digs with a backyard, where Michael and I could frolic idyllically with our offspring, but soon found that an actual house was out of our teetering rock-and-roll price range. Although he had always been Mr. Privacy, Michael agreed that we needed a roommate to help pay the rent, so I got on the phone to get the word out. When I called my old traveling partner, Renee, I found out that the girl she and I visited in Wyoming a few years earlier had tired of farm life and had just arrived in Hollywood. The arid flatlands of Wyoming had been

And then there were two. The five original GTOs—Lucy, Christine, me, Sandra, and Sparkie. Three of them have gone to rock and roll heaven. Somehow Sparkie and I lived to tell the tale.
MICHAEL CRAVEN

My sweet, supportive mom — Margaret Ruth Hayes Miller. Daddy carried this photo in a handmade frame all during World War II.

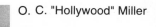
O. C. "Hollywood" Miller

Our wedding, October 29, 1977. Michael got there just in time to say "I do."

Me and my honey-hubby, not afraid to flaunt it

All we could afford at the Elvis auction: the King's toilet-seat cover
JULIAN WASSER

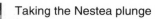
Taking the Nestea plunge

Eight months pregnant—and the
reason why NORMAN SEEF

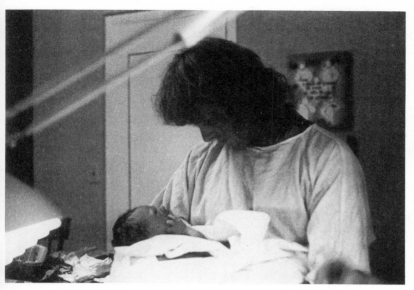

Michael bonding with Nick—three minutes on the planet SPARKIE PARKER

Michael, Jimmy Page, and Steve Jones—one of those nights PAMELA DES BARRES

The Sex Pistols' Steve Jones teaches Nick a few chords. BOB MATHEW

Nick came out of the womb a rock fan. With his fave band "Sparks" on his third birthday—Ron and Russell Mael
PAMELA DES BARRES

Nick and his grandma
PAMELA DES BARRES

Father and son—striking
a striking pose. Nick was
pushing four.

Melanie, Kathy, and I after trudging up Jane Fonda's mountain

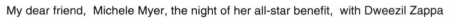

My dear friend, Michele Myer, the night of her all-star benefit, with Dweezil Zappa

my refuge when my then-boyfriend, Don Johnson, met sweet-teen Melanie Griffith on the set of *The Harrad Experiment* and illicit sparks had started to fly right in my face. I wasn't ready for romantic frost-bite, so Renee and I hitchhiked out to the wide-open spaces so I could escape the inevitable consummation. Give me land, lots of land under starry skies above, don't fence me in. There in the Middle America brush I ate gnarly homegrown vegetables and practiced complicated yoga positions under the twinkling Big Dipper, trying hard not to think about the virginal miss and the two-timing hunka hunka burning love. Renee's old friend Denise "Dee Dee" Della-quilla, the lady of the ranch, was a down-to-earth Italian girl who would now become the Hollywood roommate of Michael and Pamela and baby Des Barres. It's a small world after all.

Dee Dee and I got together and pounded the pavement in search of a three-bedroom palace in the heart of Hollywood. I didn't even think of living anywhere else. No matter how decadent and sorry Tinseltown had become, I still envisioned cavalcades of movie stars draped in shimmering evening clothes parading arm in arm down Sunset Boulevard: John Barrymore in a constant profile, ravishing Hedy Lamaar waaa-aay before they caught her stealing laxatives in a Florida drugstore, Bette Davis looking snottily down on us mere mortals, swashbuckling Douglas Fairbanks with a gold band stuck through his ear, Marilyn Monroe taking short, gasping, breathy breaths. Mickey Rooney and Judy Garland, hand in hand, forever pubescent. With any luck, you could be Donald Duck, hooray for HOLLYwood. . . .

After scanning a bunch of dumps, Dee Dee and I were wearing thin when we saw a tiny hand-scrawled FOR RENT sign hiding in a bunch of overgrown bushes, gently announcing the availability of a cool old wooden house on Vista Street. We wandered around the empty pad marveling at the redwood ceilings, thirties tiled kitchen, and overgrown, flowering passion fruit trees tangling up the back-yard, determined to grab it for ourselves. It turned out the landlady, Mrs. Finagle, a knotted, ancient white-haired crone who spoke like she had a scabbard down her throat, lived right down the street. Dee Dee and I started in with the convincing and promising, but after patting on my slightly showing bubble-tummy several times, the old dame consented to rent us her pearl of a house. After showing us a long list of possible rental candidates she'd been compiling, Mrs. Finagle tore up the names as we signed the lease agreement. It happened so fast! Dee Dee and I reeled with joy. When she finally asked about the bubble-tummy's daddy, I told her my husband was in the music industry and waited for the usual reaction, but she didn't seem to mind. She probably pictured a guy in a dapper suit behind a snooty desk, signing stacks of contracts for the Royal Philharmonic, but I promised to bring Michael over to meet her later that day, knowing that even with his long, tangled ringlets, he would charm the sagging girdle right off our new landlady. As we unstuck our thighs from the plastic-covered brocade couch to leave with our precious lease agreement, Mrs. Finagle proudly produced pictures of her great-grandchildren. She seemed more interested in my due date than checking bank info, qualifications, or credentials. The old gal loved babies, and we lucked out.

We introduced Dee Dee to Detective's piano player, Tony Kaye, they became an instant item, and we all moved into the Vista house together. Luckily, Tony had a mechanical mind, which came in extremely handy, since Michael and I couldn't do much more than screw in a lightbulb with all four hands. The house was a charmer but tottering into old age and often falling into disrepair, so Tony was constantly working on some nagging, drippy pipe or a blackened, hissing death-trap outlet. He actually enjoyed it. My dad had always cracked a well-deserved happy beer after tackling a clogged-up drain or a stubborn, non-sucking vacuum cleaner. I suppose completing a menial task must give a gal or a fella a swell feeling of accomplishment, but since I can't even stand to wash a dish, I will probably forever be denied that humble thrill.

Michael and I had gotten rid of most of our moronic, modern claptrap after the brief stint in subtopia and the new (old) house had a wildly mixed-up decor. Dee Dee brought in a lot of her downhome farm furniture, I started recollecting bamboo and ordered a dumb console piano from Sears that looked like it floated off a Hallmark greeting card. I spent whole days in the baby's room, and even though my daddy thought I was having a boy, instead of blue, I painted the room bright yellow with lime green trim, dragging out all my old Disney crapola to decorate the walls. *This* kid was going to adore Mickey and Minnie, Dumbo, Pluto and Snow White if I had to swaddle it in Disneyana. I went ape and ordered really expensive custom-made turquoise blinds with all Walt's euphoric characters bouncing around on air. I wistfully posed in front of the shades with my bulging tummy exposed while Michael snapped shot after shot. I don't know how he endured it.

After the first three months were up and I was allowed to stop

being paranoid, I spent hours in baby stores, getting drippy-eyed
over all the tiny trappings and itty-bitty outfits, trying to imagine
having my very own living, breathing baby doll. I got big and fat,
even though I did yoga three times a week with Judy, the mom-lady
who taught our Bradley birth classes, which were real different from
Lamaze because there was none of that goofy panting involved. I
found out how to do Kegel exercises to keep my vaginal entrance
toned up, a practice I *still* find extremely beneficial and stimulating.
Mainly I learned all about what was happening inside my body so I
could visualize the whole experience and not be so afraid that I might
opt for drugs to deaden the pain, thereby deadening the baby's first
moments of life. I was determined to do it without that awful saddle-
block shot in the spine, even though Michael's mother had told him
that giving birth had been like taking her bottom lip and stretching
it over the top of her head. Ouch. We got so chummy with Judy
that she decided to film our birth experience to show her future
Bradley classes. The expectant couples sat in a huddle watching various women squeeze slimy infants out on 8mm, their mouths
stretched out into soundless wailing *o*s. I also invited Sparkie to take
still photos, and of course, Michael would be with me in the birth
room, which we went to visit in advance so we would know exactly
what to expect. Except for all the baby-saving paraphernalia in the
hall in case something went awry, it looked just like a regular room
at Holiday Inn.

I'd been reading oodles of books on the subject, so I knew it
would soon be time for the baby to start kicking. I couldn't imagine
how it would feel to be jiggled and jostled from within, and I was
waiting impatiently for a tiny left hook or an uppercut to the solar
plexus. Already it was difficult to eat a whole lot at one sitting because
it·felt like my stomach was being squished and mashed from every
angle. My inner ear was constantly on guard and the weensiest gurgle
stopped me cold, but when the little bugger decided to take the first
whack at me, there was no mistaking the enchanting sensation for a
gas jolt or a digestive blurp. It was a holy moment.

Michael and I were surrounded by sound, ensconced in our dreamy
plush seats at the Cinerama Dome on Sunset Boulevard, deep into
The Last Waltz, a divine documentary on the Band, when it happened: The baby kicked. I gasped, rapt with inside attention, waiting
for it to happen again. I grabbed Michael's hand, held it over the
magic spot, and seconds later he got to feel the sweet little "hello"
tap for himself. Tears sprang out of nowhere and dribbled down my

cheeks, and Michael's eyes shimmered in the dark as he grabbed ahold of me tight, whispering, "The first kick . . . at the last waltz." It was one of those rare, triumphant moments when you feel like a living, breathing hunk of ecstasy—a forevermoment. I wish we could bottle those drops of time, unpop the cork when we feel real low, and take a deep whiff of glory to remember what it feels like.

IV

I sure wish I could say that those moments of luminous joy had satisfied Michael's thirst for transcendence. Although thrilled by his impending fatherhood, my darling husband was still staying out through several dawns at a stretch whenever the demon bit him. He wasn't one of those alcoholic drug addicts who imbibed nonstop; he was a "binger," going on sprees and binges that lasted a few days, while I sat in the sweat box embroidering Tinker Bell on a tooth-fairy pillowcase, cursing his titled name. Still, my subconscious wouldn't let me smell other women on him, even when Ciara and Chloe lingered in the steamy air. I was desperate to avoid a confrontation that might crunch my costume-jewelry concept of a happy marriage. So I relied on the silent treatment while his poor body tried to snap out of the bender, and he wallowed in apologies and self-recrimination. Nothing *nothing,* NOTHING had changed.

It was record-breaking, sweltering summer in L.A., and our gorgeous redwood bedroom might as well have been a sauna bath. Despite the fact that I was in nirvana about the soul swimming in my midsection, I was HOT! It was impossible to sleep, so I was barely dozing at 4 A.M. the blistering morning I heard a commotion erupting in the kitchen. Warily opening the bedroom door, I saw only darkness, except for the eerie light coming from the refrigerator, and I saw Michael ripping out the shelves while bottles of ketchup and salad cream shattered and cans of Dr. Pepper rolled all over the floor. He was mumbling angrily, incoherently; it was totally surreal, and I was scared. Cautiously I approached him, trying to save our time-payment fridge from total extinction, but I could see in his pits-for-eyes that he didn't know who I was. Rushing at me, he shook my shoulders back and forth like I was on one of those old-fashioned fat machines, then speaking in a foreign language, crashed into the bedroom and fell onto the bed, where he stayed for two whole days and nights. I didn't even take his shoes off. When he resurfaced Michael asked what in the world had happened to the refrigerator. The man had no recollection of what had taken place.

One other time, at the end of another wild set of nights, I watched dumbfounded as he took a whole bunch of books out of the bookcase, stacked them against the wall and then put them right back in the bookcase. He did it five times. I found out a few years later that Michael had been in what is called a blackout. Did that mean he didn't have to account for shaking his pregnant wife around like maracas? That it wasn't his fault? He didn't have to take the blame? Didn't have to suffer crunching pangs of guilt? And if he didn't even remember it, had it even happened? It was the only time he ever touched me in anger, and I couldn't even rub it in.

June 6, 1978—*So, having a baby in four months—it's kicking right now! I'm sure a child will help put everything in perspective. Michael and I went through another drug thing, c'est la vie. I always pray he'll truly get over it. He starts rehearsals for the Whisky this weekend, then starts the third album, and Detective is still in chaos. I did a Nestea commercial, and I hope I can do Pampers or something baby oriented. Please! We're living in a stunning house with Dee Dee, and we have a washer and dryer, fridge, ping-pong table, basketball hoop, a real live garage, and a little yellow cradle that I bought today. We have a yard and a patio, such a thrill!*

V

Though Michael's lapses threatened to blast the conventional walls down, I was reveling in the normalcy I had created around me. The washer and dryer represented a sane way of life, and seeing orange-ringed boxes of Tide took me back to the service porch in Reseda where my mom spent too much of her precious time taking care of me and Daddy. Sometimes that pissed Michael off, and in eloquent, heated moments he called me bourgeois, denouncing the Valley as the hillbilly capital of California. It killed me when he used that word against me because I didn't understand the meaning well enough to refute it. I have since discovered that the blasted word means "middle class," and I guess that's what I was. What I am? Maybe I have middle-class roots, but back then I just stood there, the daughter of a common coal miner, lard-laden turnip greens dripping off my fingertips, a piece of hay stuck between my two front teeth, wilting into a puddle of bourgeois hog slop. Looking back, I think Michael might have been subconsciously goading me into standing up to him. Who *knows* what might have happened if I had stuck up for myself instead of wincing like I was next in line to be slaughtered. I constantly trapped myself like a poor, bellowing moo cow, eyes rolling frantically, waiting in that long line to get one of those medieval puncturing rods straight through the brain. I languished in that middle class sometimes—a secret student of coupon-clipping. I snipped twenty-five cents off a box of corn flakes. Fifty cents off a package of Pampers—putting them in the closet to be wrapped around my baby's pink bottom a few months later. I filled out the dumb questionnaires in *Good House-keeping* and had a few moments of private domestic contentment. I told myself I just couldn't help it—a prisoner of my pregnancy. I enjoyed being temporarily engaged in soothing clap-trap trivialities. Taking that Simple Simon escape route relaxed me. So there.

But in between the binges and bourgeois back-sliding, Michael and I had a lovely marriage. We went on another honeymoon to the Hearst Castle and stayed at the outrageous Madonna Inn, where every room had a different sex-drenched, romance-laden theme. We stayed in the cave room, where I stood under the gushing water in the romantic rock shower while Michael took more photos of my big blooming tummy. The daddy-to-be was hoping a little penis was being formed in there, while I knew for sure that the tiny pink dresses I had on layaway would soon be put to use. I was so sure I was carrying a little princess that the only name I had chosen was Dominique—Dominique Delphine Des Barres, or Niki for short.

I had rubbed whole bars of cocoa butter on my stomach and slathered entire bottles of baby oil up and down my thighs to prevent those ruinous stretch marks from wreaking havoc on my highly main-tained body. So the morning I galumphed into the bathroom to take the first of five dozen pees and noticed the searing red lines streaking up the sides of my thighs I collapsed into a lumpy heap and bawled. Michael came running in to make sure I wasn't giving birth. When I pointed out the dastardly imperfections, he soothed me in his arms, promising me it would all be worth it when we had our little baby and saying how he saw the stretch marks as badges of courage and glory. Battle scars. Of course, *he* didn't have to wear these magnif-icent, courageous, blemished badges for the rest of his natural life. Thank goodness they have faded to tiny, pale slivers, and he was right: It was all worth it. He missed only one birth class, and all the pregnant couples adored his hysterical, pithy take on parenthood. He took it seriously but had the knack for lightening the thirty-extra-pounds load. "All of you ladies are in the throes of your feminine majesty," he said triumphantly, bowing to the throng of waddling, sweaty women. "You'll never be more beautiful or powerful in your lives. Flaunt yourselves!" The people who had already been through the experience told us how our lives would totally change after the baby was born, but Michael and I refused to swallow this bitter pill. Our magical offspring would sleep until noon every day, oh yes.

One sweaty afternoon Michael came home from a band meeting with a giant T-shirt that had DOMINIQUE across the belly area, and I wore it to the baby shower thrown by my relatives, where I received many mundane but necessary gifts. I dolled up for the shower tossed by my pals (boys *and* girls), oohing and aahing over thoughtful stuff like a puffy, rainbow-colored, hanging hot-air balloon and a set of antique Mickey Mouse decals that must have set the kindhearted gift giver back at least forty dollars. Michael seesawed around the room making sure everyone's punch cup was filled and the dip replenished. And when the final nutcase waved good-bye, we sat together and contemplated weensy booties knitted like a pair of cowboy boots and a stack of post-hippie, tie-dyed T-shirts the size of Michael's hand.

VI

The desire to be an acclaimed actress never deserted me, no matter how pregnant I got, so when my old genius playwright pal Jim Kennedy offered me a nutty part in *Dogfight,* a musical about Howard Hughes, I somehow managed to make it to the Zephyr Theatre every day for rehearsal. Rotund and weary, I played the part of a horny babe attempting to pick up on a corny cowboy, and no matter how pooped out I was, I got the crowd roaring whenever I struck a seductive, come-hither pose. The cast was huge, and they all fussed over the baby-laden blimp-lady, fanning me backstage while I waited my turn to emote. A fascinating Latino, Edward James Olmos, played the announcer, and a hot tamale, Katey Sagal, sang raunchy lead in the *Dogfight* band, so I felt like I was in glorious company. Every night we peered into the dark audience, scanning for important showbiz casting types who could make us famous, but after a couple weeks, despite the dedication to my craft (ha!), I had to turn my part over to the understudy. I was worn out from waddling around onstage; my hot, swollen feet poking fatly out of my spike heels. I had reached the point where all I wanted was to flop down on the couch and wait. I managed to get to yoga class, the second-to-last birth class, and when Gail Zappa called to invite me to Moon's eleventh birthday party, I just couldn't say no.

Moon was holding the heart earrings I brought her way up in the air, watching them jangle and glint when I felt myself spring a major leak. It was September 30 at about four in the afternoon, and I knew exactly what was going on. Gail gave me some female paraphernalia to soak up the baby water, I got my first contraction and started watching the clock. The anticipation was so intoxicating it reminded me of the Beatle countdown at the Hollywood Bowl in 1964. When the contractions blasted me every five minutes, I called Michael to tell him to get ready, Gail put her sister in charge of the birthday proceedings, hustled the dripping mom-to-be out the door and into her Rolls-Royce. She had been through this three times already and proved to be very adept at taking charge. I reclined on my side in the backseat, remembering to concentrate and attempting to relax when the contractions hit, but I was concerned about leaking onto the leather seat of the Rolls and kept apologizing to Gail for spoiling the fancy interior. She laughed in a tinkly way and assured me it didn't matter, "You're having a baby today!" She was ecstatic and made me feel like I was on my way to collect an Academy Award or Pulitzer prize. We grabbed Michael, who had already called Judy and Sparkie, and set out for Hollywood Presbyterian. Considering he was about to become a parent, Michael seemed fairly serene and slightly detached. He was probably in shock. I had my head in his lap and as he stroked my hair each strand seemed electrified. Bzzz-bzzz. Time becomes forsaken when you're in labor. Minutes turn into weeks. It took a year to get to Vermont and Fountain, and the short ride in the wheelchair, a towel shoved between my legs, took about seventeen months. I waved good-bye to Gail, who promised to return when the baby came, and finally climbed into bed, my eyes crossed with spellbound attention to the matter at hand. I became an animal, alone with my womb; a wordless, focused hunk of primeval wildlife. Since I was about to be filmed and photographed, Sparkie gently asked if I would like some cosmetics applied. I could hardly even remember what lipstick was, let alone have it smeared across my earth-mother mouth. I waved her away, and when Michael tried to caress me, I grunted like a beast, flailing at his fingers like they were pesky flies on my fur. Although composed, Michael must have been a wreck, because when he located Doctor Zeidner at an Italian restaurant, I heard him shout into the phone, "This is Pamela Des Barres's wife!"

Dr. Z. said he wouldn't be there for awhile because it was my first baby and since I was only at three centimeters, I was likely to be in labor for several more hours. I took in this information and discarded it instantly as fiction, knowing I would prove him wrong. Even though the pain was beyond mortal thought, I wanted to feel, feel, *feel* it all wrapped around me like swaddling clothes. I pushed hard and felt something give. I could hear my darling husband, Sparkie, and Judy having a ball in the background, like a party was going on, and I groaned, "Michael, call a nurse." I knew I was in transition. The stunned angel of mercy found I was now at nine centimeters and when surprise flattened her features, I felt a divine sense of power wash over the careening agony. For a split second I was ferociously immortal. I felt like baying at the moon.

Doctor Zeidner was probably polishing off his zabaglione when the Doctor X on duty rushed in to get everything ready for the big moment. Everybody put on sea green gowns and masks, the girls fiddled with their cameras, Michael paced. The room was aflurry with action, but the contractions had become constant, so I was one with the experience; one about to become two. Me and my shadow, strolling down the avenue. I prayed for a perfect baby and shoved like the brute creation I was, sounds coming out of me that had been heard only in the wild or maybe at a very large zoo. In the distance I heard the birth coach Judy exclaim, "It's crowning! I can see the head!" That was my cue to thrust and heave with supersonic force, propelling the tiny, slippery being out into the big, brand-new world. The final push felt like a wrenching, all-consuming, full-body orgasm, with a choir of angels tossed in for good measure. Cameras captured the first breath, the first cry, my astonishment at seeing the bright pink male apparatus, Doctor X handing me the buttery bunch of baby, pressing the little bugger to my popping breast, the look of wildcat satisfaction on my face. It was over. Four hours and twenty-three minutes from the first contraction at Moon's birthday party, I was holding my little boy. Surprise! Only three days before, Michael and I figured we had better come up with a boy's name just in case Dominique didn't show up, and we chose Nicholas because it was a simple, gallant name, and Dean after the first mainstream media rebel, James. Weak and elated at the same time, smug but thick with gratitude, I handed Michael his heir and watched them bond. He was supposed to have cut the cord, but Doctor X hadn't been filled in, and Doctor Zeidner arrived just in time to stitch up a very tender, strategic spot. "Your husband will love me for this," he said, chortling, hoping his tight stitches would make up for his missing the birth entirely. The euphoria was fading and the pain was pointedly profound. Sparkie tried to take my mind off my pussy by plying me with celebration cake and OJ, Judy praised me for a job well done, and soon little Nicky was wrapped tight in a blue blanket and back in my arms. Michael got on the phone, making sure everybody knew there was a new Des Barres on the planet. Mom and Daddy were the first to arrive, followed by Gail, my old pal Michele Myer and Tony and Dee Dee. I felt like a queen. O.C. cradled his grandson, besotted, cooing to him in a voice I'd never heard before, while Mom looked on adoringly, equally smitten by the midget bundle.

Michael, Nicky, and I stayed that night in the birth room, and I felt like I was on some sort of dippy-dopey hallucinogenic. Michael was looking at me differently, a burgeoning smidgen of respect lighting his eyes. He said he had been watching me right before Nicky was born and saw a new look on my face; one of stern determination and strength. Miss Goody-Two-Shoes finally facing the hard-core music. After we cuddled and discussed the whole perfect experience, staring endlessly at our dozing offspring, I slept the sleep of a dead woman for the very last time.

CHAPTER SIX

I

Once you have a kid, any itty-bitty sound in the night will raise you, startled, straight off your pillow, alert and ready to dart. Nicky is fourteen now, but the slightest nighttime noise still knocks my personal sandman for a complete loop. Sleep had always been a welcome pal o' mine but became a manic obsession soon after the motherbug bit me.

By the time Nicky was two weeks old I was a delirious dunderhead, banging into walls, constantly aching to snooze. I had a pad of paper and a pencil by the bed so I could add up the hours of sleep I was getting each night, and it was never, ever enough. He nursed every ninety minutes, twenty-four hours a day for six months. Michael pretty much continued his life-style undaunted by daddyhood, a fact I rarely questioned or attempted to alter. Like most new mommies, I kept a baby book to remember each *waking* moment:

Two weeks—Here Nicky is, on my bed, squirming, pink, and innocent, his mouth always open like a little bird's—so sweet and soft—with a little weenie! I was so surprised he was a boy! I felt so amazing when he came out—so slippery and enormous. After he was born, they handed him to me and I hardly knew what to do with him! What a little bundle, he's so beautiful. We asked Danny G. to be Nick's godfather, and he said he would be honored.

Nineteen days—I still can't believe I have this baby. Every day he gets more human and wide-eyed. The exquisite specimen is so time-consuming—

a twenty-four hour appendage—completely dependent little rag. Michael is great with him, but he's Mom's *job. I'm a little more mobile now that we have our Wee Kare car seat and Snuggli carrier—it's a constant thing. I can hardly see, I'm so tired.*

Thirty-one days—Almost healed up. Little Nicky getting much more receptive and part of the human race. He drives me mad because he falls asleep at the tit and wants to nurse every half hour! He's a fusser but never cries unless he's hungry (which seems 4-ever). Melanie took Nicky and me to her astrologer as a birth-present, and the lady said that Nick had already achieved cosmic consciousness, was here on a specific mission and would one day have followers! I don't want to think about that right now.

Seven and a half weeks—Little precious human asleep in his cradle—he raised his head and shoulders today on his tummy, and such an expression of wonderment at his giant feat. He's turned into a real smiler, it lights up his whole face—he even laughs! He loves his grandma and his daddy, and smiles so much for them—love him madly!

Nine and a half weeks—I'm like a dead dog most of the time. He's gotten to the frustrated stage where he cries a lot unless he's being personally amused—bounced and walked around. He's so *good-looking, when we take him out, old ladies tell us how gorgeous he is. He's gone up a diaper size and is growing out of his Casper outfits—healthy little angel.*

Three months—He's lying in his cradle now, batting rattles, beside himself with concentration. He's really figuring out his hands, twining them around and staring so intently! He's taken a shine to the stuffed Cookie Monster and talks to it twenty minutes in a row like he does to Michael. He's losing his hair, and the fuzz underneath is white! *Little platinum-haired boy.*

Fourteen weeks—He's developing a personality and always smiles at strangers, so adorable. Mom got him a jack-in-the-box, and he squeals with delight over it. He's taken up my whole life and he doesn't care! What a commitment! A lifetime commitment for Mommy. I just found out Gail is pregnant, and Nick will have a little girlfriend in July!

Fifteen weeks—We had our birth-class baby reunion last night—it was so *much fun! Of course, Nicky was the prettiest and brightest; even Judy said so. We lined up all the babies for a photo and they were squirming and flailing, except for Nicky who looked calmly right into the lens. Ha, I wonder if he will ever read this and love his mom for writing it, or will he not be close to me. It's so incredible to be a mom. He comes before every-thing—not a thing can be considered without first thinking of him.*

Five months, three weeks—To think I'd be in bed every night before midnight and always have a little baby in my arms. God, I'm too tired to write.

The pedantic, gushing, age-old ramblings went on and on like Nicky was the first baby ever to splash in the bath or say "ga-ga." My entire existence was caught up in Pampers, powder, and nursing pads. It was all Mom's job, a lifetime commitment for Mommy. Nicky Dean came before everything. But where was Daddy?

I started a pattern in those new-mom days, by getting my bossy, brassy but softy-hearted friend Michele Myer, who had recently become Auntie Shelly, to come over and baby-sit if I had to go out, leaving Michael in the back bedroom to his own devil-may-care devices, every second his own. Why didn't I say, "Michael, I have to go to the gym, here's Nicky, take care of him." Why didn't *he* say, "Oh, let me spend some time with my kid while you're gone." It's always a fifty-fifty deal, remember, and I could have insisted he take care of his own son when I had important stuff to do, but I didn't. My mom had been my caretaker 100 percent, even though O.C. was around most of the time. She doled out the punishment and the praise, taking on the entire burden of parenthood. It's as if she didn't want to bother him with all the constant, mundane, unglamorous facts of sticky kid life. From very early on I didn't bother Michael either, and then it became too late.

II

Nicky helped to bring us closer, although our sex life suffered because I was always desperately scribbling on the sleep paper, adding up the precious hours of shut-eye I managed to get each night. Even when Michael and I tried to grab a few moments of long, hot sin, it often turned out to be brief and lukewarm but still all-important because I needed to feel beloved, cherished, and desirable to him—above all, desirable. My tummy, which had been hereditarily round to start with, had become seriously round, and I scraped together the priceless time three mornings a week to strap myself to a bunch of newfangled machines in order to tighten up the flubby waistline and dingle-dangle thighs.

I had put on thirty-nine pounds altogether and still had ten to lose. Kim Lee, an Oriental browbeating, death-to-blubber exercise master whipped eleven inches off me in three months, and I vowed to speed up the tightening process after I finished nursing and could give up the glory of dairy products. I had sorrowful mixed feelings about ending those serene, rocking-chair moments of connected closeness with Nicky latched onto me like he was still attached to my body, but he had already taken to the bottle, and it was time for me to get back into shape and back into acting class. I knew my titties would need strapping down tight so the milk would dry up and go away. Right after the last supper I wrapped them round and round with Ace bandages and waited for the pissed-off milk ducts to accept that it was all over. I expected a little pain, but the poor things got so hot and bothered they swelled to a pornographic size and got as hot as a Las Vegas sidewalk on the Fourth of July. It felt like I had sacks of boiling, bubbling lava inside me, and *nothing* made the steaming bulges feel any better. I had to take care of my fidgety newcomer and go on with life like I didn't have single bleeping care. I finally took some male hormone pills, hoping for relief, but all I got were several mongrel hairs growing out of my chin like stray whiskers. Then, after ten days, my misshapen mammaries got cute again, just like nothing had ever happened.

After a rare exquisite afternoon nap a few days later, I wandered out of the bedroom and heard the whir of Tony's film projector. Wow! Was Michael watching the birth film? I hadn't felt quite ready to repeat the torrid experience yet, but maybe now I could relive the sweet memory and cherish it. I peeked in the door just in time to see Nick shooting back into my womb. Out again. Over and over. In and out. Tony, with his droll, brittle sense of humor, was running the film backwards—then forwards—backwards. I gasped for air and had to go lie down again. I haven't watched the film since.

Eventually working out became a large hunk of my life-style. Way before the fitness craze, I flopped around with saggy ladies at the Beverly Hills Health Club before it was called the Sports Connection, doing old-fashioned lifts and sit-ups, which came to be those "feel the burn" killer ass pinchers and gut-grinding crunches. I also became slightly obsessed with the fine lines appearing all over my face, remembering long, hot, baking days at the beach, my bras stuffed to the brim with created cleavage, coated in ray-grabbing grease, broasting my skin to a ravishing burnt sienna to impress those gangly, zit-ridden junior high school boys. After noticing the faint, solar-created etchings around my eyes, I went to Bullocks with my plastic to purchase every product that promised to "improve the appearance of aging skin"; smearing on blobs every morning and night, making sure they sunk way into my beached-out epidermis. Through the years I must have spent a hundred thousand bucks on creams, gels, and fancy emollients for my crabby complexion. It doesn't seem fair that I went directly from pimples to wrinkles without any kind of break. Now I coat my entire being in SPF 25 before opening a window.

When Auntie Shelly wasn't available, I dragged Nicky to the gym with me, where he ventilated indignation from within his expandable play cage. And, of course, we regularly visited my lethally damaged daddy, whose time on the planet seemed to be running out.

February 16—My daddy is suffering so, and I pray to the Gods that when his time is up he is taken swiftly and easily. Poor Mama, she's so strong. She had to go look at coffins today. How I stay so damn sane and happy most of the time is hard to figure out. To think that we all come here and live our silly lives and have to die—usually with agony. How can we be spared it? Is it all preordained? It's such a complicated life. Signed, the Questioning Queen of Housewifery.

The king of our menage was suffering his own bum trips. Detective finally hung up their badges, and Michael got involved with KISS's bass player, Gene Simmons, who had high and mighty hopes of becoming a mogul. Despite Gene's grand intentions, it was one of many liaisons that didn't work out. Record executives were imperious, meetings got canceled or went nowhere real slow. Always angry because he felt like he was constantly compromising himself for some fathead's dirty dollar, Michael either seethed or went out and got bombed. He would come home from watching a new band like the Clash and mope around for days, feeling his life slide by without being able to harness his brilliance. He signed another management contract with a bright but coked-up bozo who put on rock concerts, and even though this guy gave us money to live on, Michael called himself "a kept prop star," emanating sorrow like rays of radiation and had dark, loathsome thoughts about his battered integrity.

Finally, in frustration he decided to get back into acting, the craft of his youth. At eight years old he had been on posters all over England as the Nux Bar Kid, hyping the crunchy chocolate bar on telly and radio. In fact, he had done a bunch of kids' TV shows before landing the part, at sixteen, as the hip guy wearing sunglasses in the sixties movie classic *To Sir with Love.* The first time he heard Rod Stewart's "Maggie May," he said "Now, *that* sounds like fun," and was inspired to sing, dropping his acting career in favor of nasty, filthy rock and roll. Now that he lived in the show-biz capital of the universe, why not do both? The problem was, How many parts were there for a pole-thin, British, would-be pop star with very long strawberry blond ringlets? On one of his wild rampages, Michael ran into an old English music mate, Jimmy Henderson, formerly the bass player in the fabulous' Tucky Buzzard, and found that his wife, Kathy, was casting a new sitcom, *WKRP in Cincinnati.* She had already given Jimmy the part of a guy in a rock band and was looking for the rest of the group. Michael snatched the coveted role of Dog Boy, and as a last favor to his former band mates, brought the rest of Detective in to play Scum of the Earth, a raving British punk band that wreaks havoc on the radio station. Kathy adored Michael's wacky portrayal of a barking singer and also cast him as a rock star in *The Rockford Files,* which caught the attention of an agent, and so began his second career in America. He was stuck playing rock guys for way too long, but soon made enough dough for the family to take a trip abroad so his eccentric (to put it gently) parents could meet the royal offspring.

III

We arrived after an eleven-hour flight with a bundled-up fifteen-month-old baby in freezing England, where Michael's manager had booked us an ancient but elegant hotel smack in the bygone heart of London. Nicky still mixed up the words "hot" and "cold," so when we set out on a little jaunt to the King's Road, he kept shouting, "Hot! Hot!" when snowflakes hit his rosy cheeks and reached out into the ice-cold air like he could break off a piece and hold it in his mitten. My precious little boy mesmerized me. Ooh, Ahh, isn't he smart, isn't he special, brilliant, adorable! I marveled at Nicky non-stop, like he was the ninth wonder of the stratosphere.

Due to the time change, Nicky's sleeping pattern was all mixed up, so when Michael went out on the town, I was stuck in the tiny (but elegant) hotel room, chasing after my rampaging toddler at 3 A.M. I found myself feeling edgy and impatient, and I actually acknowledged that it was unfair that *I* was the one who had to stay in at night while his nibs had the run of London. I acknowledged it to myself, but not to Michael (as usual) and had to be content to dash out for a Cadbury's Flake while hungover Daddy stayed with napping Nick during the afternoon. But we did get the chance to meet up with old friends, buy some trendoid punk duds on the King's Road, and even got to club it up one night while Nick stayed with an old chum, Geraldine, who had a couple babies of her own. We hung out with Pete Townshend at a dive called Dingwalls, and although I was held in his thrall along with several other Who admirers, I was surprised to see how combustible he became as he poured it down, knocked it back, sucked it in. Dry and amusing at first, seemingly in high spirits, he gradually started poking fun at himself, then took jagged stabs at his own jugular. "I haven't done anything *im-portant!*" he raged blindly, "Nothing of any *consequence* what-so-evah!!" I begged to disagree but remained silent for fear of being slugged. He seemed severely disappointed and disgusted with himself for some ungodly reason. It's got to be a devilish pain in the ass to be a living legend.

We spent one bizarre all-nighter with Zeppelin's hefty manager, Peter Grant—holed up in his stuffy castle—protected from intruders by a rippling body of water and an honest-to-God moat. He sent a limo for us in the pitch-black night and we wound up deep in the British countryside at about two in the morning, waiting with several cups of tea for Peter to come down the stairs. We passed the time by counting the hidden gargoyle faces in the rock fireplace, then Peter finally greeted us with his dreaded black doctor's bag and led us into his screening room to watch live Zeppelin footage.

Poor old Bonzo had recently fled the planet and Peter needed some understanding company to revel in his late drummer's mad majesty. Over and over, we watched Bonzo cream his drum set. Stop frame again and again. "Look at that—a better drummer was never born." Peter wept openly, and every twenty minutes or so he and Michael took a little walk around the grounds in the zero-minus cold. I knew they were snooting a bunch of coke and I tried to stay in my right mind. This has to end sometime, I said to myself, and after the gray sun had been up for over an hour, we crawled into the plush carden and rode silently back to London. I wondered what Michael was thinking about, but my curiosity was coated in icicles and I kept quiet.

After a few days in swinging London we took a train out to the dismal, flat seaside of Brighton to meet up with Michael's parents at a once-charming, crumbling resort that reeked of mildew and brief, antique dalliances of a former time. World War II, maybe? We peeked into a faded, vacant ballroom where shiny shoes must have clicked on the floors and chiffon dresses flew. World War I? Gilded wallpaper peeled in the hallways, and dampness impinged on the hissy steam heaters as we wandered through the quiet place, calling out for Philip and Irene Des Barres. It was way past eerie, verging on a Clive Barker dreamscape. One of the doors flew back, and a scary Irene leapt at Nick, crying, "The new Des Barres has arrived!" and attempting to wrest him from my arms, but he squawked in shock and Grandma fixed me with an icy stare, like I had goosed his diaper. Behind Irene wobbled Philip, who had shrunk a foot since our last meeting at the pub in Oxford Circle when he flaunted the teenage girl and spilled Tuinals all over the seat. Meek and dishev-

eled, he loitered in the background while Irene ushered us into the
dank winter retreat.

After hot tea, sweet biscuits, and much fussing over Nicky, she
continued the browbeating of her husband, which I assumed, had
gone on since Philip crawled back to her not long after our first
meeting at the pub. "You meaningless old fool," she chanted
wickedly after he humbly attempted to enter the conversation. "No
one is interested in what you *think* you might have to say." She
withered him further with a vile gaze tinged with arsenic, then turned
to fix a loving smile on Nicky, who gnawed innocently on a jelly
biscuit. I was appalled, and Michael was bent over with shame, but
Irene took no notice, and whenever the opportunity arose she
dropped rank bombs on Philip's bald head, and never once did he
talk back like a bad boy. Why did they get back together? I wondered.
What happened to the nymphet girly? I suppose the twisted karmic
union of Irene and Philip had to be played out. Her venom was
ceaseless, and it seemed the old fellow was past caring, past being
able to care—his high-class, aristocratic air reduced to dribbling-
down-the-chin rubble.

Their misery was excruciating to witness, and my devoted heart
went out to my husband, who was trying to maintain a semblance of
dignity during the two-day trial. In between brief snatches of insightful brilliance, Irene complained to Michael about *his* tawdry,
commonplace behavior, and they wound up arguing to the point of
snippy, all-too-precise one-liners. I wrapped Nicky up warm and
walked back and forth on the frightfully empty beach. We sat on the
damp sand and did pat-a-cake and "How big is Nicky?" "Soooo-big"
until his little nose was crimson from the cold, and we would wander
back in and sit by the steam heater. On the second day of our visit,
I had just gotten Nick down for a nap and was looking out the
window at the charcoal sea, pondering the vast loopholes in life,
when Philip appeared, wan and trembling, to ask me for pills. I told
him I didn't have any, but he went through the list anyway, "Seconal?
Tuinal? Placidyl? Nembutal?" On and on it went. I kept shaking my
head no. It was harrowing. I pictured him as a tiny baby and wished
I could rock him into a peaceful sleep. Lullaby and good night.

Michael needed a massive escape from reality, so when we got
back to London, after a wacky dinner with Nick crawling around
under the table, he went out wild with our pal "Legs" Larry Smith,
a magnificent character I had met many years before in the Bonzo
Dog Doo Dah Band. "Legs" is a true eccentric, an artist that very
few people understand, try as they might. Glory-rock dudes like Eric

Clapton and George Harrison take him on the road for comic relief. He makes you laugh so hard that nothing comes out and your eyes cross, his insights are cringe-fests, though most of his snappy wizardry goes sailing over everyone's head. He was a pent-up, underappreciated genius on a slide at this point in his life, so he and Michael were gone 'til the dawn's early blight and then it was time to catch the plane home.

Michael was still wasted as we dragged our baggage and squalling baby down the steep stairs of our hotel. The front door creaked open and we were stunned to see Irene appear out of the mist with a giant bag, which she flung down in the foyer and then disappeared like an apparition. Michael ran after his lost-soul mother, but a cab had been waiting and was already down the street. Had she taken a train all the way from Brighton? Or had she taken the cab? How did she afford it? The bag sat there, and we were almost afraid to tamper with it. What was so important that she would come out in the pit of night to hand deliver? We looked at each other warily while Nicky wailed, and then Michael finally peeked inside. The bag was full of things for her one and only grandson: a colorful handmade quilt, bright picture books, a yellow sweater, stuffed toys with happy faces, candy bars, and packs of English "sweeties." Silently, his face full of pain, Michael picked up the bag, our overstuffed suitcases, and went out in the early morning drizzle to hail a cab.

We came home to our tizzied life, after thirteen hours of trying to keep Nick amused at thirty thousand feet. He crawled from one end of the airplane to the other, chasing ice cubes kindly provided by a smitten stewardess. "He's going to be a real lady-killer," she burbled, and I knew she was right. If I had had buttons down the front of my dress they would have burst with puffed parental snobbery. Michael flopped into bed, and I put Nick in the stroller and walked down our charming Hollywood street, hoping he'd nod off. As I walked I kept repeating to myself that life was grand. Well, it was, wasn't it? I took for granted all the humming hubbub surrounding me, all the everyday madness that became mundane. An objective observer pulling aside the curtains of my life would have seen a chaotic, stimulating, hair-raising, cliff-hanging, unique, and totally fascinating existence, but when you're in the nearsighted eye of the storm, it sometimes seems all too serene.

IV

January 5, 1981—*I really enjoyed the holidays, little Nick knew all about it and tore into his gifts with* abandon, *always wanting* more. *My mom*

*went nutty and bought a million wonderful things. Daddy is feeling really
bad again, and we all pray he will get better this time. Michael and I loved
each other's gifts. He got me a sexy black dress; I adore that he sees me that
way. I was writing in my journal the other night, and he suggested I write
how I feel about the world right now. I told him I don't know how I feel.
I've been devoting a huge chunk of myself to Nick, and I do enjoy it, but I
think it's time now to come back to myself. I feel good that I never stopped
exercising, it's like I've been "on hold." I get spurts of confidence and spark,
but they don't last—I have to push myself into creativity. Just DO IT,
instead of thinking about doing it! Don't know exactly what it is. I feel
a void somewhere inside me. (Can you feel a void?) I fluctuate from happiness to unfulfillment. I can see how women just "give up their lives," it's
so easy to slip into. I'd like to make some money; Michael works so hard to
keep it all together. We hope we can afford Nick to start preschool in March,
he has such an exquisite imagination. When I put him to bed last night
he said, "I love you, good-night." I just wanted to roll over and swoon. I
went on an interview today and he said, "Mommy looks boo-ful, Mommy
so pretty!" This guy is two years old!*

Yes, I was a worshiping mom, and a worshiping wife. I knew I
was over the top and even started calling Michael "sahib" on the
many occasions when I served his needs before he was even needy.
I transferred some of the devotion to Nick, and he got used to sitting
on a throne, where I can sometimes still find him if I bend over
backwards too hard. Poor Nicky. I kissed his small butt so indus-
triously, he came to expect it from everybody, and when it wasn't
forthcoming he got confused and belligerent. Little did I know that
with my ceaseless acts of worship and smother-mothering I was in
the early stages of creating a mini-monster. He indeed got to go to
preschool, where he climbed up on the table during color time,
pretending to play guitar, speaking swimming circles around his
peers, and cantankerously demanding constant attention. He was
such a quadruple handful, in fact, that by the time he hit three years
old, the headmaster suggested he be tested at UCLA. They surmised,
perhaps, that it was boredom making him act like Damien from *The
Omen.* He spent a lot of time in the corner, where I'm sure he mulled
over upcoming creative outbursts, but the little charmer had such a
sweet way about him, he got off light most of the time.

He made friends and started having play-overs, dragging his little
record player with him so he could turn unsuspecting tykes on to
his favorite band, Sparks. When he was two and a half, *Kimono My
House* was his fave album, and he could sing along to all the nutty

songs. He had an early penchant for art and got into cars in a big way, even teaching himself to read so he could find out particular makes to include in the steering-wheel drawings he made on dozens of paper plates. After creating these amazing replicas of assorted steering wheels, he would drive around town with me in his car seat, changing vehicles at his whim. The first time I realized he could read, we were cruising along in our big, white bomber Ford station wagon when he pointed to the shiny black car next to us and said, "Look, Mommy, another Ford. F-O-R-D." I pulled over, intoxicated with his brilliance, and he gleefully read the brand of every car that drove by. For his third birthday Tony and Dee Dee bought him a real Pontiac wheel at a swap meet, and he was momentarily mesmerized before returning to his own ever-changing batch of Porsches, BMWs, and GM trucks. He would race across the room, making growling car noises, and I was paralytic with mama-lion pride.

Nick's third birthday was absurdly massive for such a small boy. I dressed him up in a little bitty blue suit and made him a Cookie Monster cake from scratch. Our friends from the Knack, KISS, Blondie, and a motley assortment of other long-haired weirdos stood by and cheered when Nicky sputtered at his candles and blew them out, squealing. He got so many gifts he went into overwhelm, and when his two major heroes—Ron and Russell Mael from Sparks—came through the gate, Nick just stared at them unbelieving, his face full of frosting. Russell picked him up, and I snapped a quick Polaroid. The expression on Nicky's face is serene, but he was really in a mini state of shock.

V

Beneath the domestic sheen I was still a creative soul and my time was nigh, I just knew it. The agent I had been with got old and retired, leaving me stranded on the Love Boat, lost at sea, already thirty-two years old and a big fat nobody. I found a series of lumpy successors who did very little for me, so I flogged lovely eight-by-tens all over town, sat for asinine commercial photographs in various *bourgeois* middle-American poses, hoping to sell a can of Campbell's pork and beans to the average consumer, bounced my little kid on my lap while learning yawpity-yawp lines for acting classes. Dragging my Sylvester Stallone screen test behind me like a booby prize, I offered to show it to anybody with eyes. I had wet dreams about bigwigs at ICM or William Morris coming to one of my dopey avant-garde plays and yanking out a contract right after Act One. It didn't happen. I knew I was doing everything possible, but I still couldn't make a scratch, much less a dent into the sanctified business of show. It remained an elusive, invisible trick of light; a sad optical illusion, like an Academy Award hologram I could stick my hand straight through. We needed money, so I took an ordinary dumbo job selling framed posters for a (now defunct) joint called the Graphic Encounter while Nick drove the preschoolers around in his paper-plate cars. I went with forced gaiety through big office buildings, asking to speak to various managers who might want to beautify their surroundings with the all-too-common posters for ten times their worth. It wasn't nine-to-five, but it felt like twenty-four-hour quackery. And as I wrote in my diary, "It sure ain't Broadway."

I harangued myself for feeling insecure, which was a double whammy right between the eyes. I moped and worried, watching the calendar days being ripped off like in the movies when time passes, but there was so much to do, I couldn't fall into a depression. I couldn't allow myself that luxury.

Besides, Michael reserved that emotional province for himself, and, sad but true, *both* of his careers seemed stymied. After several meetings with big-boy labels playing hard-to-get, he had signed as a solo act with Dreamland, Mike Chapman and Nicky Chinn's fancy new label with posh offices situated right next to the Whisky a Go Go on the Sunset Strip. As usual, the hype was high and the promises abundant. Always in touch with his talent, Michael wrote some very cool, verging-on-introspective songs, but it took months before he got into the studio to record the first album, and by then he was weary from pumping himself up, staying on that edgy creative edge while waiting for Mike Chapman to become available. The upper-crust Mr. Chapman had produced Blondie and Suzi Quatro, among many hit-ridden others, so he was highly in demand, and there was nothing Michael loathed more than being on the back burner. He did an occasional TV show, playing the parody of a rock star, which paid the bills but made him feel like the parody he portrayed. The light I had always seen around him despite his anger and addictions became a dim, slow-moving sludge. He didn't like himself or anyone else. His eyes shot daggers, and I withdrew. For the first time I felt my heart set up a protective shield, his razor-edged anguish finally filling me to the brim. He got high, he stayed out, he smelled like someone else's cheap musk oil. He spent so many nights in the wilderness, I don't know how he even stood up straight. There were enough jarring silences between us that words seemed to stop working.

Then one fine day Michael got a call from Paul Fishkin, an old coke-mate who had amazingly gotten clean and sober, inviting him to an Alcoholics Anonymous meeting. It was a short phone call, which left Michael slightly shaken and ready to change the subject. I know he pictured the swinging lightbulb and men in trench coats, and wondered, How could his cool, successful record-company president friend find peace in such a place? How could he let go of all those high-flying nights they spent together in the land of oblivion? He went out whole-cocked at ten o'clock and came home two days later, as I readied Nick for preschool. I came out of the kitchen with a bowl of fresh applesauce, and Michael was standing in front of the picture window, squinting at the annoying bright morning with unspeakable desolate resignation beaten into his face. I stopped cold, registering the moment, because it was a humdinger. Usually I would ignore him like he didn't exist, tamping down my fury with a red-hot icepick, because, as I said, I had reached the point where I had given up and given in. The fight was gone, and our love was looking down the double-barrel of a very unwieldy shotgun. "Are you okay?" I asked. He shook his head no, absolutely, positively, without a doubt, no. But then he got into bed just like he always did, with his clothes on, and I went on my way, dropping Nick at school, selling some moderne posters to a lady entrepreneur, bugging my agents, reading a new play, moaning to my girlfriends on the phone about the state of my life, picking the kid up, making a vegetable casserole for dinner, sort of on automatic pilot, not expecting Michael to surface from his purgatorial hibernation for another day or two. Nick and I were in front of *Sesame Street,* counting up to twenty-five, when Daddy came through the room on his way to the phone. He swept Nick into his arms as he made the call that altered our lives forever. "Hello, Paul. I was wondering if you could take me to one of those Alcoholics Anonymous meetings tonight?" The double-*A* words seemed to stick in his throat and hurt when they came rushing out, but the sentence hung in the air like a line of clean clothes.

I was too stunned and overjoyed to jinx the idea by over-praising him. Besides, who knew if AA would make any difference? But an itsy-bitsy spark of hope started glowing in the closed-up pit of my heart. Michael had admitted only one time that he had a problem, but this was *very* close to the confession I'd almost stopped dreaming about. When Paul came to pick him up, I waved good-bye like he was off for another night of revelry but got down on my knees when the door closed and prayed for a *real* miracle.

CHAPTER SEVEN

I

Days turned into weeks, and weeks into months (which is what usually happens), and Michael didn't have a drink, smoke a joint, drop a pill, or inhale any powder. He followed the rule of going to one AA meeting a day, and in the first few weeks he often went to two or three. Some upstanding soul would honk the horn in front of the house, he would kiss me good-bye, and take the "big book" out into the much safer night. He took to the concept like the dying man he was, getting a sponsor right away: Ed Begley, Jr., who had two or three years in the program and a firm faith in sobriety. We got all chummy with his wonderful family and spent many fun-time hours at dinner bashes and on kiddie outings. Ed seemed to know the entire world and shared all his show-biz friends with us like he was passing around a very special bowl of candy. He was the first in town to get the Trivial Pursuit game, and one lovely night I had Tom Cruise on my team, right before he became a household hunk. He was so good-natured and generous that our team lost by a humongous margin. He blushed easily and grinned nonstop. I found myself in yet another new element, tête-à-tête-ing with Rebecca De Mornay about the hazards that fame can bring to a relationship (she was with cutie-pie Tom at the time) and sidling up to Jeff Goldblum to hear his views on the naughty interference of the press.

I was really on Michael's side, proud of his three-month chip, and totally behind, beside, and in front of his newfound life-style, cautiously commending his decision—hardly able to believe my eyes, ears, and heart—but when he suggested I attend some Al-Anon meetings, I balked big-time. Wasn't *he* the one with the problem? Here comes a super-duper serious regret: I didn't become his partner in recovery because I had absolutely no idea that by loving Michael—an alcoholic drug addict—I had been part of the problem myself. I did go to a couple meetings, agreed with what everyone said, then went home and thought I had done my wifely duty. I thought I had done enough for him, gone through enough with him, and I wanted to wash my hands of floundering, heroic intervention. Let *them* pick up where I left off. I didn't realize the Al-Anon meetings were for *me.* I needed to know *why* I drew Michael to me in the first place, why I put up with abusive alcoholic behavior but was content to wave good-bye at the door and welcome him home with a hot cup of tea. So I remained part of the problem.

A snotty-haughty, throaty-voiced actress became one of Michael's AA buddies, picking up the non-driver and bringing him home, sometimes very, very late. After meetings there were gatherings that took place in trendy restaurants, lasting well into the night, and knowing this, I would go to bed, and when I felt him crawl in at 3 A.M., I was grateful. At least he wasn't comatose. I had started to acknowledge my stirring suspicions, but since this broad was such a self-serving swankpot, she intimidated little wide-eyed me into inviting her over for dinner and letting her sell worn-out Rodeo Drive dresses at my yard sales. I was always trying to be nice and believe the best, even though her reputation for eating married men for brunch was well known. I didn't have the fallopian tubes to rub my wedding ring along the highfalutin, Chanel-powdered ridges of her high-assed cheekbones, even when she bought Michael a fancy pair of cowboy boots that some poor ostrich had to die for. I kept my suspicions to myself and, as usual, she passed into history. I was doing a TV show when *I'm with the Band* came out; I believe it was *Sally Jessy Raphaël,* and one of the guests was an old AA friend of ours. She and I were gabbing it up about old times in the back of a limo, and she said, "I don't know how you put up with Michael and that witch having that affair right in your face. I was at your place for dinner one night and they were making out in one room while you cooked in the other." The old pal assumed that since Michael and I had broken up a few months earlier, I knew all about the tawdry tryst. As we pulled into the studio, I was flooded with hazy images of serving stuffed trout with green grapes to the conniving, strumpet cow, but I didn't let on that the antique fling was news to me. I didn't want to make my friend feel red-handed and guilt-ridden right before a national TV show. I had always known down deep anyway, and it was good to get my feelings confirmed, despite the shooting sting, like Bully Toilet Cleaner being pumped through my veins.

II

Even though my darling philandering man was finally sober, I had started to feel something amiss and went on a seeking binge, not realizing that Al-Anon might have quenched some of my Death Valley thirst for inner self-savvy. While storming around my local cosmic bookstore, the Bodhi Tree, I came across some fascinating hit-home literature from the Church of Religious Science. As I sat in the incense-sweetened room, sipping tea made from straw, scouring the stack of volumes, all of my many frustrating spiritual quests started taking form and shape in the Science of Mind. Krishnamurti's seemingly complex ideas were laid out in simple, direct language that jumped into my aching head as (gulp!) the *truth*. Concepts I had gleaned from Paramahansa Yogananda's Self-Realization Fellowship lessons, Swami Muktananda's books, tons of Tibetan and Buddhist literature, and of course, the original "big book," the Holy Bible itself, cohered into something I might actually be able to *use* on this planet, in this lifetime! I bought reams of tomes by Ernest Holmes and Emmett Fox, spending way too much dough but feeling like I was onto something mighty. I soon discovered the Hollywood Church of Religious Science and the formidable pastor, Dr. Robert Bitzer, and every Sunday I sat in the front row for my weekly bolt of spiritual lightning. It was a contemplative atmosphere, no screaming out to be spared from hellfire, no pushing on people's guilty buttons. I took it in, drank it down, like a tall, icy bottle of Dr. Pepper. The knowledge seeped slowly into my heart and did battle with the little devil jabbing his poison pitchfork into my smoldering brain. I worked on tuning out that frightened, picky, nagging voice ("This won't work, it's all hype, it's too good to be true") until it became a whispered litany of jibber-jab. I acted "as if" again, until it absolutely was. If a yucky thought or nerve-racking worry passed through, I would look at it and let is dissolve, without giving it a smidge of energy. I learned how to reverse the offending brain wrinkle by seeing a big, giant eraser rubbing the damning thought right out of my head.

Ever so gradually I came to accept that the mind is creative and we actually create our entire world with our thoughts. We can direct our thinking to create crap or glory. We can make love, money, health, and success in our lives by willing it so, by believing we can. I started to realize the only person I was responsible for was myself, and I had to well and truly love myself because the power of God was hanging out within me. I could use the sparkling mass of stuff as I saw fit, turning it into diamonds or cubic zirconias. Dr. Bitzer told us that when Jesus said, "Turn the other cheek," it was to get another point of view, not another slap in the face. That insight was a relief and a revelation to me. How we respond to things that happen to us and how we react is *our* choice. We can wail or laugh, lie down and rot, or dance all over the problem like it was a shiny tabletop.

I yammered at Michael until he joined me at church one Sunday morning. I inflicted my inflated rubber soul upon him, jabbing him delicately in the ribs or sending out knowing, gently piercing looks when Dr. B. hit upon one of Michael's obvious, unattended Major Problem Areas. I was still so bowled over by the vast significance of what I was hearing that I had the subtlety of a ton of bricks covered in tar and feathers. Michael understood all too well what was being said, but I'm sure he resented my blatant pushing and shoving attempts to nurture his needy soul.

I really should have gone to Al-Anon. Really and truly. But by this time I think Michael was just as happy to have me stay at home. Happier, actually.

It certainly did appear that the fates were against Michael, if you believed in that sort of thing. Whenever he made a little headway, it seemed a monster foot would haphazardly stomp him flat. Dreamland Records and Tapes went out of business right after the release of his solo album, and then he hooked up with a feisty female hit-maven, Holly Knight, to form a short-lived duo called Knight and Des Barres. They had a tempestuous creative relationship, but Holly and Nicky became best buddies. In fact, his very first overnight was at Holly's house, where she allowed him free rein over her many synthesizers. He became enthralled with the keyboard and Holly gave him his very own mini-version, a Casio that he carted around everywhere in an important-looking carrying case. Michael and Holly cranked out song after song, some of which sounded like real, live smashes but Michael and Holly bickered nonstop. After these Knightmare temper flare-ups, he would come home in sodden rage, bemoaning his lowly place in life. He saw much grander things in

life for himself and was either bemused or infuriated. While he spit
and snapped at those higgledy-piggledy powers that be, I came along
behind him with affirmative hot air. "Think of this as a challenge,
Michael, one of those learning experiences!!" I tried to wiggle
through his ear and think positive thoughts for him. I might as well
have tried to change his diaper. You just can't change someone's
mind for them, but I didn't know it yet, so I continued to bang my
head against the wall like it felt good. A cup of Krishnamurti, a dose
of Bitzer, and how about three rounds with Mickey Mouse? That'll
fix you right up, honey!

*September 8, 1982—On the verge of my thirty-fourth year, I've been
reading my old diaries, and they were so full of ideas, hopes, and crazed
dreams—the hopes were so high in those days, I was always such a seeker—
tho' all the way through it seems I had an unworthy feeling, like I didn't
deserve the great things in life but somehow kept expecting them. My constant
hope seems to have diminished, but I know I could change it in a snap! So
why don't I? I spoke to Miss Lucy yesterday, she sounds so full of life.
Always a nutter, but so ALIVE and living it up. She's having another
baby! I love life too, I must be more open, tolerant, and loving towards
Mikie, the world, and MYSELF! Nicky is glorious. He uses such big words,
so bright, clever, and perceptive! I almost forgot, old flame Chris Hillman
called today, always such a thrill to speak to him. He stopped getting bombed
two years ago and is pumping so much iron that he called himself "Chris
Swartzen-hillman." I'd like to check those muscles out—something about
him still tears me up. Aah, I was such a little girl when I loved him, and
I'm now a grown-up woman grappling with expansion, looking for the door
out/in. I know I can clear the way with my mind, even though negative
thoughts creep in sometimes. I used to put myself in the hands of fate. Let's
create fate!*

III

My soul may have been coming out of bondage, but my body was
doing menial labor. I actually cleaned friends' houses to make those
damned endless ends meet. Scrubbing toilets was good for humility
but it assassinated the ego. I had to deal with Danny Goldberg's
crotchety landlady, a B-minus, aging actress who treated me like I
was a maid without honor, despite the glaring fact that we had both
been in that spectacular opus *The Carhops* a few years earlier. One
day I found a fangs-bared, heaving rat in the kitchen cupboard, and

when I complained, the bitch snorted contemptuously like I had planted the nasty beast just to give her grief. I put off calling the exterminators until the gnawing sounds drove Danny nuts, and when the jovial murderer-for-a-living arrived with his lethal spray gun, I wept for the idiot rodent and his doomed family.

My next *Mad* magazine—type job was a real kettle of piranha fish. It sounded completely legitimate, and that's why I did so well the first few weeks. I had to sit on the phone in a room with seven other prattling salespeople, call various companies, and in a chirpy, this-is-your-lucky-day voice, offer the employees two days and three nights at a fabulous resort in Las Vegas for two, for the mere pittance of $39.95! One of my early paychecks was $706.09, and it felt swell to be able to spend hours at the swap meets and flea markets, pulling Nick in a little red wagon, on the lookout for grimy treasures disguised as trash: serene masks from Africa, handpainted silhouette fairies, exquisite lace shawls wadded into a ball for two dollars and fifty cents. I'm such an innocent geek that it took me awhile to realize it was a time-share situation, and when the poor slobs got to good ol' Lost Wages (using up their hard-earned vacation time), they were treated to a three-hour hard sell for a time-share condo in the middle of the desert, complete with little slips of paper they could trade for a free dollar keno ticket and a frightening fake-shrimp cocktail. I felt real bad about the semi-deception, but my daddy was sure impressed with my paychecks. He loved the idea that his little girl was making good. I would show him the aging trinkets I found at swaps and garage sales, gleaned from the bottom of someone's barrel, and he would commend me for my keen eye. Underneath it all, I ached to make him proud of me.

IV

My daddy is the guy who turned me on to the glory of collecting junk. He took me to the Saugus swap meet when I was barely in a bra, and we poked through people's old, dusty, rusty stuff, hoping to score a masterpiece for fifty cents. He had the highest hopes of anybody I know, and my mom always said that I was born with his optimism and ridiculous hope for the future. It must be genetic, because at the time his pipe dreams appeared to be just so many frustrated, bungled attempts at grasping for that star-spangled, gold-plated brass ring. Not only did he miss it most of the time, he crash-landed so hard that we were constantly in debt and eating potato soup. It was delicious but redundant.

In his early days in Lancaster, O. C. Miller ran a gas station, where he cut off the tip of his finger slamming the hood of an Edsel, and he wasn't able to play guitar or banjo anymore. Good-bye highfalutin dreams of show biz. He fixed vacuum cleaners and big American cars, then got a job bottling Budweiser, thanks to Mom's heroic, valiant attempts to settle him down and coax him into normalcy. Those blasted Budweiser labels littered our house, their backs waiting to be covered with my childish stick figures and girls' pointy-nosed profiles or Mom's notes for recipes. I even passed boy-notes on them in school. Still, Daddy schemed and dreamed, gambling our modest fortunes on several gold digathons down in Mexico, convinced there was treasure in them thar hills. He actually did find a thick, long vein of gold way, way down past Mazatlán but didn't have the cash or connections to have roads built to get to the mother lode. I still have a snapshot of him astride a put-upon mule, his feet dragging the ground, a look of obstructed, fading glory in his green eyes. He brought back a small canning jar half-full of nuggets, which he would gaze at bleary-eyed after they pulled our perfect house in Reseda right out from under us. And we had just gotten wall-to-wall. Mom wouldn't speak to him as we packed our worldly goods and headed for a cheap apartment in North Hollywood. But by then I was swimming in rock and roll and dying to get back to the Sunset Strip where I could cavort with the Iron Butterfly. It was a sorry scene.

Oren Coy Miller was born in 1914 in North Carolina to a hot-headed, Napoleonic Pilgrim Holiness preacher and his downtrodden, saintly wife. In his rebel youth O.C. was already working in the coal mines, going down, down, down, bringing home the bacon to subsidize ten siblings while his banty-rooster father roamed the hollers, dragging sorry souls to Christ. He had a mess of sisters who were devoted to Jesus and were always out to trap his soul behind those heavenly, pearlescent guilt-stained gates. He ran the other way until the very last minute. Daddy was so damn gorgeous by the time he was twenty years old, looking so much like Clark Gable that people started calling him Hollywood, and he stayed an aloof, tempting playboy until he met my stunning mom, Margaret Ruth Hayes, ten years later. She has since told me it was a serious mismatch but she had been determined to entrap the guy-most-likely-to-remain-a-bachelor-forever because of the enticing challenge.

He called me, his only child, "punkin' " and "birdlegs" and took me swimming at his divorced friend's fancy house in Sherman Oaks. When I think of the fifties, I always see Emil Decker's twinkling,

Technicolor, sun-drenched swimming pool, I smell the exotic, pungent chlorine, I feel the dripping wet suit clinging to my scrawny prepubescent ribcage as I fly through the air off the springy diving board. I was usually alone in the pool while Daddy played poker with Emil and his buddies. I could hear big laughter and shuffling cards, clinking ice cubes, and Dean Martin's lazy promises of *amore* while I paddled around in the sparkles, wishing I could look just like Jayne Mansfield with her sucked-in tummy and stiff white pageboy.

When I was a little girl I did Daddy's nails for a quarter. When I got older I did the job for free while we watched *Bonanza,* using an emery board and a nail clipper to bridge the gap between us. Our fingers were exactly the same, long and thin with weird, flat thumbs. I fiddled with his hands and he was content. O.C. was from that wretched phase of men who weren't allowed to show their love, their sorrow, or their pain. They were very much allowed to be pissed off. He would look down at me from six feet tall, a towering, mysterious male smelling of dangerous sweat; his crinkly green eyes slightly curious. I would look back up at his contained rage and curiosity from my confused, pubescent female perspective, wondering what he thought of me and why did his temples pound so? Did I have anything to do with it? I never did doubt his love, even though he wasn't able to warm me up with it like I secretly dreamed he would. Mom made sure I knew my daddy loved me but spared me from his all-too-human, foibled, frustrated, furrowed brow.

Daddy and I argued about black people and Vietnam. When I started having a left-wing mind of my own, he was stunned and appalled because he was an American all the way. He was a solid navy man whose ship got blown in half during World War II and who survived to proudly tell the harrowing tale. When I insisted on having a black, gay roommate, he threatened to disown me, his growly voice splintering with embedded prejudice. But Mom, to the eternal rescue, placated, cajoled, and explained, "This is a new generation, Oren, things have changed," and when her soothing words didn't work, she finally had to give him one of the three ultimatums of their married life—"Don't ever ask me to choose between you and our daughter, because you would lose." His temples stopped pumping with angry dad-blood soon after. We quarreled and clashed on a constant basis, but his mighty, whooping laugh, somehow full of hope, always reminded me that we had the same blood careening wildly within.

V

O. C. Miller smoked two packs a day way before the surgeon general made his nightmarish proclamation, and he continued to do so even after he started hacking great gobs of black goo from his lungs on a regular basis. After many endless coughing spells my mom finally convinced him to see a doctor. He dreaded the day and put it off because he feared "the Big C." That's what John Wayne called it before he withered up and rode off into the sunset for the last time.

I have always had a ghoulish fear of cancer myself. One lazy summer night when I was eight years old I had my head in Mom's lap, sort of dozing while she and my auntie gabbed it up on the front porch. I didn't have anything to do the next day but skate up and down Jamieson Avenue and change the diapers on my Tiny Tears doll, but what my beloved aunt blabbed to my mom changed that adorable innocence into an obsessive red fear that took years to get over. Aunt Edna was a janitor at a grade school, and that very afternoon an old man had scuttled into the playground with a shotgun, howling and groaning, and within minutes blew off the top of his head. If this wasn't hideous enough to freak out the impressionable, imaginative eight-year-old, wait for what came next. "Edna, do you think Pam should hear this?" "Oh, Margaret, she's sound asleep." "She hears *everything,* Edna." My aunt went on in a hushed tone that hardened the gruesome facts into stone. "The top of his head went sailing out into the yard and landed on the chain-link fence," she whispered loudly, "brains were everywhere, and would you believe that a big buzzard flew down and landed on what was left of that poor man's head?" My mom was appropriately shocked and asked why someone would do such a thing, and in front of the children, too. "Oh, before he shot himself he said he couldn't live with the suffering anymore. He had brain *cancer.*"

The Big C.

I kept the noxious fear inside me until I couldn't think about anything else, couldn't sleep, read, play, or watch TV, much less blithely skate down the street or wipe a rubber butt. I saw that old man's head sailing through the air with the greatest of ease over and over and over again; spinning like a wet red top in the blinding Valley sunshine. Mom thought I was getting the flu until I finally asked, tight and petrified, "Mama, what's cancer?" She told me gently about the awful disease but reminded me that Aunt Edna exaggerated profoundly and told me to try not to think about it anymore. "Can children get it?" Can children get it? Can children get it? CAN CHILDREN GET IT?????

Twenty years later we waited for my dad's tests to come back without saying the (big) "C" word, and all those grotesque fears floated through my mind like the ruined old guy's head-top, but since I had delved into cosmic consciousness by then, I really worked hard at staving off that ancient, gleaming memory. So when the tests showed that he didn't have the Big C but *did* have black lung disease, I had an irrational mixture of relief and rage that temporarily twisted my sanity.

O.C. took this meaty news in the same stride he took everything else, with stewing anger and hearty optimism. After smoking two packs a day for fifty years, he put the Marlboros down and never looked back. He had to quit working at Budweiser, since his breathing had become shallow and difficult, though this, of course, did not inhibit his imbibing. He considered drinking several beers a day a healthy practice because of the hops involved. Even after he quit Budweiser, he went to the side door every Friday and got his case of comfort at half price. The TV took on major importance: the trusty *TV Guide* his reading matter of choice. He pored through the classifieds, still on the search for an elusive magic bargain, haggling on the phone for hours with other "collectors" to take his mind off his hurting inhalations. He was forever strapped to an oxygen tank, his tragic lungs failing him more every day. He detested the bedpan, and the fact that my mom had to deal with it shook his manhood to the core. Even when he finally had to get that damned wheelchair, he made it to his card game puffing, panting, coughing, and hacking all the way. He still had a Cadillac, his only status symbol. We always had Cadillacs; never new, but long, sleek, and shiny just the same. Mom wheeled him to the Caddy, packed up the chair, and he grunted and groaned behind the wheel, driving ten miles an hour, determined to get down the street to Astro Aviation where Bruce Baker or Ed Eudie would meet him at the other end, unpack the chair, and wheel him into the far end of the factory where the chips flew and the ice cubes clinked.

On top of the daily grind, O.C. had a mysterious overnight personality change that made Mom's life temporarily unbearable. All of a sudden, the goulash he had always relished became tasteless and dull, the game shows he usually enjoyed were full of stupid, ignorant sluts who never knew the correct answer, and a streak of unattended dust made him sputter with indignation. After enduring the onslaught for awhile, praying it would end, Mom started varying the scads of medication Daddy had to deal with every day, and found that a day without prednisone was a day with sunshine. The doctor switched the monster-making drug for another one, and Daddy snapped out of it, never knowing he had been a complete and utter boor.

When someone you love is really sick, there is a constant sorrow behind everything you do. Even when great things happened I would think, Wow! Isn't this wonderful?! Oh yeah, except for the fact that my daddy can't breathe. Still, he stayed around longer than the doctors expected, and a whole lot of his stay-around strength came from little Nick. He would sit on my dad's hospital bed and watch him take apart a little motor or fix a dusty, old broken watch and laugh with glee like a miracle had happened. He called him Da, and for four years he had a grandpa.

Since my mom was used to the longtime routine and the gradual decline, she was so exhausted that the big picture eluded her. I knew my dad was about to face the final curtain before she did. Toward the end O.C. finally stopped drinking beer and playing poker. Coughing hard and constantly had taken precedence. There was no more mighty, hopeful laughter. His beautiful fingers had become twisted knots, and his color was way off because there was no oxygen getting inside where it counted. His lungs had become lumps of coal. The TV was on, but he wasn't watching.

VI

Michael was in San Francisco with the newest band he had put together, so Nicky and I decided to spend the night with Nana and Da. Good old Aunt Bert was visiting from Dayton, and I thought Nick should get to know her. It was the day after Thanksgiving and even though Daddy hadn't eaten a whole lot, he seemed to really enjoy this extremely rich chestnut cream goop I had concocted the day before, and that's all he wanted for dinner. I sat there with him, watching him struggle to eat, but he didn't want any help. We never pretended he was about to run the triathalon, but he didn't like us to dwell on the fact that he would never get out of bed again. I tried to squeeze in a little spiritual info as we chatted about the inconsequential nonsense that lightened his weighty load. "Let me know what's going on over there, Daddy," I would say. "When you see that bright light, be sure to follow it." I told him I thought Mom

Miller would probably be there to meet him with her sweet smile, but he said that when you die, it's like turning off the TV; everything goes blank. I trembled to the core and pointed out passages in my spiritual books that tore that concept to shreds, but I think he was looking forward to the blankness. Too worn out to squabble with me about the hereafter, he had even conceded to all the aunties who had been trying to save his soul for several decades by accepting Christ as his savior on Thanksgiving Day. He did it for them, and I thought it was such a gallant gesture. They wept with relief and evangelical joy, but I knew Daddy was still totally confused. He kept the Bible by his bed, along with all the love-laden literature I had bombarded him with, but he really wasn't a reading kind of guy. He had always lived his life with his hands, and they didn't work anymore.

My old GTO friend, Sparkie, met me on Lankershim Boulevard for a spot of sushi, and I told her I thought my daddy was on his way out. She was a little horrified that I could tell her this so casually, but I didn't feel casual at all. I was in touch with something beyond what the eye can see. O.C. had been sleeping so much he was probably halfway to where he was going already. This was an opinion I didn't share with my aunties. They would have checked my forehead for a fever.

Science of Mind had brought my many varied and incoherent beliefs into a clearer focus. I truly believed that death was just another step in our vast and immeasurable journey and that it could actually be perceived as an adventure. I wish I could say that I conveyed some of this to my darling Daddy. I tried, but he was hurting so bad, suffering so hard, clinging to his mortal coil so desperately that my newfound faith trembled under the weight.

It was about nine o'clock when I got home from sushi with Sparkie and had a panicky urge to tell my dad what an inspiration he had been to me and how much I loved him. He nodded. "I know the first thing you're going to do over there is take a big, huge deep breath," I told him, and he smiled and closed his eyes. I asked if he wanted some of the chestnut goop, and he whispered, "That's all right, baby, that's all right." It was the last thing he said.

Since Aunt Bert was in from Dayton, we set up a roll-away bed in the living room, where I was going to sleep, and I put Nicky down on the couch and read him a story. All was quiet in Daddy's room, except for the wheezing of the oxygen tank. After Nick conked out, believe it or not, Mom, Aunt Bert, and I got into a quiet discussion about the pros and cons of lard. I saw no pros at all in the use of pig fat, whereas Aunt Bert had cooked with it her entire seventy-five years and with the exception of a stick-out tummy, she was fit as a squeaky old fiddle. Even though she was quite adamant about the many fine uses of lard, she spoke in hushed tones. Old folks seem to tiptoe around death, giving it a wide berth and a lot of respect, peeking at it between their fingers like it's a real scary movie. If we're quiet enough, maybe it'll go away.

We had all gotten into nightgowns and jammies, and I wanted to check on Dad one more time before heading into a fitful dreamland. The sight of him took all my air out and made me feel invisible. He was curled up on his side, eyes rolled back into his head, bent hands clasped, gasping, wrenching final air into his failed lungs. The death rattle is real, and it stings the ear like a hive full of defiled bees. Instantly I thought of my sleepy mom, rubbing lanolin into her cheeks in the bathroom, Aunt Bert thumbing through *Reader's Digest,* my little Nicky, who was losing his grandpa and didn't know it, sleeping peacefully. I had an absurd, agonizing desire to do Daddy's nails in front of the TV one more time, innocently watching Hoss Cartwright kick the butt of a bad guy, but pressing up against the wall, digging way inside myself, I grabbed ahold of my unbeaten, invincible spirit and pinched it, hard. Pushing myself to walk over to the bed, I took hold of his crumpled hand. "Daddy?" No response whatsoever. His lips were blue, his eyes seeing into another realm; ragged breath, rattling in and out, in and out.

With deep dread I had to call my mom in, and I guess the tone of my voice shook her up. She rushed in confused and fatally frightened, her eyes telling the thirty-seven-year-old story of courtship, love, marriage, betrayal, pain, heartache, acceptance, more love, understanding, profound compassion, and finality. When she saw Daddy she let out a scream I'll never forget and fell on him—"Oren! Oren, no, don't go yet . . ." Aunt Bert came running in, tears flying, her little lady's voice chirping, cracking, calling to Jesus. Daddy never moved, just that loud, ragged breathing signaling his imminent exit from the physical plane. "He can't go yet, Pamela," my mom whimpered in a sore, unfamiliar voice. Daddy's favorite sister, the talkative Aunt Edna, was called, and since she lived around the corner, here she came a few minutes later, being held up by Uncle Ronnie. Seeing her wild-tempered, beloved little brother with his eyes rolled back in darkness, hearing that god-awful sound demanding release, she let out a shriek and grabbed my mom, "Oh Lordy," she wailed, taking in the whole sad situation, "he could be like this for a week!" At that point I came out of my shocked stupor, vowing he would have his release way before the night was over. Relief, respite, deep, never-ending inhalations, hopeful laughter waited on the other side, I knew it. My mom was being comforted by the family, so I took a seat across from Daddy, closed my eyes, and started speaking to his spirit, "It's time to go, Daddy, it's time to set yourself free, take a deep breath, let go, let go, let go, my darling, sweet daddy." It was a precious litany from my soul to his, and after about thirty minutes, I realized his breaths were coming slower and slower, and even though I knew it was for his infinite good, when the final breath was pulled in and never let back out, I collapsed on the bed, curled into him, and felt the living warmth drain away. I stroked the back of his neck where soft gray hairs grew, I inhaled his Daddy scent over and over, until my face was soaked with tears. Mom and my aunts were on their knees, keening; I had never seen my mom entirely out of control before, which gave her a new, vulnerable dimension that made me cry even harder. Uncle Ronnie was the ultimate rock for them, for which I was truly grateful. After my daddy was gone, I kissed his cheek one last time and joined them in their sorrow, praying for O. C. Miller's terrified soul on its gigantic, swooping journey.

VII

Daddy spoke to my mother the morning of the funeral. She was wandering in the backyard, too scattered and sorrowful to know what to wear, when she heard Daddy's voice. "Put on that pretty blue suit that Pam bought you," he said softly in her ear. Mom is very much a realist and certainly did not expect to hear from my dad, but feeling much better, she went right into the house and put on the blue suit. When she told me about it, my faith spiraled and I grinned into the gray skies.

Daddy was buried on a high hill far out in the San Fernando Valley. I was shaken up, so my oldest grade-school friend, Iva, drove us to the funeral. Iva is full of freckles, and my dad had always said to her, "Hey, Iva, have you been standing too close to that cow again?" Every time he said it he hollered with laughter like she hadn't heard the dumb Southern expression two dozen times before. We reminisced about Daddy's corny sense of humor all the way up the long green hill. I didn't want to look at him in the casket, but Mom did, and I heard her cry, "Don't let Pamela see him! He wouldn't have wanted to look like this!" She called out to me in a bedraggled, strained voice, "Pamela, don't come in here, don't." Sitting out in the flat, empty foyer, I tried real hard not to conjure up any images. Michael held Mom close beside him, and I held her hand as we all straggled to the grave site, where Aunt Edna's nice Christian preacher spoke gently of heaven and forgiveness. O.C.'s poker buddies brought a huge royal flush made out of flowers and stood grimly in a row like See, Speak, and Hear No Evil, looking like sad, uncomfortable, overgrown boys. Mom and I each placed a rose from the garden on the casket. Almost overly stalwart and straight-backed, I felt like I had to be shatterproof for my mom, who was finally letting all those years of wounded strength come tumbling down.

Daddy spoke to my mom a few more times, and even though it's beyond amazing when she hears his lovable growly voice, we're still waiting to find out what it's like up, out, over there. She was in the backyard picking some white bell-shaped flowers to take to his grave site one morning, and he said, "You know I never liked those, why don't you bring me a piece of my fig tree?" The old coot was still pretty ornery. The next time he came out of the great nowhere, Mom had been arguing with one of his sisters and it was about to drive her nuts. Pacing around in the backyard under his beloved fig tree, she asked him what she should do about it, hoping absently for a reply. "Fuck 'em," he announced in her ear, and it was really just what she needed to hear.

Just recently I was digging around in Mom's cedar chest still full of faded paper dreams and frothy lace dresses Aunt Bert sent me from Dayton in 1956. I was trying to locate my floor-length Flying Burrito dress, the checkered purple one I wore to all their Palomino shows, when Mom and I came across a beribboned stack of Daddy's storm-tossed letters from the the middle of the Pacific, where he was serving his country during World War II. I scanned a couple of them; they were factual, homesick, full of longing for his young wife but resolute and unafraid. Mom and I took turns reading some of the most endearing passages, and when we closed the cedar chest, she left the stack out so she could climb back into 1944 after I left. Nick spent the night with her, so I could go to the Palomino to see the band I manage, wearing that Burrito dress, and when I came back to pick him up the next day, Mom seemed far-off, like her eyes were seeing right through me. "Your daddy spoke to me last night," she said quietly, sort of awestruck by his reappearance after such a long absence. We had assumed he was so far away he wasn't able to make contact anymore. I was beside myself to find out what he had to say. "All he said was, 'Hi Sweetie," but I had the feeling he wanted to get something through to you," Mommy told me as she took a folded piece of paper out of her pocket, "and since he spoke to me in the bedroom for the first time, I felt like he wanted me to find something to show you." She said he led her to the pile of Navy letters and among them she found a note he had written to me while I was doing that dumb soap in New York. She handed me the letter and I looked at it with wonder, like it had floated down from the farthest heavenly realm. It was from a hotel way down in Apatzingán, Mexico, where he was scavenging for gold, and here's what it said:

Hi sweetie,

Just a little note to you. I've really had a rough time the last month here, so much walking and working in the rain, have lost so much weight that friends here in town didn't hardly know me after being gone for five weeks. I'll have to get smaller clothes, mine are mostly wore out anyway, am back to my coal-mining days, with a 30-inch waist. I feel real bad about the hard times I have caused you and your dear mother, and if hard work will make them better, then they soon will be. I see you most everywhere I go; one picture up here at the hotel, one up in our house at camp, and one up in my favorite restaurant. I tell them you will soon be famous, so don't make a liar out of me. No one understands my Spanish so good, so they tell everyone you already are, so keep doing the best you can. I hope one day you will be as proud of me as I am of you.

Love,
Ol' Dad.

He found a way to let me know he had been proud of me then and was proud of me now. I held the letter and cried a whole bunch of grateful tears, blessing his soul for reaching down to show me that there really is such a wondrous thing as undying love.

CHAPTER EIGHT

I

Now that Daddy was gone, I mentioned to Mom, "Maybe I should start writing that book I've always talked about." The one about the glorious heyday of rock and roll, traipsing around love-ins with barely any clothes on, my all-girl band, Girls Together Outrageously, touring with Zeppelin, taking psychedelics on the Sunset Strip—the book Daddy wouldn't have been able to accept. She nodded. "Yes, dear, I've always thought you were a very talented writer, go ahead." Go ahead. Did she know what she was saying? Uh-oh, I had been given the ultimate permission. Still, it would be a whole year before I got the mammary glands to search Mom's garage for the bargain typewriter that Daddy had gotten cheap after some Sun Valley storage building burnt down to the ground in 1976. After I got a new ribbon, the thing worked great, but it always had a slightly sooty odor.

Very soon after my daddy died, Michael got a threatening, lunatic call from his mother telling him his father had also passed away and was about to be buried in a "pauper's grave." After borrowing the money for a trip to London from Danny Goldberg, Michael set off on his harrowing journey. I worried if he would be able to keep a handle on his newfound sobriety under these hazardous circumstances, dealing with the unstable Irene, attempting to get the funds from his father's estate to give him a decent burial. He checked in with me every few days, completely sober, praise God, but under such a grotesque strain, my mind boggled. I longed to comfort him, but it was way beyond my capacity. His father's body sat in a room for days and was finally interred in a pauper's grave. There was nothing Michael could do. His mother thought her only son had come to town to get his hands on Philip's estate and had actually called him "Judas" before turning her back and disappearing forever. Through the entire ordeal Michael kept a journal—calling it *Treasures of Every Sort*—and it saved his sanity.

One consolation for Michael was his new band, Chequered Past. And the band members' pasts were checkered, indeed. Blondie had dissolved a few months earlier, so Clem Burke and Nigel Harrison joined him, along with my old flame, Tony Sales (who had recently recovered from a humdinger of a car accident where the gear shift had gone right through his chest and he had to learn how to walk, talk, and read all over again), and an exhilarating newcomer to Los Angeles, Steve Jones, the guitar player from the earth-altering Sex Pistols. A mere five years earlier the Pistols had stormed through the soporific, stale music world and pounded it flat, injecting pissed-off poison darts and a heavy load of jagged nuts and bolts into the humdrum banality that was passing for rock and roll. They reminded the right people that rock and roll should never, ever be safe. And that was rockin' good news.

When the Sex Pistols dismantled, Stevie had roamed around London in rude and sullen confusion, getting into trouble with the law, which ultimately led him to the sunny Southern California shores where he met up with Michael and slid into Chequered Past. They already had a slick, tongue-in-cheek, hard-rock, soulful sheen, and Steve gave the band the required balls and thumping danger element it needed to compete in the snarled-up, crippled music industry. Hugely overproduced bands like Journey, Asia, and Styx topped the charts while the post-punk, new-wavers continued to redefine everybody's life-style. Hopefully there would be room for some pure-assed straight-ahead rock and roll. Danny Goldberg had started his own management company and added the band to his roster. Things seemed on an upward swing.

Since Tony and Dee Dee got married and moved away to their own private digs across the street from the Roxy, there was room for the Sex Pistol to move in. Kind of scary. For Christmas Michael and I gave Stevie a gigantic box full of the many essential items he lacked in his life: a toothbrush and toothpaste, deodorant, several bars of Dial, shampoo and conditioner, mouthwash, a few pair of underpants, and a couple sets of socks. It was as if we had spent a million bucks on him, he was so grateful and thrilled. He still hadn't gotten a dime from the Sex Pistols; Malcolm McLaren got all of it, and it would be several more years until Steve got the dough that was owed to him. He went to AA meetings with Michael, was attempting to get legal, and seemed ready to get his life in some sort of order.

January 10, 1983—Steve Jones has been staying with us for six weeks, and it's so mind-blowing I don't know where to start. He was a junkie for seven years, a thief convicted sixteen times, wanted all over England, ill educated, unschooled, but since he's been with us he's a new man. Tonight he told Michael he's never been happier and how he loves us so much. He opens up more daily. I feed him every meal and give him every good vibe I can; I like to see him happier every day. He's never had a normal life and is like a little boy in a lot of ways. I'm learning so much from him. He's always right there with you, living in the moment, with no expectations, no bullshit. He doesn't know how to be dishonest, I've never met anyone like him. It's wild. He and Michael are writing some killer songs, and Chequered Past are doing demos for RCA next week. A deal is imminent.

II

With one of the Sex Pistols living in the house, I decided to become a Mary Kay consultant, one of the great dichotomies of my life. My acting career had been reduced to a dim lightbulb that was about to sputter out entirely, and I was so damn tired of fraudulent sales pitches and splattered toilet rims! So after nowhere near enough contemplation, I sold our rarely played, Hallmark greeting card piano and bought a massive pink Mary Kay display case full of corny American (pipe) dream promise. Stevie was kind enough to let me practice cheekbone and lip-liner applications on him until I got it right. Sometimes he resembled Margaret Thatcher in drag, sometimes he looked just like Princess Margaret on one of her better days. I hunkered down and studied all the pink-Cadillac-pledging-gung-ho literature, attended pep-rally, rah-rah meetings with cardboard cut-out ladies in pink suits showing off diamonds (I kept expecting a pink-swathed guru to toddle in and teach us to contemplate our blush-on), and started torturing all my girlfriends into having Mary Kay makeup parties right in their very own homes!

The first patsy was my sweet mom, who corralled all the aunties and little local ladies into her kitchen where they sat uncertainly around her maple table, before them their pink plastic pallettes full of dibs and daubs of color, selected by *me,* the Mary Kay Consultant, *just for them.* "Oh! Aunt Edna, that's *your* color!! Opal, just look what that *shade* of peach does for the *shape* of your face! Mommy! You've never looked so beautiful! Has she, Joanie?!" After smearing globs of goop on their faces and accenting brows that had been neglected for forty years, nobody purchased any products except Mom, and she bought way too many pink-cased items from her only child.

My next party for was for Eddie Begley's wife, Ingrid, and it went A-OK; so well, in fact that one of her guests, Patti Goldblum, wanted a facial bash at her place the following week. I arrived at a big pale pad in the San Fernando Valley hills with my corpulent case and was met at the door by Patti's husband, the unique, very tall actor Jeff Goldblum, who hovered around the creamed-up ladies all afternoon, offering bits of odd makeup advice along with the nicely prepared finger sandwiches. Jeff was such a swell guy—so attentive and interested in the frothy female goings-on—that I felt really bad for Patti when he ran off with Geena Davis, but I sort of understood, because he and Geena were just about the same size, and Patti was a tiny little woman. Then a few years later Hollywood's tallest couple broke up, so I guess size isn't everything.

I had my five Mary Kay parties within the allotted time frame and received my Perfect Start pin in a convention room at the Bel Air Sands Hotel on Sunset Boulevard. As the higher-up, many-pinned, pink-decked lady presented the tiny gold-dunked trophy, I was caught up in waves of thunderous pink applause. It was somehow unsettling. Did I deserve to bask in this overwhelming ovation for selling somebody a mauve eyeliner? I received another gold-plated pin for bringing poor Ingrid Begley into the Mary Kay fold as a new consultant. I apologized to her later.

I flubbed around with the products for another short chunk of time, accepted the sorry fact that I had made a blunder and could *never* be that normal (thank the Lord), and sold the pink case full of corny promise to a cute chicana at my next yard sale. I told her the hefty case of cosmetics cost me five hundred big ones, and she got herself a nice, hearty laugh. I got fifteen dollars.

What ever happened to my acting career? My agent never sent me out, and when she did, I was either too young or too old, too short or too tall, too cute or not cute enough. I could no longer afford to spend countless days and nights doing plays that didn't pay, so it seemed that my life in front of the footlights was basically over. Tragic, but true. I made a chart featuring the pros and cons of continuing to take rejection on the chin. The cons outweighed the pros by sixteen tons.

Acting Pros

1. It feels undeniable when you are actually *doing* it.
2. I've invested many years and untold energies toward acting.
3. I have *trained* to be an actress and it's what I do best.
4. Camaraderie on projects.
5. The elation I experience when I do a good job.
6. My respect for the craft. (puke)
7. Nothing else exists when you're into it.
8. I don't want to have to admit failure to my far-reaching childhood dreams. (not that I *believe* in failure)

Acting Cons

1. I haven't made any money in acting for three years.
2. I haven't acted *at all* in over five months!
3. I've plugged away for fifteen years and am still *totally* unknown!
4. In order to "continue" my career, I would have to put a scene together and send photos to agents and casting people—actively seek a new agent. (*very* difficult)
5. I signed with my "new" commercial agent in October and have been out only four times. No callbacks, no contact with agency, no respect from agency.
6. Almost thirty-five years old—not a time to "start" a career in acting. (all over again!?) Do I still feel the urgency?
7. In order to do a play, there's about five nights a week rehearsal, a lot of baby-sitters, then I work four nights a week and make no money for the work.
8. The rejection barrier that has to be put up like a wall when they don't call back. Repeated rejections can kill someone.
9. The consistent feeling of being an "out-of-work" actor. "Have you been working?" The constant "No"s. The feeling of worthlessness at your craft because you're unable to do it most of the time. Very few people take you seriously.
10. So many times I've wound up "on the cutting-room floor." It makes me feel like quitting each time.

But I wasn't quite ready to relinquish my star-stacked hopes. Even though those repeated rejections could have killed me, I decided to carry those anvils around on my shoulders for a little while longer by joining a theater group for the handicapped. I thought I could kill two Byrds with one Stone (what happened when Mick Jagger's limousine ran down Roger McGuinn and David Crosby? Ha.) and keep up my skills while possibly doing some cosmic good.

My first scene was from *Coming Home,* the tear-dripper that starred Jane Fonda and Jon Voight as a paraplegic Vietnam vet. My partner was a quadriplegic car-accident victim who happened to be an amazing actor. In fact, I saw him on some TV docudrama just the other night, and he was top-notch. When we rehearsed in the donated high school gym, I had to turn the pages of the script for him until he learned his lines, and when we did the scene for class, I heard people sobbing and sniffling all the way through. They actually cheered when the imaginary curtain came down, and I was overcome with a satisfaction more complete than any I had gotten from taking my own bows—that rare feeling that life is a gift, a new, special present to be opened every day, wrapped in happy paper and tied with rah-rah ribbon.

I had always kept a fearful, respectful distance from the "handicapped" or "disabled," intimidated by all they had to deal with, and now I was seeing firsthand how bright and shining strong the human spirit could be—against all odds in a big way. My next scene was with an adorable, incredibly upbeat blind girl named Vicki. We played a couple of sisters on a sib-style rampage, even though she was black and I have been called white trash more than once. Vicki had moved away from some Midwestern state with her magnificent guide dog Daisy and into a pretty rotten neighborhood downtown, but she never seemed to notice. Not only was she blind, she had diabetes and had to inject herself twice a day. I watched her make her way around the itsy-bitsy apartment, where she cooked dinner for me one evening after we rehearsed. She made Campbell's Vegetarian Vegetable just for me, and spread mayo evenly on the white squares of bread before placing the turkey slices just so. I watched her make the sandwiches with awestruck amazement, like she was doing a perilous sky dive from two hundred feet. She told me how it felt to go blind, how the light got dimmer, like a shade being pulled down a tiny bit each day, until she was forever in the dark. She said she tried to hold onto the final fleeting images, but all she remembered were multicolored lights and her mother's face. I listened to her argue with her mother on the phone from that faraway Midwestern city. She wanted her daughter to come home, but Vicki wanted to be a star. After I left the acting group, I heard that Vicki had passed away from her diabetes. I remembered her blazing desire to succeed, to wage battle with her "handicap," to make her life into something daring and special, and I sent a bolt of love to her sweet soul.

I learned all kinds of things about the strength of the human spirit but at last felt I was ready to give up on acting, which seemed to already have given up on me. I pondered the decision incessantly for several long days before taking all my head shots, resumes, *Dramalogues, Hollywood Reporters,* commercial composites, and scene-study books and dumping them into the garbage in a lonely, solemn ritual. I actually put a match to the mess because I wanted to make sure I wouldn't be able to change my mind. I read the list of "Acting Cons" aloud while the trash can blazed. I wept. Jesus wept. After everything was ashes, I sat on the porch expecting to feel like an arm had been severed, like a weakling failure without an Oscar nomination, but instead I felt such a surprising, delicious relief surge over me that I wept again with joy and laughed and felt those sixteen tons slip off my shoulders and turn into feather boas. My many hours of preaching positive thinking and erasing negative thoughts were paying off. I thought about how Dr. Bitzer at the Church of Religious Science would see what I had done. I was making room for something new—not *failing* at anything! I was letting go, not giving up! Bully, bully, *bully* for me! But where was my standing ovation?

III

I certainly wasn't getting one at home. I still held down various nutty jobs, drove Michael everywhere, took care of the finances, the household, the bills, the meals, and the pets. And despite the fact that I loved Michael madly, our sex life had gradually diminished through the years, seemingly to the point of no return. It stung me to have to admit that he might not find me desirable anymore. I hadn't let myself go, in fact, I took such good care of myself, it bordered on an Estée Lauder nightmare. I agonized about what to do about the situation, almost deciding to accept the chilly fact that after a certain period of time the mystery and excitement in a romantic relationship turns mundane and ordinary. You get to know each other too well to dredge up the former wild lust that used to rack your body like an orgasmic spasm at the mere thought of your beloved's crotch area. I *almost* accepted this notion, but the fading image of an earlier me, prancing down the Sunset Strip, headed for a horny liaison, titties bouncing, wriggling all over—a sexual creature personified—kept me from accepting this atrocious, all-too-commonplace syndrome. I had fought hard for the right to my sexuality for too long to give in, give up, and get old. I had previously casually mentioned to Michael that I missed our horny closeness but was met with a noncommittal shrug, and since confrontation of any kind was nearly impossible for me, let alone a possible maelstrom of stamped-down passion, I used my straight-laced Virgo power and swept the concept under the already worn-out rug. And life, as they say, went on.

Nothing will stay under that rug forever, so I forced myself to step into the deep end one night after Michael and I turned out the lights. I so much wanted to capture that faint heartbeat of waning desire before it became extinct like the sixties flower child, but after I attempted to seduce my husband and was rebuffed like a pesky gnat, I fell into a comalike lethargy and resigned. Checked out. I lay there in the dark room, shaking all over with a mixture of female embarrassment, disgust at myself, and loathing for Michael as he slept unpeacefully on the other side of the bed-chasm, filled to the brim with his own private angst. The next morning was like a death rattle. I lumped around making coffee and heating bran muffins until Michael decided to deal bravely with the issue. He said part of the reason he wasn't able to feel aroused was because I came to bed with cream smeared on my face and wearing an old T-shirt, and it was a turn-off. I told him the cream kept me looking young and pretty, but he swore it was the culprit. That night I dolled up in lingerie and lipstick, went to bed with rust-colored cheekbones, and we made love like hot, wicked strangers. The next glorious night he carried me up the stairs in my lace baby-doll like Rhett Butler gone mad—and then it was over. Even though I tried to entice him with two different sets of garter belts, everything went back to "normal" after those two blissful, naughty nights. I floated on air and then landed back on Wonderland Avenue with a loud, ugly thud. If we just could have grabbed that moment and gone to a sex shrink. If he could have told me the *other* part of the reason he wasn't able to feel aroused. If I had tried to *make* him tell me. If I had gone to a blasted Al-Anon meeting. If, if, if.

Getting sober hadn't improved Michael's midnight moodiness

either. At one point he had to take some penicillin for an unnamed reason, and was allergic to the shot. His rear end where the needle entered bulked up like a shiny red rubber ball, then his poor penis swelled up to the size of an Oscar Meyer weeniemobile, and he was entirely miserable. I played super-nurse and listened to his blustering outrage at being chosen by those sadistic powers that be for this hideous affliction, and I understood, I really did. It *was* a grotesque situation, but there was *nothing I could do* to make him feel better. I trundled around, trying to make him more comfortable, but I was a helpless buffoon in the face of this blasphemy. To top it right off, he was feeding the cats and sliced his pinkie finger almost to the bone, and when it got infected and oozy, he was so on-fire infuriated I thought he would combust and disappear in a puff of self-induced smoke.

March 30—*It's been mesmerizingly crushing around here lately. Michael's persona is so gigantic and strong* anyway *that when he's got any kind of physical or mental problem, it's like having ten people around with the problem. And it's me who takes up the excess, of which there is a ton. It would be easier for me to sympathize, empathize, and be tender if he could accept the pain for what it is and not put labels all over himself. It's been so hard on me. (I know how hard it's been on him—he suffers harder than most, like everything he does.) But I, in fact, could be called the victim in this case. I really do my best. I have no time for myself, with most energies directed toward Michael, and of course, Nicky (who is going through some very weird changes). I really feel "put upon," knowing, of course, through Science of Mind that I put myself right where I am. Sometimes I have trouble with that concept. How could I have anything to do with a penicillin shot Michael got? I suppose it's my attitude about the situation. I say positive affirmations over and over again to keep going, but where is my creativity? I push out the negative thoughts, but where is the success and joy? I am happy with a large part of my life, but there is a* lack—*and I'm not even supposed to think that. Oh, Lordy, I need to get the creative me out of the shadows. I'm just not up to peak. (I'm not supposed to say that either.) I don't allow myself to be clear and work from my center, and then I'm guilty about it. AAAaaaHHH! I miss my great big daddy.*

In that desperate diary entry I told a humongous truth: I saw myself as a *victim*. Even though I was attempting to slog through the obvious crappy situation to the best of my flailing ability, I wasn't going to get very far by seeing myself as a stooge. It was like finally coming across the Door, and finding no knob, latch, handle, or keyhole. By seeing myself as being victimized, I threw away any power, any strength I might have been trying to create directly onto the dung heap. Also, I seemed to think my creativity was playing hide-and-seek with me somewhere out in the murky shadows. Somewhere *out there*, somewhere outside *myself*. Somewhere over the fucking rainbow. Come out, come out, wherever you are, you peek-a-boo bitch. I'm down on my knees, begging you please, to come home.

IV

To complicate the brewing nightmare even further, my little boy was starting to have serious problems at preschool. It was almost time for kindergarten, and anything he might have learned in ABC Land was history to him already. If the rest of the world didn't see things his way, he just didn't understand and either flipped his tiny lid, ranting and seething, or went into a doomy funk that lasted way too long for such a little guy. Michael and I took him back to UCLA, where we found out he was (gulp) "gifted," and needed (oh no) "special attention." I remember walking down a long corridor with a bespectacled serious science type. Peering over her glasses, she said, "Mrs. Des Barres, I think you should know your son is one in twenty thousand." Interesting odds, lady. What do you say to that? What was I supposed to do about it? Nicky went into therapy once a week with a genuinely sweet graduate student named Cynthia, who tried in vain to figure out why he was so intense. He never opened up to her, preferring to stay petrified and withdrawn all by himself. He had started to say "I hate myself," and "I wish I was dead," when the teensiest little thing went wrong. He paid too much attention to fine details, and if they didn't go according to his plan, all Hades broke loose. He kicked and bawled and banged his head on the floor. The drawings that had once given him so much pleasure and satisfaction now tormented him unless they were *perfect*. He shredded his artwork if it didn't measure up and then went into a wild rage or catatonic despair. He became agonizingly shy, he began to stutter, and I fluttered around him like fifteen confused mother hens. Sometimes his adorable cherubic glory shined through and his ever-expanding vocabulary would amaze all our friends, but I knew something was severely amiss, and I could hardly bear it. He took piano lessons with our friend, Prescott Niles from the Knack, he treasured the KISS records given to him by Gene Simmons, playing them over and over, memorizing each lick. But his little brow was always furrowed, his shoulders bent. I asked him one day what his biggest problem was, and he looked straight at me and said, "The state of the world."

How did this happen? Miss Goody Two Shoes, Pollyanna, cutesie-poo, Snow White, Minnie Mouse, heart-lady had a stunning little blond boy with a head full of deep, dark, dangerous thoughts, and he wasn't even five years old! Could the tragic Des Barres lineage have anything to do with Nick's complex and unruly confusion? Could there be some genetic factor contributing to his early self-doubt and sadness? If so, what then? Michael and I were both at a loving loss to comprehend the seemingly fathomless depth of our little boy's pain. What did his worry stem from? I had been a big worry-wort as a kid, remembering my fanatic pangs of all-consuming grief about the "Big C," but Nick's inner torment seemed vast and impenetrable. I tucked him in at night and his eyes said "Mommy, help me," but I couldn't get in.

I watched him sleep; the sweetest platinum-haired angel boy that was ever born, and prayed so hard for him to be happy. My pillow was soaked in tears, and once again I beseeched all the holy saints who had helped to make Michael sober to smile on my innocent son. I'd always had a very hard time saying no. I thought that if I kept saying, "No, you can't do this, you can't do that," it would be too much negative input and might squelch his free-flying soul. And now I doted on Nicky like Abraham Lincoln had never freed the slaves, hoping that by my drenching him in attention, flooding him with love, and *doing everything for him,* he would regain his sunny, lamblike babyhood grin and enjoy life like I did. I still put on his socks and tied his shoes. I bought him whatever he wanted; anything to give him a few moments of little-kid pleasure and to see his eyes shine.

Remember that dumb line about a baby not being born with a guide book? I truly wish one had been included with the merchandise.

V

Consumed as I was with taking care of Michael and Nicky, about all I was doing for little old me was working out, an obsession I found I could parlay into always-needed cash. I started teaching exercise part-time with my friend Buddy, using those machines I had first discovered with Kim Lee; the ones that helped me tighten that baby flab I had acquired along with Nicky. I also cleaned the studio in exchange for free use of the wondrous machinery. One spring evening I was hard at work, making sure Ted Danson and Marilu Henner were tightening their abs as hard as they could, when Buddy blasted through the studio door carrying a thin black puppy in his perfect pumped-up arms. "Look what I found about to get killed on Sunset Boulevard!"

The large puppy romped directly at me, wagging all over, and grinned like I was covered in Alpo. It was double love at first sight, so I surprised the entire household with a fabulous new pet! Blanche and Harry, our mother and son cats were definitely not amused, but Michael accepted her right away, and Stevie and Nick puppied her to pieces, so she was instantly spoiled. We called her Sunset Nellie Blue, and she was the first dog who ever spoke to me. I could get her to make sounds just like a whining, whimpering, happy human by rubbing her tummy in a certain spot. It was uncanny. Steve took a particular shine to Nellie, and she always sat all over him like a lapdog even though she eventually weighed thirty pounds and we found out she was mostly pit bull.

This divine canine addition to our lives forced us to leave Vista Street in a hurry. Apparently our lease said no dogs, and besides, now that Nick was way past the baby stage, Mrs. Finagle had lost her goo-goo interest in him. Once again I pored through the classifieds and cruised the streets, finally coming across a two-story winner at the top of Wonderland Avenue in Laurel Canyon. Aah! the glory of God's golden backyard once again!

We all moved into the tree-shaded retreat a couple weeks later; Mikie, me, and Nick, Steve Jones with his girlfriend, Nina, and of course, Nellie and the cats, Harry and Blanche, who headed for the hills in ecstasy. The lease came with a warning: The house was for sale and could be bought at any minute. But the idea of living in Laurel Canyon far outweighed that looming possibility. Nicky started first grade at Wonderland Avenue School, right down the street, skipping kindergarten altogether for obvious reasons, and I became school mom, attending PTA meetings, baking cupcakes and dumb casseroles for various functions, trying really hard to *fit in,* so that he might *fit in.* Maybe we could all make a fabulous fresh new start!

CHAPTER NINE

I

*H*aving unfamiliar cupboards and closets, different color walls and tiles in the kitchen makes you feel like something new is going on, and this time we were surrounded by layers and layers of green; Mother Nature was our neighbor on all sides. Overly optimistic (is there such a thing?) as usual, I felt the promise of a new day dawning! Good things were about to happen! The only way was *up*! Up the long and winding, scalding green hill of Wonderland Avenue.

Two things happened right about this time to confirm my heartening suspicions: I started a writing course at Everywoman's Village, a lib-type ladies' school in the Valley that specialized in yanking out artistic female expression, and I got a call from dear Danny Goldberg about setting up an interview with a friend of his who was writing a book on Led Zeppelin.

The class consisted of me and six other frustrated ladies looking for an outlet, a way to *express themselves. PLEASE.* The wonderfully eccentric teacher who wore long gray braids and Indian print skirts, set an orange on the table and asked us to describe it in three paragraphs. She had us write a three-page sentence, using no punctuation, and then concoct a poem about the death of a pet. Our last assignment was to take a day out of our past and bring it to life. I relished this one and wrote two and a half pages about the day I waited in that long, teen-scream line to see the Rolling Stones back in '65. The teacher flipped her wonderfully eccentric lid, and on the last day of class told me I was really onto something. She encouraged me to continue with my story, adding that she enjoyed my "voice." I didn't even know I had a voice, so this was spectacular news indeed. Then Stephen Davis, who was about to wreck the rep of Zep by writing *Hammer of the Gods,* came to the pad in Laurel Canyon to quiz Michael on the heaviest, most enigmatic of rock bands and to pick my brain for titillating groupie stories. He turned out to be a very charming, easygoing gentleman and the source of some excellent advice for me. "Hold on to your stories," he insisted. "Don't tell them to anybody until you're ready to tell them for yourself." He also suggested that I get a cowriter and gave me a couple of names. I had to lie down on the couch after Stephen left and stare at the blank ceiling for twenty minutes to contemplate the vast implication: A published author and a writing teacher both thought my little tale was important enough to tell.

So I finally plugged up the negative holes so those mischief-making doubts couldn't get through and poked through the dusty, musty, slanted rays in Mom's garage, looking for the old gargantuan box of diaries/journals. I went way, way back into my past, starting with the first diary I ever wrote at age ten. Mom had stuck the blue, plastic Deb-U-Teen in my stocking for Christmas, and I felt obliged to write in it dutifully every day:

January 1—*Dear Diary, I watched the Rose Parade. After it was over, Harvellee came over to play ball and with balloons. She is a poor sport, she was grouchy. For dinner I had steak, mash potatoes, and Marvo-Mix. Well, so long.*

March 16—*Today the teacher read our grades. I let down on four subjects. I was very sad after school. I went to Iva's and we traded comics. I was reading* Little Lulu *before I wrote in you.*

April 2—*I stayed home from school and watched* Our Miss Brooks, Amos and Andy *and many more. Lassie was fed some poisoned meat by a mean little girl; she made Lassie lose the race. She got sick right in the middle of it. I got some M&Ms. I picked one up off the ground and ate it. It wasn't dirty.*

June 10—*I had to dance with Jonathan for the square dance, and I had "Jonathan and Pamela" written on my leg, so I went down on the floor and hid it, but before I did that I wiped as much off as I could. I wish he would kiss me on the mouth. Guess what? Harvellee and I made up a new style: one braid and one ponytail. We wore it to school today.*

October 26—*I was talking to Daddy in a funny language like Donald Duck. Boy, did he laugh. After school, I tried Harvellee's paper doll's doll* *clothes on her paper doll, then she chased me all over trying to touch the pink dots on my chest. I ran. My parakeet Sunny is sick.*

December 12—Sunny died of cancer in his liver. Cancer had eaten his liver away. I was really crying. Gosh, when I was trying to get him to take a bath a month ago, stupid ol' cancer was eating Sunny's liver up. I always look at the cage he was in and cry.

The Big C again. And if sinless, little budgies can get it, *can children get it?* And what about Harvellee? On top of being a poor sport, she tried to touch the pink dots on my chest on more than one occasion. I would fend her off, using Barbie's pointy toes as a sword and call to my mom for help, but when she came running into my room with a dish towel in her hands, Harvellee's halo appeared like wide-eyed, innocent-kid magic every time. Even her freckles glowed.

After getting filthy with prehistoric garage grime, I found the ragged box full of the dumb notes about boys, passed back and forth in school. I found my goofy, pained adolescent poetry, so proud of myself for saving every scrap of that teen nonsense for posterity. I came across many crucial, babbling documents—a dreamy wish-letter written to me from me with someone else's signature:

My Dearest Pam,

First, me luv, I must explain a few things to you. Don't think for one moment that I enjoyed those weeks in the Virgin Islands with that ruddy Jane Asher. Oh luv, it was pure misery! She's crackers and drained me of my pay 'til me and Ringo were both skint! Natchally, as you knew, she only went along for publicity. Wouldn't any jobless actress do the same? Please believe me, me beluvved, you're the only one in my heart.

If you don't know by now, I'll tell you: I wrote your favorite song "World Without Love," for you and you alone. Oh luv, the night I helped John write those words, I needed you so! I need you now! Oh, luv, I've told you how much I love you in every song we've written. I hope you know that. Every song speaks of my love for you.

All My Loving, Paul

And I found a crumpled, stoned-out letter to Marlon Brando:

My dear Marlon,

Your name was just mentioned in an insane conversation be-tween a bunch of my lunatic friends. I'm sure everyone I know is a genius in one way or another—most of them fulfilling their creative need. I never really have totally expressed myself creatively, but at times I feel my friend's success as if it were my own. Let's face it, I'm usually frustrated. Unless one totally reacts to any given situation exactly the way one feels about it, confusion occurs, due to the block that is created by the thoughts in between the event and the reaction to it. If you withhold your immediate reaction, then there is a block. Unless you react without thinking first, it's too late and any reaction is false and useless. EVERYONE has some paranoia—due to circumstances, twisted energies, and misunderstandings of meanings and words—I so want to bring mine under control. Oh yes, I forgot to tell you the circumstances in which your name came up. Led Zeppelin got dressed up in drag last night, and the roadie said, "I don't know about the rest of you guys, but you can find me at Marlon Brando's house." He must have been reading my mind. I wonder when I'll ever get over this groupie phase. My photographer, Lee, says I'm about to get my Ph.D. As soon as I feel I am contributing to the happiness of this poor race, then maybe I won't try so hard to reap my rock friend's trips. I'm doing this play tomorrow at Actor's Studio, it's my first real BIG HOLLYWOOD EXPERIENCE. I called to let you know what time to show up. I hope you can see it. I'll bet you'd wished you had. It's such a thrill to open up and CREATE with your entire being. I am ready for absolutely ANYTHING that comes my way. There are so many times when I've almost stopped smoking grass. There must be a saturation point. I'm so full of it that whenever I get high it spills out of me and seems to SOIL MY BRAIN. It has become a social thing, like the nine-to-fiver's cocktails. I have been really overindulging on the earth level. I was so drunk when you finally spoke to me on the phone that I must have garbled on a bit. It was so kind and gentle of you to have concern for someone you do not yet know. I read Stevie Wonder's palm tonight and he said I was "very good." What a thrill. As soon as I forget the "I" in all of my life dealings and realize it's all for the entire whole, things will fall into place. I get so bogged down in small details. I'm sure the only place they exist is in my turmoiled head. Ah, Life.

Heavy shit, man. I found I had a lot of material. I had chronicled love-ins, hanging out backstage at Jimi Hendrix concerts, dancing on mescaline to Janis Joplin at the Whisky a Go Go, recording with my all-girl band, the GTO's (Frank Zappa at the helm), cavorting on stage with the Who, the Stones, Zeppelin. Wouldn't people find that stuff interesting?

For the next few months I dripped chunks of yesterday's dramas and dreams, like Miss Mercy GTO used to drop scarves, tarnished jangling belts, and wildly flamboyant articles of clothing everywhere she went. It became hard to hold a conversation about the present, immersed as I was in my torrid, traumatic, transcendental past, referring to long-gone incidents as if they just happened and speaking of freaky pals on the Sunset Strip as if they had just been over for tea with lots of honey. It drove Michael mad, but he sanctioned my new project. Although I was reliving my raging flings with more than a few rock-god dogs, he was outrageously open-minded, and for that I was truly grateful. Without his tower-of-strength spousal support, I could never have started writing—never mind stick with it for five long years. And now a voice within me piped up, muttering, "Maybe writing could take the place of your fumbled, sad-sack acting career!" Maybe, maybe, maybe, baby.

II

I was intently recalling the way Paul McCartney's long, slim thighs made me feel hot and bothered, getting it down on the page, when the phone ringing yanked me out of the panting Beatlemaniac reverie. It was the sweet, high-pitched voice of Melanie Griffith inviting me to her husband, Steven Bauer's birthday party. "I know you'll want to be there because Donnie is bringing Patti D'Arbanville, the girl who just had his baby," she said, giggling breathlessly. Donnie Wayne Johnson—one of my only True Loves and Melanie's first husband. Melanie and Don had smashed apart a few years earlier, and I had been the one to move Melanie into her swell new Hollywood apartment while she bawled her eyes out. I think Warren Beatty had something to do with it. Since then, she had married another hunky actor, Steven "Rocky" Bauer, and seemed content and semi-domestic.

I hadn't seen Donnie since we bumped into each other (literally) at a liquor store when I was eight months pregnant with Nick. All charm, he had said to me, "I always knew you'd be big as a house when you got pregnant." Such a way with words. But he and I checked in with each other every six months, so I already knew about the impending offspring and was oh-so super-duper curious about the mommy. "I can't wait," I said to Melanie and started planning my ensemble. Patti had been a semi-legend in New York and was courted on the coast by some of the same rock gentlemen who had wooed me in the West. For the rest of the day the Cat Stevens song "My Lady D'Arbanville" was spinning around my head. The line, "her heart feels like winter" made me a little nervous.

The night of the bash out in Malibu, I wore a tattered black suede mini-dress, high patent-leather spikes, and tall, teased hair the color of blood on fire. I had recently become a redhead and found that it suited me fine and dandy. After greeting Melanie and the handsome, boyish birthday boy, I clung to my stun-o-rama husband out on the breezy veranda overlooking the crashing, thrashing waves and scanned the crowd for Don and his new *amore*. There they were, D.J. and My Lady D'Arbanville looking way too good with her yards of wavy blond hair. Thumpy-hearted, I started through the crowd, and when Donnie spotted me, he grandly stood up and, laughing, opened his arms for me to run into. He told me how gorgeous I looked and introduced me to Patti, who sort of snarled at me like a taunted, ticked-off cat. Oops. After attempting some trivia talk with the two of them—with Patti glaring at me as if I was about to unzip Donnie's pants—I excused myself to find Michael, hoping that a glimpse of my real live husband would make Patti retract her claws. Besides, Donnie and Patti were recently sober, and I thought Michael, who was now three long years clean, might provide some invaluable assistance for the former drug beast and his catty concubine. As you know, maintaining a close bond with my T.L.s has always been paramount to me, so I hoped we could get along. Michael and Don forged an instant sympatico sobriety bond, and as the men intensely rambled about the difficulty of staying sane in those excruciating early drug- and booze-free days, I hung onto Michael, making sure to gaze adoringly, and I could feel Patti finally start to relax and soften. I wasn't a threat, after all.

Gradually she began to gab. "You wouldn't believe what just happened," she confided. "Right before you got here, Jan Michael Vincent's girlfriend trounced over and stuck her tongue straight down Donnie's throat, just to say hello." I was appropriately appalled, telling her about all the salacious howdy-hi's that I had had to get through. We commiserated about the shameless, wanton behavior of the desperate Hollywood dames we both had to contend with. Tsk tsk tsk. Patti was excited that Michael and Don could possibly hang out, and the idea that Michael could be a good influence on anybody, let alone my former passionflower, made me realize just how far he had come from those dastardly coke-couch days, so I swelled with wifely pride within my tattered suede. By the end of the night, Michael and Don had figured out which AA meetings to attend together, and Patti and I had a lunch date the very next day.

A new friend! Meeting a new girl and hitting it off is almost as thrilling as falling in love. In some ways it's even *more* rewarding because romantic passion and honey-devotion can be back-breaking, feverish work, whereas female kinship is a constant, consistent, uplifting experience you can always count on. Also, the part of the heart that winds up aching like gangrene rot is usually not involved, which has a lot to do with it. On the other hand, when a true-blue girlfriend does you in the feeling of shocked betrayal is like someone blowing their nose all over your face. Intentionally. Real hard. With malice.

III

I was reveling in my fabulous new friendships. I'd spent the years since Nicky's birth as the do-it-all hausfrau for the mad ménage. Even though we had various capable rock-and-roll roommates, someone had to shop, clean, schlep, and baby tend—and that was me. But with my newfound club-a-dub, bonhomie attitude, I felt like the tiger scratching out of the bag, like the social creature I used to be had returned from an arid, isolated mountaintop overlooking K Mart. It had been the right thing to put so much love energy into Michael and Nicky, I knew that for sure, but now Nicky was older, and I realized my own life had been neglected (by *me*). Writing a little about who I had been, remembering that effervescent, ever-loving, hope-filled flower child made me realize that lack of self-trust and self-love had begun to set in like hardening cement. Before the concrete dried, I needed the balancing encouraging energy of my own friends and my own fun.

I remained close with Melanie and Donnie, who had stayed sticky, itchy friends. Though they never really reconciled their destroyed, bedraggled marriage vows, a truce had been silently declared since they had both fallen in love with other people. They got along with a shot of sideways bitter humor, but at least they got along, and I thought the effort was grand. Patti and I became inseparable even though it seemed we were from two different planets, and I suppose we were; she from the kick-ass streets of Manhattan, barely raised by a wild bohemian mother, and I from the coddled, clean sidewalks of the San Fernando Valley. Three wholesome meals a day, drive-in movies, flannel PJs, getting tucked in every night. I found it fascinating how she spoke (yelled) her mind and took nobody's bull manure. If some fool dared to flip her the bird in traffic, she had no qualms about getting right out of her car and pounding on his windshield, demanding an instant retraction. She didn't back down and never backed off; she stood up for herself defiantly, and I watched her like a newly hatched hawk.

One of our greatest forms of jovial kicks was Trivial Pursuit. The game was really just like a deck of fifties playing cards, the bridge or poker of the eighties; a perfect setup for the festive, high-old-time social intercourse that I hadn't even realized how much I missed. After a few outrageous bashes Don, Patti, Melanie, Rocky, Michael, and I started calling ourselves "the Face Pack," after the newly coined Hollywood upstarts "the Brat Pack." We were so clever and cute, weren't we? Corralling a mess of smarty-pants people at least once a week, the games took on a private clublike atmosphere, each unhinged session lasting many hours. Eddie and Ingrid Begley, Steve Jones (who cracked up everyone when he read the questions in his full-tilt Cockney accent), old friend Elliot Mintz (personal publicist for only the grandest of stars), newly sober (for the first time) Ozzy Osbourne with his new wife (and our old friend) Sharon, Gene Simmons and sometimes Paul Stanley from KISS, Sparkie GTO, Malcolm McDowell and his cutie-wife, Mary Steenburgen, Tatum O'Neal, Bud Cort, along with lots of interesting fly-by-nights, would-be could-bes, and various up-and-comers who would drop in and out of the games, but the nucleus was always the Face Pack. Everyone brought some sort of food or drink and the festivities would last well into the jam-packed, fun-filled, brain-teasing night. Sometimes the guests would find questions about themselves or, in Melanie's case, her mother. "Which actress was presented a doll version of herself in a coffin, by Alfred Hitchcock?"

One by one, amazing stuff started happening for each of the fabulous Face Pack. Things were heating up madly for the Bauers. Rocky's film *Scarface,* directed by Brian De Palma, was ready for release, and once in a while the seemingly oafish chubby Brian would arrive at the game with some sort of big pie, wearing the usual baggy khaki hunting jacket, take his place at the table and whip our butts with his vast razor-brain. The night *Scarface* opened the Face Pack sat with Rocky in the theater and watched his magnificent performance as white-powder Al's goofy, sweet-faced best pal, and we all held onto each other and sobbed when he got blasted into smithereens. By then Melanie was filming *Body Double,* also with Brian, playing the platinum-blond hooker with the long, lean gams, which would start her climb onto the covers of many, many magazines along with a big fat Oscar nomination.

Fame was closing in on all of us, I just knew it! I was about to find a buyer for my book, Chequered Past would soon be a million-selling household name, Rocky was already at work on another movie, Patti had regained her svelte shape and was knocking them dead at her acting auditions, and Donnie would grab the world with his charm any minute now. He had always had a ton of self-confidence, and I didn't see any sign of it letting up. He certainly had mellowed since he became a dad and stopped inhaling and imbibing, but his faith in his talent never wavered. I adored them all—my stew of talented, quixotic, slightly damaged yet brilliantly *alive* friends.

IV

Even our dog Nellie had gotten a new lease on life, becoming queen of the canines on Wonderland Avenue, romping all day and night through her own private Canyon paradise, so it was a cruel blow when our creepy, owl-eyed landlord sold the house out from under us with very short notice.

The next pad I found was on Gardner Street, right off Holly-wood Boulevard, an old-fashioned beauty with a great big front porch and a sundeck in the back that we turned into Nick's room. I hoped the cheery brightness might help him see the cheery, bright side of things. He still had a penchant for cars, so I found a pair of vivid red drapes full of Corvettes and got him a bed in the shape of a nondescript, flashy race car. I think it was supposed to be a Trans Am.

The move wasn't so bad, because Stevie and Michael gathered the rest of Chequered Past and a big load of AA helpers, and our latest mess of bamboo furniture didn't weigh very much. It was a glorious sunny summer day when I placed my typewriter on the funky yard-sale desk in my cute, new, little office/den and swore to complete my book in that very room. Ron Bernstein, an agent friend of Danny Goldberg's, had loved the first chapter of my book and was shopping it around. Rejection slips started coming in, but since I was used to rebuffs from my acting days, I wasn't all *that* mortified. One of those rejection letters from a giant publishing house said, "This is a well-written document but would *never* sell as an entire book, maybe an article for *Rolling Stone*." A couple years later, when I got my first batch of hardbacks, I sent this oh-so-wrong fellow his very own autographed copy, but I never got even a thank-you note. Some people.

So every day I hunkered down to work, summoning the right words to appear. After writing a couple pages, I would pore over my self-help, Science of Mind, spiritual, and religious tomes, attempting to get a handle on that seemingly elusive concept: Peace of Mind. It was terrible to grapple with the constant self-doubt and its stranglehold on the soul. Certain truths worked for me: the fact that we are in fear or in love, that fear is what people call the devil, and love is God. And as I got more creative—working on the book, opening that channel—I saw very clearly that imagination is the Holy Ghost; bright sparks appearing straight out of the vast and empty stratosphere onto the page, like heavenly magic. But, of course, if I took *too* much notice, the flash of splendor would disappear and turn into a crumpling pumpkin. My jittery chatterbox brain got in my way even as I kept repeating, "Be still and know that I am God."

Gardner Street School had no idea what to do with Nick, so skipped him into the next grade way before he could handle it emotionally. I was in and out of ugly, beige public school offices, listening to underpaid, bored officials tell me my son needed help. He came in second in a citywide art contest, but it wasn't first place, and in his mind it wasn't enough. I started taking him to the Self-Realization Lake Shrine out in Pacific Palisades, praying a big dose of Paramahansa Yogananda would infuse him with some much-needed self-love. We sat feeding little chunks of bread to the swans, gazing at a beckoning statue of Jesus, discussing why we were alive. Shouldn't he have been watching after-school cartoons, laughing his small ass off instead of contemplating the afterlife? I encouraged soul study because it seemed to give him solace when nothing else could. His perfectionism had reached the place where nothing he did could satisfy him, so he began to lose himself in all kinds of books, which, thankfully, gave him temporary escape from his ever-intruding inner battle.

Fending for Nick and filling the empty pages with my past weren't filling the empty spaces in my life. I had divine friends, a brilliant son, and a husband who could never seem to relinquish his infernal devil-may-care ways. When he wasn't on the road or rehearsing with his band, he was out with the boys or at an AA meeting. Our sex life continued to diminish, and I was pricked with frightful hints of his philandering. The sad thing was when we did take the time to spend some alonemoments, it was always a rekindling of mutual adoration. I knew he loved me and I certainly loved him, so what was going wrong?

Since Michael was gone so much, I spent more time with my sweet mom, shopping, hanging out in her garden, reminiscing. One afternoon while we planted some rosebushes along the side of her triplex, I couldn't help but notice that the young guy who lived in the front apartment with his mom had grown into quite a stunning hunk of stuff. He had gone out of state to see his father for a couple of years and had come back a few inches taller, loaded with muscles and newfound sexy charm. Since he was so much younger than me—the very married woman—I struck up a flirty chat with him that day, which turned into a horny platonic friendship that made me feel hot and gorgeous again. We went out for a drink, and he confessed that when he was fourteen I had been his fantasy doll and whenever I walked by in my spike heels to visit Mom, he would dash into his room and do what growing boys do best. He said it went on for a long time and that he still thought I was the best-looking hot dish around. I almost wept with pent-up female ego-relief. We had a drink now and then at a darkened Valley bar, and just the way he looked at me helped my womanly pride make a mighty return. I was thirty-six at the time, an unwieldy age when you can let it all slide or look to Jane Fonda for inspiration. I started working out even harder, I discovered the Tova face mask, got rid of all frumpy clothes, and vowed to keep my heart young by staying young at heart.

This inside vow-job was making it harder to accept that I was one half of a perfect marriage. I needed more from Michael but didn't know how to ask for it, so picked up the trusty old journal once again and cut loose. My husband had been on the phone behind closed doors, out too late every night, and my new feminine trust told me there was somebody else on his mind.

October 9, 1984—In the throes of ending a long life cycle, I feel not quite on the verge of a very different life, but it's looming. I didn't realize the extent of the submerging of my self into Michael; the wifeness. Without Michael being obviously demanding, I allowed my self to take second place all the time. Writing the book and my friendship with mom's neighbor have brought me out again. I've done a lot of growing with Michael but have been feeling very much alienated lately. I've decided not to accept our relationship the way it is. When I want to discuss a certain incident (major or minor) he squelches it, stomps down on it, making me the instigator, the villain. Or he says I'm paranoid like he said today. Luckily I have stayed centered (mostly) these last few months. I don't want to feel so alienated from what our life together used to be, and I have changed so much that I'm not sure I would be satisfied with the relationship before he got so unhappy and distant. I feel alone a lot of the time. I'm pretty sure he's "seeing" a girl in AA, Janet. I'm feeling so mixed about it all, and so tired.

Michael did something he hadn't done since we first met: He read my journal. I think it's because he felt me withdraw and it scared him. For the first time he was forced to think about his actions and how they were making me feel. And for the first time I was admitting to myself that he might be romantically involved with another woman. Not quite a complete admission, however. Since I couldn't truly accept it all the way, my heart felt injected with morphine, and all Michael's soothing, placating attempts to woo me back to the way I was fell on a numb love-thumper. Janet's name was never mentioned even though it hung in the air above our heads, but Michael stayed home more, and family life resumed in a semi-content way until Nicky found a syringe along with one of his baby spoons, bent and blackened. "Look, Mommy. What happened to my spaceman spoon? What is this funny needle for?"

Stevie was at it again. Loving him like a brother couldn't keep him away from his addiction—heroin. Since he had disappeared a few nights before, even missing a gig in Santa Barbara, Michael and I suspected the worst, and we had been so sadly right. It was doubly hard for Michael because he and Stevie stayed straight together, and Michael had invested so much time and energy attempting to keep his guitar player in a sane, safe state of mind. Steve had slipped a few times before, but only briefly and never at home. We waited days for him and finally had to clear out his room and drag his belongings onto the back porch in black plastic bags. The bags stayed there for two months, getting damp and moldy while Steve roamed the miserable, dark world of strung-out misery. They were still there when we left Gardner Street because we couldn't afford the eleven-hundred-dollar rent without him. Awful stories surfaced about his bent and punishing purgatory on the streets, which made us angry and full of sorrow at the same time. I thought of Stevie holding Nellie in his lap, opening his first Christmas presents, so happy about a toothbrush and a pair of socks. When we packed our things one more time, Michael discovered that Stevie had taken two of his leather jackets, and it killed him. It was a brand-new year, 1985. There was no more Chequered Past, and we had no place to live.

CHAPTER TEN

I

My darling mom offered us her one spare room, but since Michael and I had thirty days to somehow find our own pad, we actually prayed together for a miracle. That very same week Donnie went up for a part in a TV pilot about two hip vice cops—one black and one white—to shoot almost immediately in Florida. He had just completed a movie called *Cease Fire* about a damaged Vietnam vet, so he seemed primed as the next member of the Face Pack to "go places." Donnie was about to go someplace all right, straight to Miami, without looking back, which left enough room at their small house in Santa Monica for the five of us: Michael, Nick, Nellie, Harry, and I to crash until we could get another place of our own. Harry's mean old mama, Blanche, had disappeared into the wilds of wonderland and was sorely missed. Donnie had gotten the adorable little pad eight years earlier with his best friend, Sean Walsh (remember *Arizonaslim?*). They had taken it over from a den of angeldust dealers and had been there ever since.

The house was clogged. Not only was Patti there with Jesse and their Irish setter, Jones, she also had a nanny who resided in Jesse's room, and the closets were already stuffed to the hinges with all of Donnie's things. We'd brought only our barest survival items, but they still got underfoot, and Michael withdrew into gloom, spending most of his time away. Nicky felt totally threatened without a space to call his own and treated Jesse—who had an entire room filled with kid-crap, though he was only two years old—with hideous disdain.

After each cantankerous outburst I desperately devised schemes to make Nicky happy—keeping him out of the cramped house, at the local mall or library right up until bedtime—instead of giving him what he needed and cried out for: discipline. I wanted to avoid wreaking hellish havoc on the household, so didn't punish him, even though Patti encouraged it. The only thing she and I argued about was how to raise a kid. But my codependency was at full throttle: If you kiss everybody's ass enough, all will be well!

Then a fat bully started to torture Nick at his new school, Roosevelt, yanking him unseen into hallways and threatening him with all sorts of bullshit, sometimes pinching and poking to crank up the fear level. Nick refused to go to school, actually making himself sick to avoid the monster. I saw the principal, had meetings with the teacher, tried to reach the fat kid's parents, all to no avail. After seeing Nick curled miserably on the couch and listening to me moan, Patti decided to take action. Surprise, surprise. We waited at the school gate one afternoon, followed the kid home, and after a few minutes rang the doorbell. The poor slob lived with his ailing, decrepit grandma who could hardly hear in an overstuffed, hot apartment. The big troubled kid vehemently denied any wrongdoing and got right in Patti's face, cursing and spitting at her for daring to suggest that he had bullied Nick. I grimaced, waiting. Nobody, not even a blubbery eleven-year-old does that to Patti. She grabbed him by the neck of his shirt, actually lifting him off the ground, and told him to lay off or *else*. And he did. However, the damage had been done to my sensitive child, who seemed to have become even more withdrawn because of the experience, more closed in, closed off, and unhappy, expecting to be bombarded from all sides by ass-wipes who wanted to hurt him. School, which had been uneasily tolerable, had now become the enemy. He even dropped out of the school orchestra, where he was getting past the screech phase on the violin.

Nothing was working for him. He couldn't understand unfairness; he needed his Libra scales to stay perfectly balanced, or else. We found another soothing therapist, whom Nick wrapped around his pinkie, and the search was on for the perfect private school. After several aggravating gab fests with headmaster/mistress hierarchy, Nick landed up on Mullholland Drive in an elite, expensive yuppified school called Westland. On top of the six-thousand-a-year tuition (which we had to take out a loan for) Michael and I had to lend a hand twice a month helping out in various capacities. My first duty was to trim a mammoth, smelly tree full of contorted pods, despite the fact that I had never held a pair of clippers in my life. Nick tried tentatively to fit into the school program but battled with his perfectionism, especially in the many adorable group projects, which the concerned, trying-but-not-quite-hip teachers at Westland seemed so fond of.

II

We were seriously beholden to Patti, but she never, ever rubbed it in. In fact, our crammed-up circumstances strengthened our friendship, as we girl-talked incessantly over mug upon mug of spicy tea loaded with caffeine. While she wailed about cheating rumors that were drifting back from Miami, I confided my discovery of an insidious VD-type infection that had been brewing within me. After my visit to the doctor, I roamed the house with a blustering gray cloud over my head, trying to knock out the adulterous fact that Michael had once again been on the loose with a loose woman. This time it turned out to be a loose girl, but who's counting? After vehemently denying any philandering until presented with my telltale bottle of medicine, he grudgingly confessed to flinging it up with a seventeen-year-old named Heather in Vermont. Heather. Such a yuppie-puppy name. After long weekends spent in the lush Vermont greenery, he returned with talk about the grandeur of the trees and purple mountains' majesty, when all the while he had his face buried in a very different kind of bush. It hurt so bad. After I raged, wept, and imploded, he swore to lay off the yuppie pup, but my skin got thicker by the day, like the bark on all those grand trees in the state of Vermont. *Whatever happened to "forsaking all others"?* my inner voice whispered. Any respect Michael might have once had for me had obviously been buried deep like one of Nellie's bones, and she always forgot where she dug the damn hole.

Speaking of the fabulous Nellie, the first time Donnie came back for a few days off she took a dump right in front of him as he prepared to say grace over Sunday dinner. I cringed and bowed my head even further down while Don pointed his masterful finger and she was relegated to the backyard for the remainder of his visit. Even the poor mutt was feeling the impending magnitude of Sonny Crockett.

Sadly Heather wasn't Michael's only conquest. As Patti and I walked home from the market one winter evening, we saw Michael entranced on the phone through the picture window, but when we walked in, he was busily changing the channels on TV. "Who was that, honey?" I asked sweetly. "Oh, Steve Jones," he answered non-chalantly. Butter wouldn't have melted in his pants. Stevie had recently come back into our lives, clean and lean, sober as a judge, apologetic for his stoned-out transgressions, but still, something about the virtuous look on my husband's face made me look at the clock, remember the date and time, and carve it into my subconscious until the phone bill came. Luckily (or unluckily?), since we were out at the beach almost every call was recorded for posterity. Sure enough, the bill told the truth: Stevie's number was nowhere to be found. After some Patti-assisted digging, I found he had been chatting intensely with the newly sober wife of an aging British rock hero, a girl whom I'd often blabbed with about babies, the glory of henna, and ways to stay beautiful for our men. I thought we had a certain rapport.

This time I attempted a real confrontation. When I blurted out that I knew it wasn't Stevie that he'd been talking to, a black cloud formed over Michael's head. "How *dare* you check up on me!!" he fumed, breathing heavily. "She's a married woman!!" Not "I'm a married man." Oh no. He went on to chastise me for infringing on his privacy, which made me feel like a mere blip of humanity. I would up apologizing, beseeching, and begging his forgiveness.

Later, of course, I found out that he had indeed been boffing the wife of the former rock legend. I saw the shameless coquette at a party and burned holes through her head like I was wielding a blowtorch. She couldn't look at me. She fidgeted, suddenly noticing something in the thin air in front of her and stared at it, fascinated—almost cross-eyed, grabbing ahold of her husband's hand like it was a protective device. I thought of blabbing it all to that poor sot wearing the wedding band, but what good would it have done? I said this over and over to myself, like a litany, while the hubbub swirled around us—trying not to feel so hard-core ferocious and vindictive. Forgive them, Father, for they know not what they do. Forgive me for seeing blood-red, and let me live in the whitest of light. Please, please, please, *please,* to quote the mighty James Brown.

Eventually I made up with Michael, but acidlike erosion had flattened my heart and made wretched little etchings in it. I know how artistic that must sound, but it was more like when Van Gogh cut off his ear and sent it to Heather—I mean to a hooker. Simon & Schuster turned down my manuscript, Random House did the same. We didn't even hear from William Morrow. My agent, Ron, had taken quite a beating and even though he believed in the idea had to move on, telling me he had done all he could and not to lose heart. Since it was flat and covered in acid etchings, I hardly noticed.

III

It was a truly dismal time for me, and due to a severe lack in my romance reality I fantasized about Bruce Springsteen, rattling on in my diary like I had once done over Dion and Paul McCartney:

> *After seeing Bruce live, I've been in ecstasy. Many years have passed since I felt that high and happy. Nothing exists but Bruce, and you never want it to end. He's so happy up there, which makes the audience so happy and united! Not to mention the guy's ass! Many fantasies occurring—but he'll be gone in a few days, and my brain will clear out. I'm finding that FAN part of me never dies—my groupie spirit lingers. Very few people bring it out in me anymore, but what an exception this is! My palms get itchy and I start imagining getting my sweaty hands on him. I'll bet my "visualization" helped me get near those rock guys I went nuts for in the old days.*

It was all quite sad really, but I certainly loved the music. It saved my grace. Music still gets right under my skin and becomes one with my bloodstream. If I find myself feeling melancholy, in a tizzy, or hot under the collar, I can snap straight back into my god-self by listening to Dwight Yoakam, Etta James, or Sam Cooke, the Kinks or Merle Haggard, John Lennon, Janis Joplin, Van Morrison, Elvis, Prince; reeling in that inspiration, mainlining it like a drug that can never, ever hurt me.

For awhile it seemed that music would save us all. The one ray of glory during this time came from Michael's difficult writing stint with Holly Knight. A song they wrote called "Obsession" was recorded by a new band, Animotion, and had climbed into the *Billboard* Top Ten. But it took a while for the dollars to trickle down, and, as always, we were pressed for cash. So I got yet another bizarre job with a local screenwriter gal in Brentwood, as her sort of "personal assistant." Her name was Susan Berman, and her dad had been the head of the Jewish mafia in Las Vegas during the fifties. She wrote a book about her unusual childhood called *Easy Street,* so when she read my two chapters and encouraged me to continue, I got a momentary creative buzz. If she can do it, I can do it! Yeah! Yeah yeah yeah. Yeah, right.

Meanwhile, I was her dutiful servant, buying all her gifts at Saks

Fifth Avenue, printing out stacks of screen pages, having her cutesie poodle trimmed just so, purchasing its food—the expensive lo-cholesterol kind, of course—picking up fancy-schmancy meals at restaurants that Frank Sinatra had probably haunted in his slay-day and delivering them hot while Susan slaved over the typewriter. She was fascinating and infuriating, with a brain inside her head that oozed out of her skullcap, it was so damn large. I've always worried about people with IQs that topple the charts; I consider anything over 120 a tragic badge of honor to be dealt with tiptoe carefully. Handled with care. Fleece-lined kid gloves perhaps?

Susan canned me one day after I inadvertently lost her eccentric fiancé's very important black leather jacket. I had taken it to a seemingly reputable tailor's shop in Brentwood to be mended, but when I went to retrieve the wicked heirloom, the Yugoslavian weirdo owner told me that it had already been picked up by someone else and I owed him one hundred and twenty-five American dollars. I sputtered, stammered, and threatened to sue. The enraged Yugoslav cursed loudly and had me forcibly removed from his piddling little shop while overdressed onlookers cluck-clucked at the gall of the deranged chick who refused to pay the bill. I knew what the jacket meant to Susan, so when she bawled and fired me, I wasn't surprised. She said the jacket had been *priceless* and that the whole thing had been a *plot,* a *scam,* perpetrated by the evil foreigner, who probably sold the biker item for a thousand dollars. Somehow we remained friends, and when her fiancé-turned-husband killed himself a couple years later, I thought about his important black leather treasure that had been such a blatant object of thievery, and felt real, real bad.

IV

After we had lived with Patti in Santa Monica for what seemed like forever, sleeping on a fold-out couch in the living room, with Nick snoozing fitfully on a daybed across from us, Donnie came back into town for a screening of his brand-new Florida pilot, *Miami Vice.* The only people in the screening room at Universal were Don and Patti, me and Michael, Donnie's agents, and a couple of massive bigwigs waiting for the lights to go down. Don was unusually nerveracked and edgy, but after two hours of watching all those glinting guns and muted pastels chasing down fleeing dealers in Miami, swallowed whole by a supercool rock-and-roll soundtrack, it was blatantly obvious that we would all be spending a whole lot of time on that other balmy coast. Michael and I were overwhelmed by how good the show was, Don's agents had pea-green dollar signs in their eyes, and Patti was wistful and dumbfounded all at once. Everything was about to change.

Miami Vice was picked up almost instantly, and all of a sudden Donnie was highly in demand all over the country, on the cover of the *Star* and the *National Enquirer.* We still can't figure out why they singled out him to gnaw at in the rags. Donnie had a way with the dolls; a glamorous stud with a reckless, flagrant, drug-laden past— the perfect fodder for those dirt-hungry, salivating slimeballs to shred for the panting public. Which they did with menace for the next several years.

Instant success meant that Don had to relocate *right now,* leaving 90 percent of his belongings behind for Patti to deal with. It truly happened so fast, his life altering forever right in front of us. He never saw any of his old clothes, furniture, or lifetime of accumulated crap ever again. He bought everything sleek, shiny, and new in Miami, never even mentioning his hippie tree-trunk coffee table or the gigantic, macho canopy bed he made with his own hands in 1979.

Patti decided to stay behind in L.A., since Jesse was just starting school and she was hoping to revive her acting career. Donnie bought her a big trilevel pad in Studio City, and before she split to higher haciendas, she tossed a yard sale in which she sold off all Donnie's seventies *Stayin Alive*–type suits, big-collared shirts, mismatched mugs, and hand-carved male furniture. There were even a few pair of colorful jockey shorts, soon to be replaced with pure silk undergarments. We almost put up a sign saying, SONNY CROCKETT'S CRAPOLA 4 $ALE, but we thought better of it.

The Des Barres family was on tenterhooks (tender, piercing hooks) waiting to see if we would be able to remain at the abode in Santa Monica. Nick was firmly ensconsed at Roosevelt, and I had come to love the amazingly clean air, the safe neighborhood, and the cozy little house itself, which was built in the late teens with a real live backyard and a fireplace that burned real wood. Finally Donnie said we could stay until Nick's school year ended, and for awhile I could inhale deeply of that salt-sprinkled air. *Miami Vice* was raging, D.J. was fast becoming a household name and fashion plate. It didn't look as if he would ever want to move back to the sweet, late-teen beach pad, so I had sincere, grandiose hopes that we could stay there indefinitely.

Patti moved into her palatial Valley digs, and I was finally able to take my beloved antique dresses out of boxes and hang them in my very own closet. As usual, Michael got the biggest closet in the bedroom, while my duds languished in the hall, but once again, I did not say, "How about if *I* get the big closet this time, or maybe we could *share* it?" I saw these ignominious acts as generous shots of love, which ultimately backfired on me. I longed to close the grave-pit gap that now sundered the lovey-dovey tightness that Michael and I once took for granted. He still left me beautiful, tender notes that I clasped to my bosom, wishing they were him. And we still had our harmonious sidekick moments of long-term understanding that only long-term couples can understand. Ha! Our dumb, cutesie-coo love-language stuck like super-glue, whether we were at odds or evens, and we also dealt with Nick as a unit, never disagreeing about what was best for him. To tell the truth, we stumbled around in the scary, maternal/paternal dark together, having no idea what really was best for the little bugger. We were struggling blindly with Nicky and with each other. It was so convoluted and ill, but maybe all relationships are diseased in some way. Give and take. Swallow and burn. Grin and bear it.

The last time I picked up my journal for over a year, I wrote:

May 6—*Taking it day to day. I'm poking along after a gross bout with food poisoning (infected tuna sandwich in the car) and a forty-eight-hour migraine. I didn't think I would allow myself such a major slump, but the vibe is so sorrowful. Michael says he's getting mixed signals from me and doesn't know what I want from him. I don't know either! I do know I've got to get myself creative, find some self-esteem, and get rid of these second-class-citizen feelings.*

It was music that gave my disharmonious marriage a much-needed reprieve. I was hanging out with Nick in his new bedroom, setting up his Transformers and Go-bots, decorating the walls with Japanese posters, when I got an intriguing call from Michael, who was visiting Donnie in Marshall, Texas, on the set of *The Long Hot Summer*. It seemed some upper-stuff New York promoter had tracked him down and wanted to fly him to New York to meet with a hush-hush rock band that was looking for a replacement lead singer. Despite Michael's smash hit, "Obsession," he had been concentrating on acting but down deep felt he hadn't fulfilled his rampant rock-and-roll potential. He had previously been offered gigs with upstart or old fart bands but refused to compromise himself for the easy dough, the way he felt he had done in Detective. (It was actually very *hard* dough.) He usually referred to his former band as "Defective" and preferred not to refer to it at all.

When Michael got to Manhattan he still had no idea where he was headed and whom he was going to meet. With intoxicating secrecy the silent limo driver had taken him to the Carlyle Hotel, where he sat around in luxury, eating grapes until there was a knock on the door. His mysterious guests were John Taylor and Tony Thompson, who explained that Robert Palmer had dropped out of Power Station summer tour at the last instant and they were hoping Michael might be able to step in. Chequered Past had opened for Duran Duran a few months before, and Andy Taylor had remembered Michael's way with a microphone. The next morning Michael was on the Concorde to London, where he went straight to the studio and sang his ass off, spent the evening with Andy in a cloud of pot smoke, and returned to New York in a daze with a tape of all Power Station's tunes to practice, practice, practice. They were going to give him a huge hunk of money for his services, and he would be onstage at Live Aid in front of the largest audience in the history of the universe. Michael was agog with visions of dollar signs, long overdue recognition, and legitimacy.

When Nick and I picked him up at the airport, my soul was surging with hope, desire, and longing for the good life with my chosen man. We had been through such up- and down-heaval for so many years. Maybe, just *maybe* we could work it out after all. Michael was always happiest when he could drown his beaten-back cares and woes in his work, and if that work could bring him adulation from the impersonal masses, just *maybe* he could live without adulation from the personal misses. For the next few months I put bandages over all the heart-hurts and shoved the bubbling bitter stew on the back burner, totally determined to make this yet another new start for all of us.

We made love, I cooked wonderful dinners, we took Nick to the park and watched him swing high in the air, happy and laughing. Then Michael packed his bags, put on his helmet, and went off to war. Packed his bags, put on his mascara, long white linen coat, and lace-up boxing boots, and went off on tour. Private jets, suites at the Ritz, fancy fresh fruit baskets, limo city personified with the hoity-toity stars-since-they-were-teenagers-Duran-Duran-spoiled-brat-baby-boy-multimillionaires.

Actually I came to adore John Taylor and Andy Taylor. John was a ravishing slab of serious trouble, elegantly charming—almost swashbuckling in a genteel British way. His lips were real red, he had a hearty, naughty laugh and a very improper look in his sparkly eyes (though he always treated me like a true lady). During the tour Michael had woven a sober spell around Andy, and he was making a glorious effort to stay off the booze. He was a mischievous, flirtatious gnome; a cute and sexy, cheeky, smarty-pants superstar. He had lo-oong hair, a quiet little blond wife, and an adorable baby boy, Little Andy, who grabbed my Ray Bans one night and pounded them into dark green granules.

By the time Power Station came to play Los Angeles, Michael was fully integrated into the grand world of superstar heaviosity. He even walked cockier and held his head at a jauntier angle. His new road wardrobe was flowing chiffon—red, black, and white, the Power Station colors—carelessly tossed together with a cocky, jaunty flair. Michael always had an exquisite sense of style, and now he was able to use it dramatically, to the hilt. When Nick and I went to visit him at the hotel (he stayed with the band during the L.A. stint) I actually felt intimidated and excited, seeing my husband in this successful, nonchalant, world-weary mode. Despite the fact that he was inundated with interviewers, butt-licking liggers, record company cretins, newfangled, fangs-bared groupies, and various heavy hitters, his AA humility remained intact—joyous gratitude shining through the platinum-plated excess. Nick took to the fruit baskets and brie plates as if to the manner born and expected the snazzy life-style to continue nonstop. The family languished by the pool, eating strawberries out of a pineapple shell while people peeked through the bushes at the new singer for Power Station, watching his every cocky, jaunty move. God was giving Michael the magic rock-and-roll moment in the sun that he so richly deserved, and for that I was once again truly grateful.

It had been a long time since I had been locked within that very small world inhabited by much-desired, coveted rock gods. The whole thing made my cheeks red despite the fact that backstage was a totally different experience than it had been during the heydays of yore. No visitors were allowed—just the band, John's model-girlfriend, and parents, a few other band family members, me, Patti, and the road crew, who ate chunks of Cheddar and took photos of each other. I suppose the former backstage pizzazz had been destroyed by charmers like John Hinckley and stupid duped groupies who jacked off peon roadies to gain entrance into the hallway next to the dressing room. Gun-toting security guards had taken the place of fun-seeking, music-loving "in"-crowders. I briefly mourned the old days while sitting in the new inner sanctum, sipping Pellegrino, waiting for my husband to entertain the hungry crowd. A couple years later when I went to see Robert Plant at the Forum I was the *only* girl allowed backstage, and while I felt momentarily privileged, I missed the feather-boa glory of the sticky, sweaty, heady sixties when rock was young. Corny, but too, too true.

I watched from the side of the stage while Michael drove them wild, feeling pride mixed up with sorrow. He was so damn good at what he did, and it had been such a struggle for him that I cried while he pranced around on the giant stage, his long red scarves billowing, the girls screaming, bright lights hitting him, and loud, thunderous music wrapping him tight in its powerful, baptismal spell. I loved him so much. I felt his turmoil and ecstasy, almost passing out from the crashing weight of it. Nick stayed with my mom so I could spend the night with Michael in the hotel. I carried his wet clothes, I wrapped a towel around him, held him close in his illustrious moment, and loved the needy little boy inside that had been hung out to dry and given up for dead by his twisted, selfish parents. I tried so hard to forgive them like Jesus said, for they had no idea what they had done to their only son. Forgive them, forgive them, forgive them, for they know not what they do.

CHAPTER ELEVEN

ncredibly, amid all this exciting turmoil, I finished quite a bit of
my manuscript. The weight of my work in my hands, as clichéd
as that sounds, felt like a deliverance from the mundane, the
dryasdust flatlands where most people are content to languish,
where I had found myself more than one too many times. And
miraculously, through a bunch of nutty circumstances, a big-time
agent, Mel Berger at William Morris, had taken the project on and
actually sold it. The fact that my editors, Jim Landis and Jane Meara
at Morrow, thought it was good enough to stick in the bookstores
made me feel like shoving back my shoulders and jutting out my
chin. I felt real pride creeping in—the good kind of pride that makes
you happy to be who you are. I got heartily pissed off when people
asked me who I'd used as my "ghost" or cowriter. I had a ghost all
right. I had finally glommed onto my very own personal Holy Ghost,
tapping into it like a bee dipping into sweet honeysuckle.

I spent days on the phone, looking up photographers who might
have taken photos of me in my wilder moments, called acres of music
publishers, buying rights to the lyrics I quoted. I got charged the
most for "The Times They Are A-Changin' " by an old-time lawyer
Bob Dylan must have hired eons ago, and since Danny Sugerman is
an old friend of mine, didn't have to pay anything for the Doors'
lyrics. The Boss didn't want a dime for "Dancing in the Dark" either.
What a cool guy.

A double celebration was in order—for my book and for Michael's
tour—so he, Patti, and I got extravagant and rented a limousine to

see Prince at the Forum. Prince had become my pet fantasy-porn puppet. I even had salacious, drippy dreams about him and woke up in a delirious, carnal sweet-heat-sweat, hankering for his tiny, hot highness. As the limo pulled into the parking lot, I asked once again if Patti had any ideas for the book title. She thought for a moment and shook her head. "I'll get it, don't worry." When the limo attempted to enter the private band area unsuccessfully, I yelled out, laughing, "Hey, you've got to let me in, I'm with the band!" Patti yelped so frightfully loud it scared me. "That's it! That's it! The title for your book! *I'm with the Band*!" It was triple revelry at the Prince Purple Rain show that night. Prince slithered around under the covers onstage, setting my crotch and soul on fire—and I had a title!

▌▌

Music was about to save the world. After a decade of disco and metal decadence, rock gods—including Michael!—were converging at Live Aid to soothe the savage beast of world hunger. But first Power Station played Miami, where Mr. Miami Vice introduced the band then got them parts on the show. Michael was heartily annoyed because the boys didn't appreciate what a big deal it was. I suppose Crockett and Tubbs hadn't hit London yet, where Taylor and Taylor were the hotshots in the neighborhood. John turned up late on the set due to overindulgence the night before, so all was not a bowl of maraschinos. Still Donnie introduced Power Station on Live Aid, and Patti got to go. I didn't—I didn't even *ask*—and I regret it.

Nick, my mom, and I watched Michael live on TV as he winked at the two billion music lovers around the world, and I said thanks to God for all the money rock and roll was making for the starving masses and for letting my husband finally realize his dream. While I sat on Mom's couch, slightly awestruck, watching Michael wail, little Nick ran to the screen and kissed it, just like I had done in 1964 when the Beatles were on *Ed Sullivan.*

Michael was overjoyed that I had sold my book but frustrated and temperamental when he got home, since the days going by weren't fraught with all types of tension, thrills, and chills galore. Coming back from the road can be equated with coming down off a dose of Orange Sunshine; nothing looks the same when you get back, it's not quite grand, colorful, dangerous, or 3-D enough. It's just all too blankety-blank ordinary. He bounced off the walls like they were made of Silly Putty, making all kinds of plans to cap off his fortuitous stint with Power Station. Andy Taylor fell mad for the California beach, bought a house in Malibu, and for a fingers-crossed moment it looked as if there might be another Power Station album with Michael taking Robert Palmer's place in the studio. It was touch and go, going, gone. When that collapsed, Michael started digging around the industry for another solo record deal. He could have taken it easy because for the first time in years, we had enough money, but he was on a real-live roll. Danny Goldberg gave him a deal on his newly formed label, Gold Mountain, and he was off and flying.

Soon we were all soaring through the clouds—on Donnie's private jet. America was two hundred and ten years old, so Don summoned some of his closest and dearest to New York to celebrate Ms. Liberty's unveiling in absurdly grand style. Elliot Mintz herded us all together: Michael, Patti and myself, a few of Donnie's adoring tag-ons, and Danny Goldberg, who had recently started managing Don's musical career, because it was his birthday. Our first stop was somewhere in Texas to help Willie Nelson out with Farm Aid. Musicians wrestling family farms from the grip of greedy banks! When we landed, it was as if Elvis had come back from the dead to teach us all to dance. Screaming people reached for Don from all sides, he held his hands in the air—a blessing from the pastel pope. We got to schmooze with Willie on his bus as he and Don nodded their heads knowingly about the rigors of fame. "Sometimes it's rough, man." Yes, sirreee. I shook Willie's calloused hand and admired his newest young wife and the unpretentious way he seemed to be living his life on the road. Dogs and children were everywhere. Don announced Willie amid farm-style hysteria, but we couldn't stay for the performance and trundled back to the jet, headed straight for the Statue of Liberty, tomfoolery, and firecracker mania. Helicopters were called to get us to the place where we would board dingies and float out to the MTV boat, but after Don, Patti, and a couple of his aides waved adios at the dock, Michael, Danny, and I realized we wouldn't be shooting the shit with any MTV video jocks on that particular evening. We found a cute little Italian joint and laughed about the rigors of fame while the entire city lit up with fireworks. Happy birthday, dear Danny, happy birthday to you.

III

I was beginning my thirty-eighth year of life, and with my book completed and soon to be published began a much-needed cycle of renewal. Michael and I had an unspoken love-truce and started having a little more fun. For my birthday he and Patti threw me a feast-fete at Helena's, downtown in a gone-to-seedy area behind Silverlake. The barely opened pleasure sanctum had been discovered by that chic chick, the divine Melanie G. Former unique bohemian-freak actress, Greek belly-dancer Helena Kadianiotes ran the joint, with the financial aid of her two next-door neighbors, Jack Nicholson and Marlon Brando. "Mother Teresa feeds the poor," Helena said to me, "the rich and famous need it more." She was the patron saint of the super-elite. Helena's was an over-the-rainbow, beyond-belief, hipper-than-thou experience to be relished by the too, too few. My girlfriends dolled up to chomp on the goat cheese, sun-dried tomato special, and the double-heart carrot cake Melanie had so kindly provided. Michael toasted me, praising my efforts even though I had spared no mushy, horny detail about any of my *amores*. Bruce Willis was there with my friend, Sheri, and almost unknown cute actor, Robert Downey, Jr., came with his trendified manager, Loree Rodkin, and Patti snapped at least sixty Polaroids while the place clogged up with actors, musicians, producers, directors, tall, willowy model-types, and all the truly ravishing people.

Helena's soon became our new hang-spot. That twinkly magic man Jack Nicholson was there every Friday night, lighting up the dive. He held court in the corner, allowing only certain babes to grace the seat next to him for no more than five minutes at a time. Lou Adler was usually with him, and sometimes the old charmer, Warren Beatty came by for a glass of Evian, scanning for beauty. We got to be fairly friendly, flirting like fools, and I graced Jack's table for several five-minute slots of fun, wondering what it might be like to find myself trapped in his naughty lair for several five-hour slots of sin. Can you tell I was slowly turning into a horny beast? I guess writing about all my lovers woke up my sadly neglected libido. It's all the more sad because even the smell of Michael, the touch of his silky skin still thrilled me. But it seemed he believed the grass was always more emerald, chartreuse, sea green, jade green, lime green, moss green, avocado, and leaf green way over on the other side.

One night when the peel-back ceiling was peeled back to reveal the splendor of the smogged-out stars, Marlon Brando made a brief appearance at Helena's, and even the high-stepping cream of the swank set started buzzing. I was tempted to sashay over to Brando's table to ask what he did with all those half-naked shots I sent him back in '72 but decided to keep my cool intact. One night somebody claimed they saw Jack Nicholson and Sean Penn peeing against a wall outside, and it became a spirited topic of conversation—just to show you how really silly Hollywood-types can be. I was an observer the night Sean bopped a guy called "Hawk" over the head with a chair for cozying up too closely to Madonna. Even Prince showed up on a fairly regular basis, sitting near the dance floor with his dad and two giants who constantly kept their eyes peeled like neon grapes, peering into the dim, creamy night light. Helena must have paid a pile of loot to make the beautiful people look and feel even more bee-yoot-i-full within her precious pinkened walls. I was feeling pretty delicious one Friday night, dancing maniacally to Prince's "Kiss" in a skintight getup, when his majesty arrived wearing that very daring, belly-button-baring black "Kiss" ensemble and a pair of pitiless black sunglasses that screamed "I VANT to be alone," even though he was at the world's hippest nightspot. While I reamed the dance floor, the funniest thing happened: Just at the part in the song that goes, "You don't have to watch *Dynasty* to turn me on," Michael Nader, who played the sensitive yet studly hunk on *Dynasty*, walked through the door and stood grandly, in plain view of the entire place. Even Nader didn't get the hysterical significance. I laughed so hard all by myself, hoping that at least Prince caught the retarded magnitude of the ludicrous moment. I took a peek but couldn't tell because his shades were as dark as night and twice as impenetrable.

After just about having sex with myself on the dance floor two feet from where Prince sat, I dared to approach his table, tossing my cool and all caution out the star-roof. "I love you, I love you, I love you," I declared, forgetting I wasn't Pam Miller in Reseda, circa 1962. I stood there after the brazen preteen act, frozen to the spot, and all he did in response was to lower his shades a smidge so I could gaze at those rich brown beauties for a brief instant. I flew across the floor like hot-rod lightning and took a few swigs of my white wine spritzer. "What made me do that?" I wondered out loud. I told Patti about it and she spit her cappuccino across the table, getting a splotch on Rob Camelletti, Cher's boyfriend—the poor, innocent guy the rags called "the bagel boy"—but he didn't seem to feel a drop.

One packed Friday eve, as the stars of stage, screen, and CD bopped to the beat, a rancid odor filled the dance floor, engulfing the hipsters with skunk-stench. Scattering, they all headed for the door. Who *dared* to let off a stink bomb at Helena's on a Friday night? Helena's eyes spit fire as she blazed around, scanning for the perpetrator. I saw that unruly, outspoken diva-donna, Sandra Bernhard slyly sneak out of everyone's way, like she *knew* they just might be getting ready to leave. What a daring, villainous deed.

It would be at Helena's that December, amid tons of joviality and

Christmas cheer, that Michael would finally meet the girl of his—and my—nightmares. Where else?

IV

Our lives appeared charmed again, but the distance between Michael and me seemed to sprout wings. It was as if glittering nights and our fun-time friends were all that held us together, whether at Helena's dancing under and among the stars, or at home, the now famous site of *fab*-ulous dinner parties, *dar*-ling. After cooking little tidbits all day, I would sweep around the house, wearing some forties satin number, tasting my sweet-and-sour turkey balls, feeling *just* like Lauren Bacall. Ever-witty Michael was George Sanders, Eddie Begley was Jimmy Stewart, Ozzy Osbourne was Oscar Levant, Steve Jones was one of the Bowery Boys, Bruce Willis could have been Bogie, and Sheena Easton sort of resembled Judy Garland in a certain kind of candlelight. After all compliments about my vegetarian curry had dwindled, Eddie would begin charades or an equally HOLLY-wood fungame that kept everyone on their toes and off their asses.

Together with a few intellectual poet friends, Michael jump-started a serious re-trend among Hollywoodites: Poetry Nights at Helena's. I hadn't written any poetry since my beloved hippie stint, but wanted to get in on the act, so shoveled through my ancient pages, looking for the perfect dumb poem that recalled with fervor the love-in mentality that was so lacking in the overdone eighties. After Ally Sheedy read a tale of psychological woe, and Judd Nelson wowed the pack of Kir-sipping, would-be beats, I grabbed my banged-up book and made my way to the podium to read a poem:

November 16, 1966

Restless and burning
Our souls are yearning
Still no heads are turning
And no minds are learning

Our minds they're destroying
And this they're enjoying!
"Did *we* raise this generation?
They're against segregation
They have no discrimination!"

How can we show this aching nation
To be full of love's elation?

They're too busy with machines
Riding around in limousines
Wanting dollars by the score
So they won't be labeled "poor"
Or be classed with you and me
Being what we want to be
With our souls flying free
Frowned on by society

Too quick to hurt each other
Always judging one another
Making others weep
And not losing any sleep
Taking the name of God in vain
Doesn't cause them any pain

We cannot forget about it
And there's no way we can doubt it
While the TV tube is teasing
There are others who are freezing
And parts of this great nation
Are dying of starvation

The way of life is changing
The world needs rearranging
If all hate would cease
We would need no more police
Everyone would be respected
No one would be rejected
For the color of their skin
Or the financial shape they're in
And if we keep believing
Ignoring the deceiving
Love can lock the doors
On any threat of wars

Certainly nobody should be neglected for the financial shape they're in. Right?

Michael and I spent two looooong days at the theater with a bunch of pals seeing *Nicholas Nickleby,* and I remember one particular intermission, Patti and I trailed along behind our friend Sheri and her love man Bruce Willis. We watched Bruce's ass under a thin layer of blue silk for a few mischievous moments, then looked over at each other with the same lustful thoughts and cracked up so hard. "If Sheri only knew what was in our indecent heads," she said, grinning at me, and we pretended to be pious for about three seconds.

Donnie's rocketing celebrity was giving all our lives a new and glamorous sheen. Despite the glaring fact that all those rumors Patti heard about him stepping out with a young brainless model were true, they weathered the formidable front-page breakup and had called a truce because of their devotion to their son Jesse. Men.

Since D.J. and I went way back, he invited me to Miami, where he could review the chapter of my book devoted solely to him: "I Met Him on a Monday and My Heart Stood Still." I stayed at his pastel mansionlike pad right on the water, with its pinks, pale greens, aqua, and mauve abounding; with its marble floors, gigantic featherbed couches, high glass walls letting in the constant sunshine. Wowie. Cooks, assistants, secretaries, gofers, aiders, and abettors of all kinds came and went while we discussed the past and roared with laughter about stuff that killed us back then. And the palm trees swayed. I spent hours on the set of *Miami Vice* in the super-snazzy metal-jet trailer, eating low-fat cuisine, sitting in cool-air comfort with a stack of pages and waiting for "Cut!" so we could get back to perusing our own personal history. When it came right down to it, there were only two details he wanted taken out of the chapter: the first involved a mutual enema during one of our health kicks, and I'll have to remain silent about the other one. I was afraid I would have to fight him over certain specifics but was relieved when he realized it was all the big, fat truth, just like the diary entry in which I called his member "huge." Little did I know I would have to discuss those two piddling words—huge cock—on national television about three dozen times.

After the work was done Donnie led me to his private jet, outfitted with catered caviar and baby vegetables ripe for the dipping, and to his new two-story dream pad in Aspen. I didn't ski even though I was supplied with the newest in slope fashion. Freezing, falling down, getting real wet, and sprouting a Rudolph nose in front of Jack Nicholson didn't appeal to me. Instead I wandered around the tiny shopping area in the snow, marveling at the chichi fashions and baubles for billionaires. Aspen in late '86 was a cross between Melrose Avenue and cowpoke country. Now it's almost exclusively Melrose verging on Rodeo Drive, but it's still a beautiful place. You can bump into Don Henley at any given moment. Ha ha. Anyway, while I was scarfing illicit strawberries and honeydew melon balls in Aspen, Michael was doing the same thing back in Los Angeles, only with a luscious human female piece of fruit. And once again I was kept blissfully in the dark.

IV

The one bond between Michael and me that never wavered was our commitment to Nicky, and together we wrung our tied hands over his growing difficulties. We were becoming painfully aware that he needed a new shrink, that Janine, with all her puppet work and singsong games, was totally ineffectual. I asked around and came up with the name of a supposedly "good" child psychiatrist, for I'd begun to wonder if, as a last resort, some type of medication could help Nick's powerful mood swings. In her book Patty Duke described how her life had been a tortured shambles until somebody had prescribed lithium for her (. . . they walk alike, they talk alike—at times they even drop alike . . .). So Nick and I waited in the stuffy, tiny outer office until the great man let us in. Nick was understandably agitated, and the "doctor," who studied him like he was an amoeba under a microscope, had the gentleness of an iron lung and the patience of a demon on speed. In fact, after about a half hour of attempting to reach Nick, he became more and more red-faced and furious, until Nick climbed behind the couch, shrieking and sobbing, "Demon! He's a demon!!" After I'd coerced him out of his hiding place by promising him we could leave, the good doctor said—*right in front of Nick*—"Yes, I agree that your son is crazy, and I don't think there is anything I can do for him." The word *crazy* sank into Nick's head like a hatchet, and he cowered behind me, shaking and breathing hard like he had just witnessed an exorcism. I glared at the beast in doctors' clothing, but it was too late. For the next few years, when anyone questioned his behavior for any reason, Nick declared that he was crazy. I canceled the creep's check and wrote him a scathing letter, but I should have called the American Medical Association, taken him to court, and put his pancreas through a meat grinder. Thwarted mother-hen retaliation dies hard.

It wasn't only maternal pride that made Nicky's intellect seem dazzling. Since he was a tiny kid he had been enthralled with all

things Japanese, and at age nine was actually teaching himself
to speak the language. Our main weekly outing was downtown to
Little Tokyo, where he bought Japanese comics and browsed among
the much-coveted robots. One remarkable afternoon, as he carefully walked the fence in our front yard, he told me a wondrous
tale about his previous life as the caretaker of sharks in a "Sea
World–type place," where he had drowned after falling into the
water while feeding his shark charges. "Now you know why I don't
like to swim, Mom," he said, "so don't bother me about it anymore."

But there was a kernel of darkness in his brilliant imagination that
made him prey to haunting fears he could hardly name or describe.
He saw tortured faces, ghosts, and other strange apparitions in the
corners of his room. He saw people from other planets out the
windows. He would finish a book about scientific progress and worry
it was all going too fast. After watching a TV show about children
starving in India, he sobbed for two days. Already an eco-monster,
he clipped the plastic six-pack holders so they wouldn't wind up on
the snout of a porpoise. He mourned the vanishing rain forests. In
attempts to help him figure what in the world was going on, I took
him to the Bodhi Tree bookstore, and he pored through spiritual
tomes seeking refuge. He tried yoga, putting himself in all sorts of
contorted asanas (yoga positions), he went through a stage of transcendental meditation, oming for inner peace. We kept up our trips
to the Self-Realization Lake Shrine and the air would fill up with
incense smoke and comic books on Krishna and Shiva. Lordy, Lord,
Lord.

Speaking of the glorious Lord, Nick spent a few months at a Jesus-
oriented school after the final, final straw at Westland, in which he
tossed a chair over the heads of his classmates, almost breaking a
window, and was asked to leave the fancy, haughty private school.
I had to find a replacement fast and came up with this Bible-thumping
institution. The long-suffering, do-gooder born-agains thought it
was their Christian duty to help the pissed-off little fellow find
Jesus, and in their attempt to save his soul, he was placed in many
corners and given many hellfire-type lectures, but they never asked
him to leave. He told me about these outmoded procedures and
complained about being bored and understimulated, but I was at my
heart's end and needed some of my own time and space, please Jesus,
and I also believed it was better for him to be with other kids then
to sulk around the house. However, after a little Christian walk to

McDonald's one afternoon, I yanked him from Jesus school real fast. The class had wandered by a Far East antiques store that sold Buddhas and other religious statues, and when Nick pressed his nose to the glass to check out the merchandise, the teacher harped, "Cast your eyes away from the devil, Nicholas. Those pagan statues came straight from Satan." I realized their shallow values were so foreign to Nick that the potential for screwing up the one thing that gave him solace was too strong. I also remembered visiting my born-again relatives down in the gorgeous hills of Kentucky and the agony I felt. Guilt-stained and wracked from carrying the cross down the Sunset Strip, I found myself down on my knees in front of the TV set, praying with Billy Graham. Seeking forgiveness for being young, free, joyously wild.

Michael and I had a thousand meetings with the Santa Monica school system and state board of mental health, and Nick was put through way too many days of ink-blot and IQ testing. For one test he was told to draw a picture of himself, and Nick produced a perfect log like the one the "log lady" carried around on *Twin Peaks*. Confused by the boy wonder, the official fools could only advise us to find him a good therapist while they attempted to find us "proper placement." So Nicky returned to the local public school under great duress, and I met with many child psychiatrists, extremely wary and on guard, until I finally came upon a sweet, big bear of a man called Laurance at a children's facility in West Los Angeles. Since Nick didn't think this guy was on a mission from Hades, sent to torment him, he started twice-weekly sessions and actually seemed to be feeling a bit better about himself.

He had even made a new friend, Taliesin Jaffe, T.J., the blond little actor boy in the movie *Mr. Mom*. T.J. was an outgoing, intelligent charmer who had to work on Nick for thirty minutes to get him through his front door, but when he did, they found they were both interested in astrology, astronomy, Greek myths, and most important, Japanese animation. T.J.'s mom was a casting director friend of Michael's, and the next time we all got together T.J. introduced Nick to the spellbinding world of Nintendo—and the all-encompassing place where he could destroy the bully bad guys and control his own destiny. He soon had his own Nintendo system, followed by every game he wanted, then more systems, more games. More games. More systems. More. Sega. Genesis. Turbo Grafx CD. P. C. Engine. Sega Master System. Game Boy. Game Gear. Famicom, Super Famicom. Neo Geo. Super Nintendo.

V

Big, new weighty worries were waxing as the old year, 1986, was waning. My dear friend, Shelly—Michele Myer—was suffering insurmountably with the Big C. My brilliant, stubborn, longtime girlfriend had always cursed her mammoth bosom and hated doctors due to her truly prudish Catholic school upbringing, so had put off getting a breast lump checked out, and now the disease had spread to her spine. She was banging weakly on heaven's door. Shelly had been the black lamb in an alcoholic family, striking out the only way she knew how—through music, shoving her way up through the rock ranks slowly but surely until she booked the coolest local clubs, discovering incredible bands and making almost no money for her dedicated inspiration. She was the first person to book Van Halen, and the Go-Go's, among so many others, but still didn't have a darn-tootin' dime to call her own.

Michael and I decided to put together a benefit for Michele and called out all the dogs. We rented the Roxy, and there were lines around the block to see the Knack, a few of Motley Crüe, re-formed Chequered Past featuring Michael and Steve Jones and Paul Cook from the Sex Pistols, Charlie Sexton, Dweezil Zappa (in his first appearance), some of the Go-Go's, and a heavy-duty jam session dedicated to the "den mother of rock and roll," featuring our new pal Bruce Willis on harmonica. At the close of the show Michael crooned to Shelly, "Mee-shell, my belle," and the whole place cheered while she silently bawled, so sweetly grateful to be acknowledged. Gene Simmons and Paul Stanley of KISS came through with a hefty donation, as did David Lee Roth and Ronnie James Dio. At least she didn't feel beholden and skint while she suffered and swigged liquid morphine to curtail her ever-expanding pain.

After the benefit Michael went to that other balmy coast to cavort with Donnie on the set, where he had started to rule with an over-wrought iron thumb, and Michele stayed with Nick and me for a few days in Santa Monica. Her most surprising comfort came from the person she had loved more than life, almost all her life: Chris Hillman. She liked to say that her rock-and-roll obsession had been all his fault. Her favorite band had been the Byrds and then the Flying Burrito Brothers. I met her in 1969 at a Burrito session at A&M Records. She announced herself as "the original Burrito fan," and I let her have the all-important credit. Shelly had always underestimated herself profoundly or got severely angry about not getting the respect from the rock mutts she thought she deserved. In the old days Mr. Hillman had often ignored her desperate adoration at his gigs, sometimes just being downright mean. I had kept in touch with my first love through the years, kept track of his various musical projects, and had noticed a gradual change in his bravado attitude, so was not dumbfounded by his response to Michele's illness. "I'll come see her tomorrow," he announced, and we prepared for his arrival. Shelly camped out on the couch (she was almost to the point of immobility) dressed in her most colorful oriental robe. She had lost almost all of her hair and was on a constant search for the perfect turban. We found her a bright yellow one with gold thread running through it, and she was ready to greet Mr. Hillman.

The knight in shining armor arrived wearing tight faded jeans, carrying a bunch of flowers, and brought the house down. He spent hours with Shelly handing her such a luminous hunk of light that she felt that the whole, hard trip had been worthwhile. Then he decided to make me feel good, too. While I was making tea for us in the kitchen, he came up behind me, encircling my waist with his big arms. "I'm really proud of what you're doing for Michele. You're a good girl, Pamela." Do you ever fall out of love with your very first heartthrob? I stammered, I held his hands, I looked into his bright blue eyes and yearned for yesterday's busted-up teen dreams. When it was time to go Chris hugged Shelly tight and promised to see her soon, and I walked him to his car. I thanked him for lifting Shelly's heart. We stood in the driveway looking at each other the way I dreamed about when I was too young to know better, too far gone to care. "I've always loved you," he said. Then Prince Charming roared off in his 4x4, leaving me standing in a dewpond of ancient, unrequited desire.

VI

Shelly finally had to move back to her hometown, San Francisco, to be with her sister, and I made a couple trips north to bask in her sorrowful company and try to boost her morale. On my first trip her sister Claire lent me her bomb of a car, and I loaded Shelly and her wheelchair into the wreck for her last sojourn into the wilderness. We went straight to Haight-Ashbury, where we had lunch at an old hippie diner and found two like-new three-ring Beatle binders for twenty-five bucks each. We scored heavy and she was wearily ecstatic. She slept for hours and hours afterward, missing a show that she had circled twice in the TV listings, while I sat beside her and listened to her troubled, aching sleep. That night, attempting to find Mr. Sandman in Claire's water bed, I cried for Shelly and her bare, thwarted life full of self-inflicted burdens. She despised her giant breasts, looking forward to the day she could afford a reduction; she cursed her family, the nuns, the record industry that wouldn't recognize her potential. And even though she had a razor-sharp one-liner mind and a hidden sweet heart that came out in her "Auntie Shelly" mode with Nicky, she complained constantly about her lot in life, "Why am I alive?," her constant bitter query. I had always chastised her about shoving so much negativity into her atmosphere, but she thought I was nuts. I tried to drag her to Science of Mind, but she told me she had enough religious input from Catholic school. Still, she had her glorious moments. I remember one of my favorite Michele Myer quotes: "We know our limits—and there are none." If only she had believed it.

By my second trip she had weakened dramatically. While the game shows droned, she lay under her blankets like a gasping fish out of water—every breath labored and tight, clutching her ever-present bottle of liquid morphine, even in sleep. She had me go through all her collected, precious papers: autographs of heroes, shots of her with David Lee Roth, John Entwistle of the Who, the Go-Go's, the coveted piece in the L.A. *Times* that called her "the den mother to the L.A. rock scene." I read it aloud to her: "Myer's job doesn't end with the last encore of the night. She's a rock and roll Mother Goose, chaperoning out-of-town bands, baby-sitting for rock rookies and protecting her charges from the sharks that feed on naive young rock stars. 'Michele has a lot of heart,' said Peter Case from the Plimsouls. 'When we were really down and out, she'd take us out to dinner and make sure we were OK. She's always gone out of her way to take care of us.' Another local rocker adds: 'She has kept people alive. Who knows how many times she's propped up some kid backstage and said, 'Do you know who you are? Let's talk about it before you go out and die in the street.' " She smiled thinly and said she never knew who the "local rocker" was that gave her such celebrated credit.

She gave me her treasured Bruce Lee puppet to give to Nick, and I wept, trying not to let her hear me. I made her promise to contact me after she reached "the happy hunting ground," as she called it. She attempted to be funny, but it hurt too bad. I told her to look out for the big light, and thanked God the drugs kept her knocked out most of the time while I sat there feeling hideously inept and inadequate. I felt for Claire, who had become a constant nursemaid, exhausted and red-eyed. We talked while Michele slept. She wanted to know who her sister was, who she had turned into after she left the miserable, chaotic family nest and headed for Hollywood. She read the *Times* article, she looked at the photos of her feisty older sister with Eddie Van Halen, Bun E. Carlos of Cheap Trick, Bruce Johnston of the Beach Boys (her very first lover). Claire sighed and told me Michele had always been headstrong. A mild understatement. Nothing or nobody ever kept Michele Myer out of a room she wanted to enter. She prided herself on "crashing" any event that didn't have her name on the guest list, and she never failed.

I left San Francisco knowing I would never see Michele again. She died three weeks later, and I closed my eyes tight and asked Gram Parsons to welcome his number-one fan into rock-and-roll heaven with open arms. Nick was crushed. He still has the Bruce Lee puppet in a place of honor, next to the goldfish that has lived way longer than we ever thought it would.

April 6—*My darling Shelly went to the happy hunting ground today. Good-bye sweet angel-woman. I love you so. I cried and dazed around, called Claire a couple times, prayed and spoke to Michele on her way. I know she's floating free of her battered body, God bless her.*

CHAPTER TWELVE

I

The drama in my frazzled life felt thick and full like a spider-sac brewing a ball of black-widows—and with the terrifying loss of Shelly, the decision to have dermabrasion on my teen-picked skin, Nicky's shadowy sadness, and the looming book tour coming up, it took me awhile to realize those incessant walks Michael took with our dumb dog, Nellie, and the mounds of dimes and quarters all over the place meant big trouble.

When I finally decided I could no longer deal with the fraud my marriage had become, I felt like my heart would burst and poison my quaking guts if I didn't ask those awful questions: Where do you go every night? Are you seeing someone else? Is there another woman? Are you having an affair? Do you love somebody else? Do you still love me? I *knew* he was at it again, because my intuition never fails me. I had previously ignored the small, still voice screeching and howling, battering at my inner eardrums until it finally weakened, flopped around aimlessly, and faded away. Did you hear something? No? Hmm, I could have sworn I heard something. . . .

To make the entire typical horror show even more god-awful, I had just had the dermabrasion and was red, goopy, and scabbed with Vaseline-dripping bandages hanging off my miserable, sore face. I kept thinking I could keep it all inside until I looked and felt a little better, but once the jig was up, I had to get it out in the open. I had pieced together all the nightmarish cheating facts, and they were haunting me as I thrashed around the house, pacing, rehashing events, looking just like a Stephen King hell-hag. Is there another woman?

Nicky was at my mom's, and Michael was out walking Nellie for the fourth time that evening. I knew he was going to the pay phone on the corner to call *her*, because up until about three months earlier he never went near the poor dog. At first I was eyebrow-raised and pleased that he began to give a shit about the mutt, but it slowly began to fade as I realized he didn't take much notice of her until he decided she needed a little fresh air. Are you having an affair? One afternoon I had followed a short ways behind them, my heart slamming hard, *ka-bump*, *ka-bump*, *ka-BUMP*, just to see Nellie struggling on her leash to frolic while Michael chatted away on the public phone. I felt like Mrs. Columbo on acid. I had also started to see large piles of coins littering the tabletops, and for a man who used to throw his spare change in the gutter, this was indeed an oddity. The phone rang more often, and I got several hang-ups a day. Hello. Hello! Hello? Hello!!?! So rude. Are you seeing someone else?

I waited silently on the fake Deco couch that we were paying off on our Broadway card, listening for Nellie's delighted yapping. She was always happy to see me. She didn't care if I looked like one of the walking dead. I was petrified, shaking, but determined to confront my errant titled husband. I knew he would deny any accusations because he always did, even when faced with clean, straight-ahead facts, but I had a newfound resolve this time around. I was a stronger person, a stronger woman, and a lot of it had to do with the fact that I wrote *I'm with the Band*. Tampering with my past, studying it, reliving it, delving soul-first into all that *stuff*—turning it into a viable, buyable piece of rock-and-roll history gave me some *balls*. What is the female equivalent of balls, anyway? It gave me some ovaries? Fallopian tubes? I finally had some mammary glands?

Even in this precarious, vulnerable position, I sat there on the couch like a cross-legged Indian squaw ready to do battle. I was about to slit open my love-pump and expose that squealing baby girl, and the pain was unutterable. Pondering all that had brought me to this heart-wrenching, heart-pounding moment, I waited for my husband of thirteen years to get home from spewing gooey love words to another woman. Do you love somebody else? Do you still love me?

By the time he got home a few minutes later, I had balanced myself, ready to ask that first big question. Where do you go every night? He unleashed the dumb dog, popped on the TV to watch the news, and got comfortable in his leather recliner across from me. "So, how did Nellie like her walk?" Not quite. "Want a cup of tea?" Nope. I was pissed but still in the adoring-wife mode where I still held myself hostage. Confrontation is wicked for me. Especially when the doll-house is about to be squashed underfoot. "Where do you go every night?" He didn't answer, so I posed it to him again. He had gradually built up to about five nights a week and was getting pretty blatant: squirting on the Opium, sucking in those dramatic chiseled cheeks, making a mad dash for the door.

"I've been spending a lot of time with Stevie," he said in a strange voice, "I've been going to a lot of AA meetings." He looked every-where but at my aching face. "I've just *needed* to get out of the house."

We circled the question for awhile until I had him in a hole the size of the Hollywood Bowl. "Michael, I'm not *asking* if you're seeing somebody else, I'm *telling* you I KNOW you are." I was letting my intuition shine, speaking my mind—even though I felt like lying down in a dark room for a year—glory hallelujah. He was caught so cold that his scoffing and protests were weakling attempts to get me off the track and then he just shrugged, exhausted, and gave up the fiction. One of those unspoken agonies passed between us; the air chilled, the sun went down, the curtain closed, and the sorrow was transcendental. I had demanded the truth for the first time. I wanted to get down to the splintered bone no matter how many wounds I would have to lick later. I had always nodded enthusiast-ically when he skirted and sideslipped the truth, not really wanting to know. I had begged his forgiveness when I caught him scarlet-handed, put hazy walls in front of the facts, looked the other way, turned the other cheek to avoid the raw certainty. He had always ended the dalliance when I started asking questions, but I could tell by the crumpled misery, the cave of his shoulders, the bed of thorns in his deep blue eyes, that this time it was going to be different.

II

Michael's head had become a woebegone burden, weighing fifty tons and hanging close to the floor when he finally admitted to having another affair. He couldn't look at me and I didn't blame him. How about your wife busting you for one more adultery while her whole head looked like it had been eaten by a garbage disposal?

I loved this fucker, even at this ignominious moment. Even now I felt his pain like it pumped through my own arteries. "Who is it? When and where did you meet this bitch?" I asked, wishing I looked beautiful. It just *happened*, and it just *happened* to have happened at Helena's. Big shocker. I didn't want to, but I cried, the salt biting into my scabs. "I know about the phone calls on the corner." Oh, how he hated to admit he had been that obvious. "She hangs up on me five times a day," I went on. He grimaced, he fidgeted. Here came the humdinger. "How about when I called you in Palm Springs on our fucking *anniversary* and there was a 'do not disturb' on the line? Hmm? The very place we went for our *honeymoon*. How about *that?*" I yelled, sounding like something roasting on a spit. I shouted that his lust-crave for me had gotten up and split, probably a long time ago. And guess what? My desire for him had been flattened paper-thin like a run-over cat by his lack of desire for me. Had he ever thought of that? It took two not to tango, remember? I was boiling mad and frozen to the spot, while Michael decided to get up and pace.

"We've been together so many years, Pamela, desire fades, we know each other too well." Age-old breakup words—the mystery train gone way, way down that old railroad track. A speck in the distance.

Too much troubled water under the bridge? Too many blemishes blatant in the morning light before the chance came to daub them with Blasco cover cream? Too much sameness? Everyday, dull, ordinary life-pain? From me, too much veiled desperation disguised as overpowering love, perhaps, a cloak of pink, humid oppression that made Michael shrink, flail, go out on yet another crazed escape binge seeking a cool, hot-tempered model bitch to give him a hard time while I sat home wearing my Goody Two Shoes grin, writing out checks to California Edison, Group W Cable, and Sparkletts water?

Still, I kept pushing. On that awful night I had to know: Did he love this home-wrecking bitch and/or did he still love me?

In the past when I made it clear to Michael that he had better stop seeing a certain little miss adulteress, he would comply willingly, almost happy to be found out because he had the perfect excuse to put an end to the fling. I wasn't even sure what I hoped for this time. A sub-sleeping part of me wanted him to refute me, so we could somehow move on. I'm sure he didn't really want to hear one more sodden ultimatum from me, either. Still, I expected him to say, "Don't worry, honey, it's over," or "I'll never see her again." Then it dawned on me like the Age of Aquarius that this might actually be IT. "Do you *love* this amoral piglet?" I peeped, attempting to shield my sore face from his answer. Of course he said, "No," but I didn't believe him. I had come to know his lying voice well, even though at times I ignored it entirely in favor of keeping at least a piece of the peace, the tranquillity of fiction.

He looked at the wall and said, "I can't stop seeing her now." A knuckle sandwich straight in the kisser. What the fuck did "now" mean?

"Do you still love me?" The sound of my thin, whiny voice in my own ears made my flesh crawl like termites had infested and were about to reach the heart chakra. Michael looked at the floor. "I will always love you." It came out like a crucified whimper while I sat there like a lump of redundant flesh—weak, worn out, and hollow— the Indian squaw that had been prepared to hurl her brave's own arrows, transmuting into an ordinary trodden-down, cheated-on wife. After the longest, quietest time in the universe went by, as my heart sagged and my face throbbed, I asked what we were going to do. He suggested I allow him to continue to see this girl until the time came when he might be finished with her.

"I think you'd better move out," I said, and my voice seemed to be coming from the ceiling.

Dead silence.

Actually living, breathing, choking silence filled the room like nuclear waste. Finally I got up off the couch, went to the bedroom, and climbed under the covers. Michael went out the front door with his pockets full of change. He left Nellie behind.

The party's over, baby—why don't we call it a day.

II

I'm not saying Michael wasn't hurting over the situation; it's just that he had something to take his mind away from the hard, cold, breaking-up facts—a young brunette model. *I* had to start the withdrawal process while *his* heart was full of passion for someone else.

Since it was one of those times when the Des Barres didn't have a whole lot of dough, we agreed—with a sense of unspoken relief— that he should postpone moving out until our finances grew less bleak. His new solo record, "Somebody Up There Likes Me," had just come out, and I sat in the appreciative audience when he sang on "American Bandstand," finally meeting Uncle Dick Clark and shaking his hand. And his acting prospects were picking up—he had already done a very amusing episode of *My Sister Sam* and was up for a part in a sci-fi thriller—so the arrangement wouldn't last long. But it was harder than we could have imagined. In the beginning I hated Michael so deeply sometimes that I didn't know myself and was scared of the volcanic vehemence of my increasingly nasty thoughts. Of course, I still loved him too, even though I was so full of resentment I felt like I had eaten a sixteen-ounce steak after twenty years of living on papayas. It was all very, very confusing. Michael was equally volatile, totally on edge, looking for any excuse to go on the rampage. One evening the tension was so syrupy and thick, I was watching every move and slipped up anyway. Nick was reading a book with his tray balanced precariously on his knee, and when I set a soda pop on the tray it tumbled off and spilled all over the place. Michael exploded with rage and, going off the deep, deep end, grabbed the tray, threw it into the front yard, and stomped it, bleating about the bourgeois household he was forced to live in and how the tray incident represented all that was mundane and trivial in his life. There it was: I was from the San Fernando Valley and he was a blue-blooded aristocrat. Nick was caught in between and started quietly bawling.

III

We still hadn't figured out how to tell Nick about our separation. Such a sensitive child, he surely had been feeling his parents' strung-out friction even though I tried to camouflage it with the upbeat day-to-day trivia of living. But whenever I thought about telling Nick that his dad was moving out, the impending moment made me want to bury my head deep in the Santa Monica sand only ten blocks down the street. Instead I went into therapy.

My therapist was Aggie, a psychologist around the corner who happened to have done Nick's astrological chart. She had been pretty accurate about the little bugger's personality, also telling me the hardest years of Nick's entire life were upon us all. He was supposed to come out of the nightmarish phase around his twelfth birthday, and since he was only nine and a half, I prayed for strength to deal with it all. And I thought she might be able to deliver some equally helpful insights for me.

At first I didn't even think it was necessary to discuss my childhood. I was home free, wasn't I? After all, I grew up with both parents in the house, had never been psychologically or physically abused, and had always felt mightily loved, in a sane mommy-daddy-child-Valley life-style way. TV dinners on a colorful metal tray. Listening to the Dodgers in the sunny backyard. Bicycles, roller skates, a skate key around my neck on a red string. Hot homemade potato soup on a chilly night. A flowered flannel nightie. My mom had even let me build my doll's house on top of the TV. When Daddy complained, she made him see how important it was to little Pam. My childhood was idyllic, peaceful, joyous, serene.

But I found out real quick that the idea I had about my incredibly normal upbringing was straight out of left field. That ball is outta here! When Aggie asked me to recall my childhood memories, what wafted into my mind was a moment in a gloomy foyer, at the bottom of a long flight of stairs. I was looking way, way up, so I must have been a tiny thing about three or four years old. I was calling to my mommy and daddy to stop yelling at each other. My Aunt Bert was trying to comfort me, and I sobbed to her, "Make them stop!! Please make them stop!!" I was surprisingly shaken by the dredged-up image, and Aggie asked what the moment might have represented to me.

My mom had told me a little tale soon after Daddy died that put her in an entirely different light. It made me realize she was a real live flesh-and-blood woman and not just my mother. Forty years before, she had fallen in love with the gentleman half of a couple in our family. For two whole years they agonized, then finally decided to get their separate divorces and get married. They talked about moving away together, but the gentleman couldn't bear to leave his children behind. Just when my mom finally got the guts to ask Daddy for a divorce, the female half of the couple told O.C. that she thought her husband was having an affair. Never a thickheaded man, Daddy put two and two real close together, went across town, and beat this guy within an inch of his life. For an entire day and night he led Mom to believe he had actually murdered her lover. (The blatant fact that Daddy had cheated rampantly himself never even entered the sorry picture.) In his rage he told her, "Pam would be better off dead than to be raised by this blankety-blank man," and soon after, the thwarted lady actually threatened to kill my mother. Terrified, Mommy and her gentleman severed the relationship, and it remained a whispered subject—the Miller family scandal.

Recently—this is forty years later, remember—this couple came to visit one of my aunties. I noticed that Mom was moody and distant the whole time they were in town. She, of course, couldn't set foot on the property. She had told me she felt him thinking about her through the years, and this got to me because I'm such a hopeless— oops, hope*ful*—romantic. So I offered to slip him a note from her, so maybe they could talk on the phone, but she wouldn't do it. I even went to my aunt's for a little visit to check him out; he turned out to be a quiet, unassuming man, much smaller than my handsome daddy, and I sat there, sipping iced tea, making non-talk, trying to imagine his tumultuous past with my sweet mom. Alas, he died a short time later, and Mom never had been able to bring herself to contact him. She was quietly miserable for a few months afterward, but because she is strong and stalwart, got on with her life.

Over time Daddy and Mom slowly rekindled their marriage. She says it actually got better as a result. But what had *I* gone through? The shadowy little figure at the foot of the stairs? That terrifying moment I remembered from my childhood, wailing in the foyer, must have taken place right about the time my mom and Daddy were going through their own private hell. Every kid has to undergo all kinds of nightmares and come to grips with them later on—or not. Until I met up with Aggie, I had always prided myself in *not* feeling anger and rage. Voices raised in anger made me want to cower, cringe, say, or do anything just to make them stop. Give in, give up, give way. Take it, take another little piece of my heart now, baby. Just stop yelling! And I *would* wind up with a man who had a temper the size of Idaho. Me? I've always been Miss Goody Two Shoes for real. A perpetual happy face, the bearer—always—of good tidings. But if that was really who I was, then why did my head pound and ache when I kept something inside that I wanted to say to Michael but didn't for fear of a confrontation? Could my seemingly perfect childhood have anything to do with my newfound put-upon rage?

Who knows what makes someone the way they are? A whirlwind combination of things, I'm sure. Aggie and I started digging away at the notion that I was a product of Beaver Cleaver's household or the daughter of Donna Reed. I found out some pretty sad facts years later; that one of my favorite wise and understanding TV dads was a miserable alcoholic, while the family's adorable, prankish youngsters were locked in their dressing rooms shooting heroin. I once saw the actor who played Bud on *Father Knows Best* wearing dirty clothes, ambling down Hollywood Boulevard with matted hair down to his ass, and a long beard. Startled, without thinking, I asked, "Why, Bud! What happened to you??!!!" The filthy look I got put me smack in my place. Growing up on television must have been like walking a tightrope over a den of iniquity.

Aggie told me we *all* had a right to our pain and we had to let it out, but the process was slow. Michael stopped getting fabulous dinners made for him every night and went out on his dates with the "other woman" after kissing me good-bye on the forehead. I thought I had grown strong enough to take it but then realized, *why should I?* There was one tense night when I came across a hidden stack of photographs of a ravishing brunette model in various slinky poses, sultry, sad, begging eyes—long, skinny legs, very small chest, red fingernails. The other woman. Right under my very own bed. Michael's side, of course. I stood there shaking, studying the face of this person who obviously believed she was in love with my husband. What had he told her about me? How could she do this to another female? Maybe he had told her his marriage was over? In Name Only. Did he buy things for her? Lingerie? Perfume? Take her to romantic dinners, his purple-blue eyes half closed, glazed over with desire? I baked with rage at this amoral Jezebel floozie, trollop-chippie-tart who was putting a cheap clown's hat on my marriage. Michael happened to have been out for the evening, and Nick was already in bed, so I took all the modeling cards, succulent eight-by-tens and lighthearted snaps, and lined them up on the table so he would have to face them when he opened the door. The next morning they had disappeared; Michael made me a lovely cup of coffee and never mentioned the indelicate mistress display. I never mentioned it either, so it went under the rug with acres of other unspoken atrocities with claws.

Michael soon went back to pretending to be married to me—at least when I was in the room. There were even times when we reverted to our comfortable spouse roles: watching TV, admiring the same cutie-pies up on the big screen, laughing at dinner parties. We never stopped touching, either. Hand-holding, hugs, and kisses are hard to give up. I had gotten a shimmer of reality in therapy and saw that I was still firmly entrenched in that victim mode. But I was determined to take an intergalactic pickax to those cracked, outdated, cream-puff ideals that were holding me back, making me a wimpy, weedy, cowering kiss-butt. (But I would still be a nice, sweet, well-liked person, right? Right? *Right?*)

IV

I paid a fortune to Maria, a fabulous Greek psychic, who told me I would be separated from my husband by August, my book would be a best-seller creating an entire career for me, and that it was good that Nick ate a lot of junk food because it kept him grounded. Somehow this info cheered me up; life wasn't so bleak after all. I always had the thrilling hope of tomorrow and tomorrow and tomorrow, didn't I? Always on the search for enlightenment, I started classes with Maria to pull out my own hidden abilities. The first thing she had us do was to make out a very specific list of exactly what we wanted in life and expect it all to happen:

1. I want a totally healthy body from head to toe—now and always.
2. I want a best-selling book (*I'm with the Band*) all over the world.
3. I want a successful and brilliant writing career.
4. I want my son Nicky to be happy.
5. I want my husband Michael to be successful and happy.
6. I want my mother Margaret to be healthy and happy.
7. I want to own a four-bedroom house with a guest house in Santa Monica.
8. I want to own my own 1987 T-bird.
9. I want clear, wrinkle-free facial skin.
10. I want several million dollars.
11. I want to find the perfect school for Nicky.
12. I want to meet Prince. (Oh, why not?)
13. I want to find the perfect masseuse to massage me at home every week.
14. I want a firm, tight body.
15. I want *I'm with the Band* to be made into a successful film.
16. I want to clear my mind and be able to meditate successfully.
17. I want a joyous love relationship.
18. I want a joyous steamy sexual relationship.
19. I want my dog Nellie to be happy and stop peeing on the carpet.
20. I want someone else to pay all my bills every month so I don't have to think about it.

What about world peace? A cure for cancer?

Maria said we are all full of potential psychic wonders, and I did have an amazing experience in class. After meditation we each took a piece of jewelry from the person next to us and were supposed to do a psychic reading on it. As I held the lady's watch, all kinds of images floated around in my head—I saw a menu, zoomed in on the man holding it, and could tell that he was considering changing the dishes, changing the concept of the restaurant he was standing in. Everything was in disarray; booths were stacked up, light filtered in through smudgy windows. I reported all this in a dreamy voice, and the lady was astounded. She and her husband had just bought a restaurant and were deciding whether or not to keep the menu the way it was or to change it entirely. Maybe I should call Robert Stack and get a job on *Unsolved Mysteries*. I'll bet I could even get him to crack a smile. But when I gazed into the crystal ball of my own life, everything was swirling and murky.

V

Michael continued to see his model, though with not as much guilty enthusiasm. At one point we decided to be the ultra-modern couple and *both* go out with other people—have one of those cheesy "open" marriages. It was a brief but très interesting decision. He would get all dressed up for his dates with the other woman, while I pondered how to meet somebody with whom to have my own indiscreet liaison. I was starting to feel my horny womanhood again peeking out from underneath years of cold-shoulder storage and checkered-tablecloth familiarity. Seamed stockings seemed in order, if you know what I mean.

Patti and I went to see *Blue Velvet* at a dark afternoon matinee while the boys were in school, and I had a surge of adrenalin peak through me like a flaming transfusion. It reminded me of the night many years before, watching the Who screech through *Tommy*, just *knowing* Keith Moon would show up large in my future. "What about Dennis Hopper?" I whispered to Patti as his character writhed around on the floor with that grotesque gas apparatus over his face. She grinned in the gleaming dark and nodded approval. The following Friday night Michael and I got our usual table at Helena's, and I wasn't surprised to see Dennis Hopper leaning against the bar when we walked in. He had just started to find himself back on the scene, sophisticated and sober after years of schizzed-out drug madness in the desert. I was wearing all black, skintight, throbbing to find some temptation on the dance floor. I got his attention by humping and bumping to "When Doves Cry," gave him a wink (*so* brazen!), and from then on his steel-ball eyes were on me while I table-hopped and cavorted merrily, laughing loudly with half-strangers, sipping expensive wine. I turned the knob all the way up. If Michael noticed what I was up to, he didn't show it. I think he was thick into his own dramatic world, living out an elegant fantasy of his own. On the way out the door that night, Dennis growled his telephone number in my ear, and I said it over and over to myself driving back home while Michael listened to Al Green. His number must still be carved on my brain somewhere—one of those useless tidbits of information clogging up the think tank.

When I finally screwed up the nerve to call Dennis, he wasn't home.

His answering machine had my hero Bob Dylan announcing: "The rules of the game have been lodged—it's only people's games that you have to dodge." Leave your message at the beep. Too, too cool.

Eventually he called back, and I could finally tell Michael that I had a date of my own. I don't think he believed me. I don't think he wanted to. He stayed home with Nick while I checked out Dennis Hopper's art collection. Come up and see my etchings, baby.

Did I really want to start an affair with the infamous genius freak from *Easy Rider*? He lived in the wilds of Venice, in the thick of gang shoot-outs and serious danger, behind some pretty thick concrete walls among several classic hunks of arts. Yes, he did show me his incredible art collection, one piece of which cast a certain shadow on the wall that resembled his very own profile. He made gallant, off-kilter chatter, poured me a cup of herbal tea, and we kissed a few times. It felt very strange to kiss someone other than my husband of many years. Then he sat down in front of me on the floor, crotch level, and gave me the best line I've ever heard from any man. "I want to worship your pussy," he said to me. Was it just a statement? Some sort of offer? A simple request? Hmmm. Wasn't it happening a little too fast? What kind of guy was he, anyway? He knew I was a married woman, so I suppose he was just getting right down to it. I hemmed and hawed, and we made out for a couple hours. While I drove through the Venice war zone on my way back home, I spoke aloud to myself, wondering what I was doing. Could I possibly play the Dating Game? My insides were still raw and bruised, I was trying to flaunt myself too soon, forcing the issue, needing male attention. I was scared shitless but hoping for some passionate heart-rage, just to know I was still capable of feeling it.

I saw Dennis and his famous art collection a few more times, and we almost did the deed, but not quite. I visited him on the set of *Colors*, and got all agitated and excited about the whole thing for awhile, but then it petered out, and now we nod and say "Hi, how're you doing," whenever we see each other at a function or a restaurant on the beach. He's got his gorgeous young dancer wife now, and I'm sure he worships her pussy appropriately.

Michael and I decided an open marriage was a bunch of shit anyway. The idea of it hurt too bad—like something had soured beyond repair, failed, just too hard to live with. His romance with the model went underground, and I concentrated on the new career I had carved out.

CHAPTER THIRTEEN

I

My old friend Danny Sugerman called to tell me he saw *I'm with the Band* in a big pile at Book Soup, a very trendy, eclectic store on the Sunset Strip. Danny's book about Jim Morrison, *No One Here Gets Out Alive*, had gone all the way to number one, and I thought it was significant that he was the person to tell me this sublime news. I hadn't been expecting it to hit the stands for another month and I was giddy with anticipation. I drove straight to town, parked in the red, and ran in. There it was—*right* next to *Glory Days*, a book about Bruce Springsteen, with one about Paul McCartney on the other side, and another on the King himself right above me! There I was, in a heap among the grandest of rock's goofballs. I pulled the Polaroid out of my purse and snapped away, announcing to all the people in the store, "Look! My book is out! Can you believe it?!?" I asked the person behind the cash register if he had sold any copies. "Sure, I've sold quite a few," he said. "Congratulations." I just stood there gawking at the stack of books with my teenage face on the cover, reeling inside. A lady came through the door, headed right for it, and started rummaging through the pages to get to the pictures of me twisting with my big, gorgeous Daddy, hanging tight to Keith Moon, standing with Mr. Zappa and the GTO's in the recording studio. It was one of life's finest, funnest fairy-tale moments. Pamela Ann Miller Des Barres from Reseda, California, was a published author. People were calling my agent for interviews, and the ball was about to start rolling.

The publicity blitz hit in the next few weeks. It had been twenty years since the Summer of Love, and *People* magazine did a massive spread on the flower-power generation, incuding a full-page shot of the GTO's out in the wild garden at Frank Zappa's log cabin. There I was, my hair in frenzied ringlets full of flowers, my hand over my heart, gazing into the air with poignant aching hope. An expression that is still found on my face on occasion. Ha! Since I had written about love-ins and the Sunset Strip, was I about to become some sort of flagrant spokesperson for my generation? Someone who lived to tell the tale? Uh-oh.

MTV called and wanted to interview me on the grand old days of groupiedom, so I sat in a booth at the Whisky a Go Go, reminiscing about Jim Morrison shoving a microphone down his filthy, black leather trousers right on the very stage in front of me twenty years earlier. In fact, I told many delightful Whiskey stories, but the one they wound up showing at least a hundred times (you can still catch it late at night if you're lucky! Ha!) was the one about stripping Jimmy Page of his dripping wet chiffon shirt after a gig, pressing the damp fabric into my face, and breathing deep.

The rock radio stations were chasing me! It seemed there was some real interest out there and the book might actually sell a few copies. Something I hadn't even allowed myself to think about, even though it was number two on my psychic want list. Some of the more macho-dog DJs had been condescending, intimating I was a groupie-pig-loose-babe trying to make a buck by dropping Jimmy Page's name along with my underpants. And I could always tell if they had actually *read* the book by the questions they asked. Real quick, I got the hang of defending myself while staying carefree and effervescent. When I wasn't remorseful about my sordid past—which, of course, I never saw as sordid—I found it really pissed them off. I enjoyed throwing uptight moral value judgments back in people's faces, listening to them sputter with frigid indignation. I took a lot of callers on the air, answering and evading all kinds of questions, which prepared me for the vitriolic onslaught I would encounter out on the road. The specter of AIDS had just taken hold of everybody's mental genitals and put the fear of death into their bedrooms. "How can you talk about your sexual exploits when this god-awful disease is raging?" First of all, my sexual exploits are only a small part of this book, and hey, man, it was the sixties when all you could get was the clap! And I was looking for love—L-O-V-E—with all those magnificent musicians! Statements like these irked the plugged-up women who wore their panties up around their necks. They thought I should be weighed down with regret and remorse for my wanton ways. My only true regret was that I had been too stoned at times to remember every exquisite detail.

The television talk shows wanted me! Along with Diana Faust at Morrow, I got my very own publicist, Mitch Schneider, who booked me for three whole weeks on TV shows across the country! Yippee-ki-yay-ki-yo!

II

Just as I was gearing up for the book tour my friend Joyce Hyser called to tell me Warren Beatty was considering buying my book as a property for her to produce. Elated, I went to the bright top of Mullholland Drive a few different times to meet with Joycie and Warren, but even though he seemed to be very intrigued by the idea, it never quite manifested. Warren was wild about Joyce, but he still held a powerful, rapt gaze whenever he spoke to me—the gaze that made many strong women fall into horny, quivering heaps. The way he listened was also magic, as if he crawled into my eyes to get the full picture the way I saw it. I know it's a cliché at this point, but he really does have a cosmically beguiling way with the ladies. He even included Joyce when he gave me a compliment; "Pamela has pretty legs, doesn't she, Joyce?" At one of the final meetings, during a healthy-salady lunch in his spotless chrome kitchen, after studying me like the clue to the universe was locked within my nearsighted blue eyes, Warren said to Joyce, "Pammie looks just like my sister, doesn't she?" People have always told me I look a lot like Shirley MacLaine, and I think it's a great compliment. I hope I can kick as high as she can when I'm fifty-five. And I would really like to join her waaaay out on that precarious limb someday. I admire her because she brought the massive message to the masses.

Soon after this complimentary incident Joycie had a little party at a cool soul-food joint on Pico, and she told me Bob Dylan was going to be there. I had met him once before at the Troubador, the night I threw daisies at Waylon Jennings's feet. I guess it was about 1970. Willie Nelson introduced us and Bob gave me that wet-fish handshake while I gazed at his Ray Bans in the dark. I stood there hopefully in my garter belt for a few lonely moments while he looked off into the murky distance, but I suppose he didn't feel like chatting. I had finally met Bob Dylan, and he didn't give a shit.

So Joycie invited Bob to her bash and I found myself in his presence once again. I've gotten over just about everybody. I've met almost everyone I wanted to meet except for Stephen King and Prince. It has taken me a long time, but I finally realized all my heroes are silly, insecure human goofballs just like me! What a relief. Still, no one on the planet ever inspired me the way Bob Dylan has, so I was happy to be in the same room with him again. When we were introduced, I got a handful of damp fish once more and assumed that the wimpy pompano was a form of protection from getting too many people in his face. Since it was more like good-bye than hello, I started dancing to some Motown, and when I dance I lose my mind. It's my form of meditation, and I go O-U-T, so imagine my surprise when I came back down to earth and Bob Dylan was standing in front of me, watching. "Do you want to dance?" I asked before I could think about it too hard. He grinned from inside his shades and encircled me from behind, where he hung on for thirty minutes. It took a couple songs by the Temptations and one by the Four Tops before I got adjusted to his sense of rhythm, which was as jarring and jangling as his lyrics. Yes, dolls, time stopped, but because I had recently become friends with his girlfriend, Carole, I didn't even have the old flirtation temptation. He did say one of the best things that's ever been said to me, however. He asked what I did for a living, I told him I was a writer, and he said, "What else do you do? I can think of twenty or thirty things I'd like to do with you." (Twenty or thirty? OhmyGod!!) He stepped back and studied me. "Yes, you could take you anywhere." Wow. What a compliment.

It seemed like all the cute young actresses were interested in playing the teenage me on the big screen, but Ally Sheedy was serious about it. I had met her a few times at various show-biz functions and saw something shining in her eyes that I recognized. Despite her brat-pack, youthful yuppie image, she was definitely leaning over the edge, peeking wildly into the abyss. Over lunch she told me she was enthralled with the sixties and had just started a rocky relationship with Richie Sambora from Bon Jovi. The whole music world was eating her up. I think she was also looking to break free of the cutesie image that had her trapped in long skirts and high necklines. And since she had just started her own production company, Nice to Mice, she was interested in producing. Ally bought the screen rights and started "taking meetings." I packed my bags and hit the road.

III

My very first big-deal TV interview was for the *Today* show. I wore a black leather jacket and told the world what Mick Jagger was really like (fun-loving, self-confident, hot). My mom's reaction to the book. (She was mortified at first, having to relive my tumultuous past, then proud of me.) What did my son think? (He's too young to care about what I did in 1969; he may *never* care about what I did in 1969.) How did my husband deal with it? (He was happy I finally wrote the damn thing after talking about it for so many years.) I got through that one—gigantic national TV. How many millions? Those pounding bright lights making me break out in a leather-sweat, seven fun-filled minutes over in a blink, wink of an eye. Michael sent me a telegram: CONGRATULATIONS YOU WERE WONDERFUL, RELAXED AND BEAUTIFUL. I didn't remember an instant of it. I had to fly straight from New York to Washington, D.C. for *Larry King Live* on CNN. I was on the second half of the show and found I had to follow Jesse Jackson. The big man got up, shook my hand, and I sat down in his place. From the sublime to the ridiculous, or was it the other way around? Larry King was very fatherly and gentle with me. I took calls about Led Zeppelin, Don Johnson, Mr. *Miami Vice*. Did I *really* cross-dress with Keith Moon of the Who? one irate lady who probably never had an orgasm raged at me from Middle America. Poor thing.

On some of the local talk shows I had to fill an entire hour by myself. Did Don Johnson *really* have a huge you-know-what? How huge was the thing, anyway? Did Jimmy Page use his whips on you? Why not? Was Mick Jagger a good kisser? Just how big were those things, anyway? Once in awhile I even got to go deep, explaining how girls from my generation felt caught between the fifties and sixties, confused as to which way to go. I popped the Pill on the Sunset Strip and searched for my identity through rock and roll—a women's libber in my own right. As brave, new, liberated females, we were supposed to go out and claim what we wanted, right? What I wanted was to take care of a man who played music, someone who might even be able to yank out *my* lurking creativity.

June 18—*Paul McCartney's Birthday*—*Oh me oh my, I'm reliving my past four or five times every day. It's so outrageous to be divulging my personal stuff on national TV. Strangers are coming up to me telling me they love the book, can't put it down—for all the right reasons.* Rolling

Stone gave me a rave, but heavy on the sleazy tidbits. Out of context they sound horrific. Oh well. Almost all of the interviews have been positive so far. I love being alive every second of every single day.

Sometimes there were excited yelling matches with the ladies who wore polyester pantsuits, then I would continue on into the day and do two or three live radio shows, a couple of newspapers, and a magazine or two—pin-eyed with exhaustion, get some dead-to-the-world, hard-won sleep, then back up at the crrraaack of dawn, starting the whole thing over in another city.

The week I got to Boston, bedraggled but in high spirits, I was greeted with the best review ever: Under the headline WHAM BAM THANK YOU, PAM, the *Boston Phoenix* spewed a full page of glory: "As a chronicle of the 60's and 70's L.A. rock scene, an unofficial history of female fandom, a sexual memoir of a girl coming of age at the height of 60's Love-Power, and the voice of a misunderstood and maligned rock subculture, *I'm with the Band* is one of the most important, revealing and unabashedly honest books about rock ever written."

After devouring a lobster and a huge slug of Boston cream pie, I climbed under the heavy brocade bed covers, comatose with fatigued accomplishment and ripe with gratitude, and slept for thirteen hours.

IV

When I was whizzing through New York I found that my very first dream-doll, Dion, was performing with the Belmonts at Radio City Music Hall. What could possibly have kept me out of the building?

When I had been a mere colt-girl of thirteen, my itsy-bitsy breasts blooming and budding under one of those growing bras that allowed for many inches of expanding promise, Dion DiMucci crooned directly to my barely teenage heart, making it spill over with sapling desire. His first solo album was called *Alone with Dion*, and as if the steamy look on his face wasn't enough, a pair of arms wearing long, pink gloves encircled his body tenderly, causing a near-riot in the lush pit of my pubescence. I wanted to put my arms around Dion, I wanted Dion to put his arms around me—sigh—but he lived far, far away on the exotic, dangerous East Coast, and even in that pulsating state I realized I was much too young for Mr. DiMucci. Besides, *Sixteen* magazine told me that he went and married his longtime love-button, Sue Butterfield. This big news caused so much baby-girl grief that it put a big, fat lid on the dewy incandescence of my near-perfect (or so I thought at the time) adolescence. Oh well, these things happen.

It took me twenty-seven years to get to this point, but where there's a will, there's a wangle, an angle, a WAY. After checking into the situation, I found that Dion's manager, Zach Glickman, used to work with Herbie Cohen and Frank Zappa in the old Bizarre-Straight days, so I called my agent, who called someone else, who called another guy, who put me in touch with Zach. We reminisced, I told him about the book and how I had written about my adoration for Dion in the first few pages, and he invited me down to the show to *meet* his client, Mr. DiMucci. Oh boy.

After sitting in a formidable threesome on the *Geraldo* show with Roxanne Pulitzer and a torch-haired sixty-year-old lady who had romped in the hay with JFK and Elvis, I sat seventh row center at Radio City Music Hall, surrounded by bouffants and quiffs, double-swooning while Dion did all his hits. As the audience swayed, singing all the words to "Runaround Sue," I clutched the book I had brought for my teen hero, rapturous tears in my eyes, anticipating the moment when I might be Alone With Dion, minus the pink gloves. It was one of those peak rock-and-roll experiences that make me want to shout loud and hard with the sheer joy of being on the planet the same time as Dion, Elvis, John Lennon, Mick Jagger, Etta James, Jimi Hendrix, Gram Parsons, Frank Zappa, Janis Joplin, Pete Townsend, Bob Dylan, Bruce Springsteen, Prince.

After Dion's show I waited in the outer-inner sanctum until Zach took me by the hand and led me over to a cute, fluffy-haired lady and introduced me to Sue Butterfield DiMucci. Real live Runaround Sue! I showed her all the Dion parts in the book and regaled her with ridiculous anecdotes about my teen-angst obsession with her husband. "Dion had groupies, you know," she said in an adorably humble way, "only they had a less flattering name for the girls back then." My peaking interest shot through the ceiling. What, what, WHAT were my brave predecessors called? "TFFs," she whispered, looking around to make sure no one was listening, "Top Forty Fuckers." Top Forty Fuckers. It was almost too much.

The twenty-seven years were up and it was time to meet Dion. Zach led me through the crowded corridors, full of an incredible number of Italian relatives that Dion probably hadn't seen in a dozen years, and into the inner-INNER sanctum, where he was perched on top of a desk, rhapsodizing about a huge mound of mozzarella cheese someone had just given him. While I sat on the couch, Zach tried to get the room cleared for my private moment with Dion, and as I gazed at the man who had made life in 1960 worth living, I felt like I was about to meet all four Beatles.

Introductions were made, handshakes, smiles. I tried to be cool and casual, but I blathered and stammered as I handed him the book, pointing out the photo of me wearing a locket that said, DION FOR-EVER, showing him the passages where he was adored and idolized. I knew he was born again and I hoped he didn't think I was a brash, breathless piglet. I just wanted him to know he had inspired me beyond the breaking point of no return. Zach brought in a photographer, Dion put his arms around me, and the flashbulbs popped. If someone had told me when I was that gangly colt-girl of thirteen that when I reached the magic age of thirty-nine, Dion would put his arms around me, I would have marked off the days on my calendar. Time stopped and the flashbulbs popped. Oh yes.

June 20—*Several cities later in Detroit, and majorly pooped out—revved up at the same time—can hardly believe I met Dion! I called Mom to tell her, and we talked about the times I dribbled all over the TV set when he was on* American Bandstand. *It's all swell out here. Philadelphia was a great city, but the travel aspects are sooo tiring.* USA Today *came out today, a big L.A.* Times *"Calendar" piece on Sunday. As my dear, sweet Shelly would say, "It's all happening!!" I hope she knows what's going on, watching over me from the happy hunting ground. Hard work, wacky gut-spilling—struggle with suitcases—but have met some cool people. I don't know what will happen, I'm waiting for sky-rocketing sales!*

In between all this madcap hullabaloo, the day came that I was invited to Bob Dylan's birthday party. I felt like I had won first prize on the planet. What could be more divine than helping my hero celebrate his day of birth? What do you get Bob Dylan for his birthday, anyway? What becomes a legend most? Another black leather vest? I spent two entire days traipsing all around town, attempting to procure the perfect trinket and wound up with an antique copper ashtray painted with real berries and grasses and hand-beaten by an entire tribe of Indians. That's what the très chic salesperson told me. She was wearing some sort of authentic-looking buckskin getup with several old Indian-head nickels down the front, so who knows? They wrapped the important artifact in unbleached muslin and tied it with raffia. I wrote something on the card about lifelong inspiration, trying real hard not to kiss his ass too profoundly. You can tell he's real sick of it.

Precious Patti was also among the chosen few to cruise down to Malibu that warm Gemini afternoon, and to say our spirits were high would be the world's most laid-back understatement. Some of that scary old peering-through-the binocular mentality threatened to rear its wicked head, but I admonished it into submission. Get lost, you lame negative thought pattern! I did the old one-two with my cosmic inner fists. Out, out, damn spot!

We got to Bob's house on time and the roosters scattered and the dust flew. It was so ramshackle on the outside, it must have been designed to keep out prying eyes, but after wading through the chicken coops, yakking ducks, heaps of old wood, cages, rubbish, it was like pulling back the Technicolor curtain to the land of Oz. Lush green all around a gigantic glass-and-wood abode, with the shimmering ocean as a backdrop; children frolicking, music playing, dogs yapping. The first person I ran into was Roy Orbison, all in black with serious sunglasses on. Hmm, there's Tom Petty, Jeff Lynne, Debra Winger, Joycie, Carole, various cool musicians, hip record-business types, George Harrison . . . GEORGE HARRISON!!! Fab Four flashbacks stung my head like blazing confetti; bobbing-head Beatle dolls, goopy teen Fab Four mush stories, a gently weeping guitar, "I'd be quite prepared for *that* eventuality." So Bob calls Patti and me over to embrace us, and we sit down with him under a big umbrella. Dogs woof, children laugh, the sun glints and sparkles on the sea, it's Bob's birthday and it's all too perfect. He introduces us to George; we are pink-cheeked and starry-eyed. "Oh, we've met a couple of times, haven't we?" George said to me. Did he remember me sinking into the blacktop at A&M Records back in '69? The brief moment in the recording studio with that nutty friend of mine a couple years ago? "Bob, have you read that wonderful book of Pamela's? I'm not in it . . . unfortunately." He laughed and told Patti that she was a legend, and she said, "Look who's talking!" It was a bit overwhelming, all very charming and tra-la. The way George said "unfortunately" was exactly how he said the word "eventuality" in *A Hard Day's Night*. I was still trying to get over the fact that one of the Beatles had read my book when the Beatle in question introduced me to his mechanic. I suppose he takes the man everywhere.

George said to me, "This is so-and-so, he works with engines the way you and I work with words." YOU AND I! He was comparing himself to me as a creative creature, and I was overcome with rapture. I shook the mechanic's hand and grinned a whole lot. Bob leaned over to me and said, "Maybe we could work together on a screenplay or something." I grinned the whole rest of the day and well into the star-filled Malibu night, dancing to cool old songs on the cool old jukebox that George, Jeff, and Tom had gotten Bob for his birthday. None of the brilliant, creative souls at the party could figure out how to hook the thing up at first. Bob stood by watching with his arms crossed saying, "Don't look at me," but Tom Petty finally plugged it in, and everybody cheered. As I rocked out to "Runaround Sue," George called me over to him and whispered, "You're really cute, you know that?" Beyond wow. Being called "cute" at forty by one of the Beatles is a truly glorious thing.

Bob seemed to enjoy his jukebox, but I didn't get to see him open the other gifts, so I don't know how the hand-beaten, berry-stained ashtray went over. I hope he liked it.

VI

The book went into a second printing, and then a third, and so after a brief dollop of duty at home, Morrow put me back out on the road. This time I got to go to Chicago, where I hung out in dingy, frantic rock clubs with my old friend, Cynthia Plaster-Caster. She is still casting semifamous rock penises, or is it peni? She was invited to come on *Oprah* with me to describe her seemingly sordid past and present but declined out of shyness. Besides, Cynthia's poor mom still has no idea that she's the legendary dick-mistress.

So I had to share the *Oprah* stage with Gene Simmons and Paul Stanley along with Jackie Collins, who had just written a no-dimensional novel called *Rock Star*. Paul and Gene were telling horny, amusing anecdotes about groupies, Jackie was regaling the angry audience with trumped-up tales about her rock friends, and I was ticked off because I had read her "rock novel" but couldn't express my opinion because a pal in publishing had smuggled the early galleys to me. Kind of a cloak-and-dagger thing. A smoke and Jagger thing. Ha ha. The audience was unamused when Gene said he had sex with two thousand women. (It's actually close to three thousand, but he didn't think they could handle it.) The would-be libbers booed and jeered when he stood up and grabbed his crotch, and started hump-

hump-humping the air. He ate it up with a sticky spoon. Jackie was alone in her upper-crust world of hype, and I was there to represent the real thing: the groupie girl. Groupie woman? (Actually the *former* groupie girl/woman. I always have to remind people of that fact.) I didn't get two words in edgewise.

In place of Cynthia P.C., the *Oprah* show had dug up the "butter queen" to spew a few outrageous vulgarities from in between two pent-up polyester matrons-before-their-time. Oprah asked her *exactly* what she did with her trademark cube of butter, and the matrons sputtered indignantly while she described her cholesterol-laden antics. I always felt bad about being lumped in with girls like the butter queen, God bless her. I like to think of myself as a romantic soul who happens to love rock and roll. I became established in that world before the notion of "favors" came into being. There were no passes, stickers, or laminates that guaranteed access to that hallowed ground, where true acceptance can never be bought and paid for. After *Oprah* I went down to Miami, where everyone wanted to know all about Sonny Crockett's massive member. It seemed I was surrounded by dicks but living like a celibate.

It was at this time that I suffered the rotten lowlight of my entire publicity glare. I had rushed from one coast to the other on a tiny moment's notice for *The Late Show*, just to be lambasted by the chilly charmer, Suzanne Somers, who asked me how many times I had gotten the clap, right on national TV. "How did you meet these guys?" She asked through a smudged veil of sweetness, "Did you stand around on street corners?" Yeah, right, smartie-pumps. Mick, Keith, Elvis, and Jimmy Page just happened to be wandering by while I stood there on the corner of Sunset and Vine. Where was Joan Rivers when I needed her? As I made a mad dash for the plane, the producers apologized, all pink-faced, and told me how well I handled myself. Thanks a lot, guys. I had been in the smoggy City of Angels and hadn't even been able to see Nick. Later on that night, too pooped to peep, back in my room in Miami, my mom called to tell me she wanted to wring Suzanne Somers's neck, and how could she get to her?

Always, some of the public adored me—thwarted rock-dollies who glommed onto my past like it was their very own, girls who told me I spoke their minds for them, guys who wished they had been there; and always, another part of the not-so-adoring public saw a scarlet letter—a raised, searing welt in the center of my forehead. Shame, shame, shame. On a live satellite show to Australia, the scum-host said menacingly, "How does it feel to be known around the world as a slut?" The world has never liked admitting that a woman can have a live-wire sex life. So when my old friend Robert Plant called from London to say he was giving the book to his teenage daughter, Carmen, so she could see what the glorious rock dog and doll days had really been like, I was pleased and strangely proud.

I spoke to Michael and Nick every day from the road, and their love and support energized me. Fortunately, Nick was too young to take much interest in the PR proceedings, but poor Michael had been subjected to hideous cracks and jibes about his wife, the groupie whore who kissed-kissed-kissed and told. How did he feel about his wife of thirteen years announcing to the world that she had slept with ALL THOSE rock-legend creeps? Always the devil-may-care sophisticate, Michael defended me to the hilt, telling people he was proud of my accomplishments and my blazing, colorful past. He said none of the revelations had been a surprise to him and he had been much, much worse in his heyday. He championed me with a big smile on his face, and I was grateful, but inside I knew he was squirming. Michael was home alone with his unhappy child, while his wife paraded around on *Geraldo* with her knickers down around her ankles, evading questions about the size of his best friend's dick.

August 14—*On the big bird headed back to L.A. I didn't write much on the entire tour—so hectic. Swell time with Donnie in Miami—we have such a special thing. I feel truly comfortable with him, so much Evian under the bridge. Lovely dinners, hysterical conversations, exquisite rides in his boat late at night under the huge full moon, mist steaming up off the ocean. He had one of his teenage no-ones with him part of the time, but we might as well have been alone. The Harmonic Convergence is occurring on Sunday, and I am ready for a transcendental awakening.*

CHAPTER FOURTEEN

I

The minute I got home, even before a nap, Michael dropped the bomb: He had found an apartment in the hysterical heart of Hollywood, very close to several of our former family love nests. He had recently completed a high-budget pilot for Aaron Spelling and had a pot of dough—and a month or two before, he had admitted having "very strong feelings" for the model (could this be love? Aaaaaaggghh!), yet seemed to lack the energy to take the next step. But now he was moving out. This was it.

Weren't there supposed to be sirens? Somber bells chiming? An announcement on the loudspeaker? A silent alarm, maybe? The next morning before dawn cracked I grabbed Nick and went to a high hilltop in Malibu, along with a thousand other seekers, attempting to still the frizzled cacophony in my head by meditating as thirteen heavens converged with nine hells. While Nick let his tortured spirit float out on that silver chord, like a beseeching kite of light, pictures of my marriage were illuminated on a magic screen behind my jittery eyes: Waiting triumphantly at the airport when Michael left England for me, our engagement announcement over the loudspeakers at Rodney's English Disco—and the envious teenage glances it caused—twenty dollars to an Elvis employee for a better seat, the first kick at *The Last Waltz*, the look on his face before he left for his first AA meeting, the broken wrench in his eyes when I asked if he still loved me. Oh, my dear Michael.

How to tell Nick? Sit him down over a nice dinner at the King's Head, fish and chips . . . Nick, don't just eat the crunchy parts, you know the actual fish has the protein. Why don't you at least *try* some ketchup on the chips? No, I don't know why they're called chips in England and fries in America, honey. Umm, you know how Daddy and I haven't been getting along that good? Sure, you can have a Coke. Excuse me, waitress, can we have a Coke? Michael, can you help me a little here? Thanks, Mikie. Nick, you know how Mommy and I have been arguing a lot lately? Well, Daddy has gotten his own place in Hollywood. I need to spend some time on my own. Oh, you'll see me all the time, honey. In fact, I want you to help me pick out some furniture, I want you to make me an art piece for the place of honor. Right, Mommy? Nicky, Daddy and I will always love each other. In fact, the main reason we aren't going to live together anymore is because we'll get along lots better living apart. We want to stay good friends. Oh, honey, don't cry. No, it's not your fault. We love you more than life, and always will. Would you like another Coke? Eat some dinner, sweetie. Pamela, I don't think he's all that hungry right now.

I know Nick, being so plaintively sensitive, had been picking up the hard-core hell of the situation anyway. And I believed real strongly that you shouldn't stay together for the sake of the kids, like couples did in the fifties, but it was HARD going. All kinds of guilt raged within me about not supplying the beloved offspring with a solid foundation, holding the family together *against all odds*. It was an agonizing, slow-moving realization that perfect romantic idealism is just so much cotton candy—smoky, sweet-spun wisps in the wind. Take Mommy away from Daddy and what have you got? Fifty percent of America. Maybe more.

September 4—*Well, my darling husband has found an apartment in Hollywood, and is moving on October one. Many mixed emotions, and I'm sure I don't yet realize the full extent. I believe I have already done a lot of the grieving and severing during the last five months. My book enabled me to get back some of who I used to be and also to gain a ton of new courage and self-worth. Even though Michael is the one who did all the deeds, I instigated the separation. I'm proud of Michael for going through with it. We shall see what we shall see. Is there another fella for me?*

The day Michael moved out, as he loaded his clothes, aftershave, and cassettes into a pickup provided by good old Stevie, there was a decent-sized earthquake that shook the foundation of the house, sending ceramic figurines and pouting African masks clattering to the floor in great disarray. It was perfect, except there should have been a few lightning bolts thrown in to add a little more drama. Actually, we tried to downplay the dramatics for the sake of Nick, who was less agitated than I would have imagined, getting ready to help Daddy set up his new place. Michael had already taken Nick on shopping excursions, and even I had accompanied them a couple of times to add my feminine-touch two cents' worth to his bachelor pad. Michael left me just about everything, taking only one piece of furniture, a leather swivel chair that he liked to relax in while watching *60 Minutes*, CNN, or himself on TV.

When all the boxes had been carted out, I waved good-bye and they drove off, Nick sitting on his dad's lap, plaintive and jazzed all at once. And there I was, alone in the house. Separated from my husband. The big bedroom closet was empty and I stared at it for about half an hour, not even realizing I was bawling my head off. I felt like a teakettle after all the water had boiled away but the flame was still burning my ass. Dry heat. Energy dripped out of my fingertips, what to do? My arms felt like dead stumps as I slowly gathered party dresses, velvet jackets, and Betsey Johnson specials out of the hall closets and into the master bedroom. Oops. Mistress bedroom. I hung the garments one by one, inhaling Michael's familiar scent. Ghost suits and silk shirts danced with my fancy frocks. I was losing my mind.

II

October 12—So, Michael moved almost two weeks ago—the first few days were solemn and weird. The day before *he moved, the fateful day itself, and the day after were horrors, but the vibe around here is calming down; it's actually starting to feel good. I've "spring cleaned." Patti and I had a yard sale and I made six hundred. My clothes have space in the closet and it feels very strange. Michael seems pleased in his new pad and proud of himself for getting it together. I know it's très important to him as a* human *no matter what else happens. Nick seems okay about it. He's a bit pissed off, as he doesn't know the real reasons behind the breakup. He sees his dad a lot; we've all had dinner a couple of times.*

The dinners were stilted and forced happy. Trying so hard to prove it was all going to be okay. Nick didn't look in our faces too closely; I think he was afraid we would crack and fall into little pieces right in front of him. He continued to see his burly, bearded therapist, and I prayed he was confiding in him. Every week I dutifully sat in the waiting room, reading ancient *Redbook*s while the well-meaning psychologist tried to crack Nick's ever-thickening shell. He had gone to Montessori summer school; Michael and I thought he would thrive in the creative nonjudgmental atmosphere, but he hated it and was kindly asked not to return. A phantom back at Roosevelt again, he was alienated from kid-kind, except for T.J., who, thank God, came over on the weekends. They discussed Atropos and Lachesis, how they wove the threads of life, and studied Japanese comic books because Nick had decided he was going to be a Japanese animator when he grew up. At least he had a goal for the future, no matter how seemingly far-out-fetched.

I felt like a tender sponge after Michael moved out. If somebody touched me too hard it felt like a bruise was being called up out of my brooding bloodstream, mottled and blue, physical proof of the heartsmash inside. At the same time a goose-bump sense of euphoria was blooming, and part of it was freedom from my own addiction to making sure Michael was happy. Putting his feelings before my own had contributed to so much spleenful discontent on both sides. Somewhere down deep I felt he *owed* me for making me hurt so bad. On top of all the sticky guilt I made sure he suffered, he must have felt I owed *him* for taking him on his own private trip through Walt Disney's Fantasyland one too many times. On a cosmic level, however, I now realize that our loved ones are our teachers, and sometimes the private lessons almost do you in.

As I had many times before, I started to write down my dreams every morning, trying to be my own analyst piecing together the subconscious puzzle, poking around for the answer when I hadn't even had the balls to ask the question yet.

November 1—*I'm in a huge American car, pulling into a big empty, very clean garage—a professional auto shop. Chris Hillman is the mechanic, and he yells at me to "turn the tape down!" I get furious with him, gun my motor, and feel like running him down. Chuck Connors appears— strong, old, tan, and leathery—representing manhood. He asks if he can take me to dinner, very casually. His fingers are very tanned and strong.*

November 6—*I was at a trendy party, and Richard Gere and I went into a dark den-type room where we proceeded to have major sex. The only real clear moment was when he came in my mouth. It felt like an explosion, and I thought it was a huge amount of semen, but it turned out to be just a few drops.*

November 9—*I was in the tub with no water, spiritual rituals going on in the background. The tub was decorated with symbols, and as I sat there the whole world started shaking and I began praying out loud* (knowing *the prayers would work*) *"The power of God in me knows perfect safety," etc. All of a sudden I'm with Nick on a metal beam in Tokyo many stories in the air, and we're attempting to get down. The building crumbles under us from the earthquake, and our first jump is successful. I know we will make it.*

November 20—*I am sitting on the couch reading a magazine, and Michael comments on how ugly my double chins are. I look down and see rolls of fat.*

November 22—*Nick and I are sharing some sushi out of a tin holder, offering some to Michele Myer as a good vibe to her spirit. We held the chopsticks high in the air.*

November 29—*I made sleazy love with Prince. It was* really *real. I was in his room—red, red lights, hidden glitter, sultriness. He had his shirt off—skintight spangly pants. We were friendly and chatting, and it turned amorous. He took out his dick—really big and beautiful—and rubbed it all over my tummy and came buckets. I remember thinking, I'm sure he can come again. I started porning out—fingers in ass and pussy. He was standing in front of me at the foot of his bed, beating off.*

How shocking! A combo of carnal delights, blubber paranoia, Chris Hillman in coveralls, and The Rifleman with leathery hands. At least I had a little God power in there, which showed me I was thumping along on the right track. Bong, bong, bong! *Saved* by the spiritual bell.

III

Thank heavens I had all my girlfriends to remind me that life was grand—even with all its high-flight ups and deep downs. Patti, who was long past grieving over Donnie, took my heartblood pressure and prescribed a dose of Vitamin F (fun, fun, fun!). She dragged me along to a full-on Hollywood bash, two hot-to-trot single babes out on the town. Since her split with Donnie, she had come under the spell of several hunks of stuff and was currently pursuing one of the best-looking men who ever breathed. He was an actor, half Indian with long ebony hair that was way shinier than mine would ever be, no matter how much Nexxus Humectress I worked through to the ends. He was supposed to be attending this particular soiree, so I had to doll up as hard as she did to trail in her hellbent stardust.

I decided to show off my triceps and abductor muscles. Why sweat and strain and not give the world a glimpse? I wore a very short, slink-snug rust-colored panne velvet job with cutouts in the middle; Patti had on layers of frothing black lace. We were a pair, for sure. We had been there for ten nonchalant minutes when I felt like I was being intently watched. I can always feel a stare, can't you? Surreptitiously I scanned the room, which isn't that easy because I'm nearsighted. Poking Patti in the ribs, I asked her to take a peek for me, and after a quick once-over, she lit up. "It's *him*," she whispered, "He must have just gotten back from New York." HIM. Hmm.

I've thought long and hard about whether or not to tell this story, and after deep contemplation, I realize I have to go into it because a lot of growth occurred, a whole lot of female hormones were brought out of hibernation and back to high-flying form, which gave me a new lease on life as a *woman*. But how? I told the person in question I would never write about HIM—he is Mr. Privacy personified, having done an amazing job keeping unwanted press at bay for many years. He is a Big Star, laden down with awards, one of those people that most everyone on the planet has heard of, except maybe some immaculate monk or monkette who has lived his/her blame-free life in a cave of seamless solitude, hidden high in the mountains of Tibet.

I had seen HIM on a few occasions at Helena's and once at the Roxy when I felt that intense gaze slapping me around. It had been one of Michele Myer's last outings in L.A. She couldn't take her eyes off the mega star who couldn't take his eyes off of me. "I'm impressed," she said, laughing. Shelly always loved people who were bigger than life, especially in person. But this guy's long-term romantic relationship was legendary, and I was a married woman so couldn't consider the stimulating possibilities. Eddie Begley told me that HE had asked for my phone number and Ed had discouraged the concept, telling HIM I had been married for eons. Still, I can't pretend I wasn't deliriously flattered whenever he sought my face in a crowd and smiled at me so wickedly I had to turn away. (This happened a couple times when I had my glasses on, so I know for sure!) And here he was—alone at this chichi party, and so was I. Patti nudged me in his direction, but I found that I wasn't ready to sashay on up to HIM and announce my availability. I hovered in different rooms, gathering steam for a possible encounter, but it didn't take place that night. I probably missed the all-important beckoning glance because of my anti-spectacles vanity. But shouldn't HE have come up to me, and where was what's-her–name? All the way back in Patti's new Accord, I berated my pussy-wimp attitude, realizing it might be fun to get to know this guy, but how often did one run into . . . HIM?

November 30—*I look different in the face, I can't figure it—some sort of metamorphosis. Lots going on but no lovers. I dreamed that I fucked Bono of U2 (in my Maidenform bra—ha!) and he kept telling me to have more faith and belief in myself. What's the correlation between sex and self-esteem?*

I was about to find out.

Three days after the flashy bash the phone rang and it was HIM. He didn't tell me how he had gotten hold of my number but invited me up to a late dinner at his palace in the Palisades, and I accepted. I wish I could say I was feeling cooooool as a hothouse cucumber, but I was a nervous wreck. I knew he was taken, I knew our encounter would be "purely sexual" and my aching-for-love stammer-pump had always come before lust. I had rarely given my pussy without at least the hope of lifelong adoration, despite the false and sleazy reputation I had gotten as "the world's most famous groupie." Ha! Didn't she sleep with all of Led Zeppelin at once?

Fuck it. You only live once in this body. I grabbed some garters and a slinky emerald green teddy and dashed over to Patti's, shaking, excited, buzzing; a post-post-juvenile delinquent ready for some purely sexual passion. I could handle it, couldn't I? Patti made me up hot, with deep, dark eyes, glamour-puss on the prowl. No mistaking what I was about to get up to. By the time I got to his door, it was past eleven and I was on a dangerous mission. You looking for trouble? You came to the right place.

"I'd just about given up on you," he growled in that voice I had heard at least eight thousand times. "The lamb is cold." Was that some kind of code? No, the lamb stew his cook had made hours before sat on the long carved table in stiff lumps, the elegant salad wilted. "I don't eat red meat, anyway," I squeaked, trying to sound provocative and proud in one sentence. "Oh, baby," he moaned, "I hope that's not the truth."

December 4—*After the briefest conversation, he tore into my mouth and I knew I was in for something new in my life. I sat down on his couch and hiked up my black cut-velvet dress to reveal the teddy and one black satin pump. I was ready for whatever he wanted to dish out. I felt like a ripe—almost overripe—piece of forbidden fruit. . . . I was so ready for* *this. . . . The smell of him drove me senseless, I was lost in him. . . . When the sun was coming up I told him that this is what bodies are for, and after more real heavy petting, before another supreme round, he said, "You're right, this is what bodies are for."*

I embarked on this flaming rocket trip to the stratosphere knowing where I stood. He never led me to believe it was anything but sexual. Purely sexual. Pure sex. I wasn't ready for much else anyway, since my heart was still a numb lump taking a vacation. You deserve a break today. The healing love-balloon did come to life a few times, attempting to climb into HIS king-size bed, but I knocked it back with a gentle reminder. Purely sexual, remember? Please, *please* remember. I found the beating thing between my legs once or twice, however, because that's the kind of person I am.

I saw HIM whenever the opportunity arose and reveled in being a woman: a temptress, seductress, vixen, tigress, redheaded Aphrodite on a half shell, succulent, edible, wanton, and profoundly female. It lasted for over a year, and I kept the whole thing clandestine because that's the way he wanted it, and HE will continue to remain HIM.

December 29—*Tonight he felt like talking. We went upstairs and I cuddled into his lap and we talked about his career, lots of funny, fabulous, and exciting stuff. He likes me, and why not? We kissed like teenagers for about forty-five minutes prolonging the wildest passion. . . . He never stops with the patter—constant, thrilling nasty words in my ear. This man was made to make love, and I'm pretty steamy myself! We kept marveling about how good it is. He read my book and loves my writing. He said I'd better not put him in the sequel. Ha!!*

You like me, you like me, you really like me! A weensy bit of self-confidence making a teensy return.

IV

I was flat on that same old fake Deco couch, breathing heavily and counting beads of sweat when my sweet Melanie strutted through the door, pulled her shirt up and her pants down to show me the incredible flatness of her concave tummy. She had called me two hours earlier from Laurel Springs, Jane Fonda's posh new spa retreat in the Santa Barbara Mountains, to ask if she could stop by (to show off) on her way home. Her enthusiastic call prompted me to slide Jane's *Challenge* tape into the VCR and wage war with my middle. After all, I had a glorious hot-tamale reason to tighten up. "I'm going

to take *you* back there with me, as a Christmas present, Miss P!"
Melanie announced excitedly (she *still* calls me that). Fa la la la la . . .
la la la la. The cost of the week at Jane's was twenty-five hundred
big ones, a stunning Christmas gift, most definitely. An opportunity
not to be missed.

Melanie was grazing the clouds, getting paid tons of dough for her
amazing portrayals of shimmering babes on the big screen. She had
just completed *Something Wild* with Jonathan Demme and was verging on mammothness, in my opinion. She had split up with Steven
"Rocky" Bauer a year earlier and was on the loose, like Patti and
me; so we both needed a soul-restoring girl-gab. We could blab it
up at Jane's for a whole week!

Almost everybody has a huge opinion about Jane Fonda. Mention
her name in a crowd and see what happens. Nobody yawns. She is
one of my personal inspirational faves. The woman is fifty-four years
old and has a waistline like Scarlett O'Hara. Many times I have
flopped around in my own living room with her grinning face on the
tube, hoisting my inner thigh up-up-up, hoping to erase those dingles
before they got a chance to dangle.

Before leaving for the retreat, I made an appointment at Jane's
Workout in Bev Hills to take a stress test and find out just how
much of me was pure flubber. While lounging in the waiting room
I saw Queen Jane in the mirror, pulling on a stretchy piece of rubber
that flexed dozens of divine muscles all along her back and biceps.
It was awesome. When she came into the waiting room and found
out I was headed for Laurel Springs, she told me to pack a muffler
and warm gloves. I was touched.

Michael agreed to come and stay in Santa Monica with Nick, and
I packed my sweats and Nikes, so thrilled to be getting away from
it *all*. Melanie drove, with toddler Alexander in the backseat happily
gnawing biscuits and bobbing off to Wynken, Blynken, and Nod
Land while we chatted up a cyclone. It felt like zero degrees when
we arrived, thirty-five hundred feet straight up to holy Chumash
Indian ground, where Jane had chosen to build her fortress to fitness.
The sun had just gone down when we were welcomed into the
cozy but massive cabin by cooks, caretakers, and Kathy, the fresh,
glowing, flawlessly fit instructor who would alter my body for all
time. After a magnif dinner of fresh bouillabaisse, oregano bread,
and a ton of kale, which I'm ashamed to say I had never tasted before,
we were sent to our rooms for a serious snooze to prepare for the
intense training session that would start before dawn. The four-
poster bed had been turned down and on the pillow was a slip of

paper with the cosmic thought for the day printed on it: LET MY LOVE SPREAD ITS LAUGHTER IN ALL HEARTS, IN EVERY PERSON BELONGING TO EVERY RACE. LET MY LOVE REST IN THE HEARTS OF FLOWERS, ANIMALS, AND IN LITTLE SPECKS OF STARDUST. My sentiments exactly. As specks of stardust twinkled through the skylight, I cozied up in the down comforter and counted my countless blessings.

I'm doubly ashamed to say I had never seriously hiked before, but for the next seven days I made up for an entire lifetime. A few times I thought I would drop dead in a patch of poppies, but the sight of Kathy's faultless calves, gleaming golden in front of me like a beacon kept me trudging ever onward and upward through the rocks. Sweat streamed rivulets down my back. I had no idea I contained so much H_2O. After the morning hike we beat ourselves to death in the unparalleled gym for about three hours, rode mountain bikes, and were rewarded with a divine passionflower-oil massage at the end of every grueling day. One evening I noticed the masseuse's hands hovering around my middle, flicking at the air. "What are you doing?" I wondered. "Getting rid of bad vibes?"

"No," he answered. "I'm releasing the negative energy." Isn't that what I said? Once I opened my eyes a slit during a dreamy massage to find Jane's errant hubby, Tom Hayden, taking a gander at the proceedings. Nice to meet you too.

By the end of the week I could see brand-new muscles popping out all over my tight, new body. It happened so fast! I had a sleek new tricep, a bitchen bicep, my thighs were rock hard, and I had stamina to spare. My skin was pink and glowing, and I had lost four pounds. I found I loved weight lifting because results came quickly, and I vowed to go right out and buy a set of weights and a rowing machine when I got home. Which I did. I had always excercised but realized I had been a lazy fraud. No more half-assed sit-ups! No more sugar, fat, white flour! What I needed was my own private trainer like Kathy! Yeah!

There were moments on our last hike, which was seven miles up, when I rolled my eyes heavenward and chanted "Om" to force one pink Nike in front of the other. It was a Zen experience, like becoming physically enlightened. The night before we left, Melanie, Kathy, and I sat outside in the Jacuzzi, steam rising high in the freezing cold air. We drank hot cayenne garlic broth as the rain pelted our faces, laughing from our hearts, singing wildly along with Prince to "Purple Rain." Ahh, memories are made of this.

V

My friend Sheri was having a small all-girl Christmas Eve fun-fest, and along with Carole Childs, Joycie Hyser, Patti, and me, she invited Barbra Streisand. I was excited, of course, but determined to be myself with the diva. After all, I had been scrounging around inside my psyche and, after forgiving my own trespasses, actually liking who I was. So why wouldn't Barbra? In fact, I had reached a pretty even keel with my astrologer-psychologist Aggie and was on the search for a *real* psychiatrist, preferably a Jungian, because the spiritual element was kept intact with God high on the list of priorities. I never trusted Sigmund Freud anyway. I don't look at a bowl of bananas and automatically think of penises (or is it peni?). Do you?

All us girls were exchanging gifts, and since I hadn't met Barbra before, I brought along a copy of my book for her, hoping she wouldn't think I was cheeky. I thought forever about how to sign it, finally coming up with such a corny line, I'm sort of embarrassed to confess to it. Oh well, I've confessed to everything else, so why not? "Dear Barbra, The way I was . . . Love, Pamela Des Barres." As my sweet little Moon Zappa said while making fun of Valley girls in the mall way back in '82, gag me with a spoon.

It was a cozy, comfortable evening with perfect, thoughtful gifts and reams of girl talk. After a brief fidget I found myself enmeshed in a conversation with Barbra about exercise, the pluses and minuses of plastic surgery, and *all* about boys. She wore tights with a big sloppy sweater, and we both moaned about having to suck in our tummies half the time. Sheri's middle was concave and we were not amused. *How* did she do it? Barbra was a regular girl in most ways except for her vantage point. She seemed fascinated with the humdrum mundanities of normal everyday life, sort of like the Queen of Sheba stepping into a laundromat, or Jackie Onassis behind the counter at Burger King. Would you like fries with that? Sheri called a mutual friend in New York and we sang "Happy Birthday" to her over the phone. I raised my voice in song with the best singer in the world. La Streisand thanked me for the book without mentioning my gaggy little inscription and promised to read it soon.

Michael came over late on Christmas Eve and spent the night on the couch so he could watch Nick dig into his gifts the next morning. I cooked us an expansive feast, as was my habit, and we all ate it up, merry Merry Christmas. I tucked Nick in, flanneled and creamed myself out, and climbed into bed, "Good night, Mikie . . ." It was so odd knowing my husband of fourteen years was thrashing around on the couch while I reclined in our former bed, alone. I could ramble on here about the unpredictablity of life, but I won't. I submerged my animosities, held his hand, watched him unwrap the stack of gifts I got for him, opened my glorious hand-picked, high-taste items, enjoyed Nick's grand time under the tree, and sent Michael back out into the world from whence he came. Holding a grudge is like a death sentence. I was really working on tossing it to the winds.

Donnie didn't have a date for the New Year's festivities in Aspen, so I flew out to hang on his arm at some ridiculous party full of celebs. We ate stuffed capon with Michael Douglas and his wife, chewed the carbs with Jack and Anjelica, discussed the slopes with several trendy downhillers, and got a stiff dose of a very angry, bombed Hunter S. Thompson. I don't think he went skiing the next day, but Donnie did, and I spent the first day of 1988 waving to red-cheeked superstars in thousand-dollar ski suits, sipping spiked hot chocolate on top of old smoky, all covered with snow. I sat in the sauna, ate lots of endive and radicchio, watched a bunch of big-screen TV with Donnie, and made a valiant, thwarted attempt not to think too much about HIM. Big stuff had been reawakened, stuff I hadn't allowed myself to ponder for too many years. It seemed I always had a slight temperature, 98.6 a thing of the past. It felt like I was walking with my pelvis thrust forward, but nobody said, "Pamela, why are your hipbones entering a room before you do?" Constantly on the verge of a full-body orgasm, my insides were shakin' like a leaf on a tree.

> **January 1, 1988, 2:20 A.M.**—*I hear Donnie wandering around up there; he wanted me to watch TV with him—the envy of millions—but I'm so tired. I was with strangers at midnight. Oh well. D.J. ran into Barbra Streisand yesterday, and she told him she was adoring my book. Wow! That's so cool. He's having "tea" with her tomorrow. Hmm. The year is about to start up again—work, exercise, money, success. Oh yes.*

When Donnie went to have tea with Barbra, he said, "I'll be back in about half an hour." Three hours later, as I went into my fiftieth sit-up in the middle of the living-room floor, he arrived grinning like a smitten goof-pot.

The blasted year that had crept in on black-widow legs was finally coming to an end. I had surging hopes, as usual for brighter dawns, dreamier nights. Could somebody crawl out of a cocoon at my age? Actually, I felt I was halfway out already, straining to stretch my wings.

CHAPTER FIFTEEN

I

Aaahhhhh! What would the new year hold? Always on the search for the psychic who might help me sweeten the existing course of fate, I was excited when Chuck Wein, my old mentor-director-cosmic cohort called to tell me about Ariana, an amazing lady from Nevada who was in town for a few days doing readings. I made an appointment for Nick and myself, praying this good lady could reach the place in him where so many others had been denied access. He had gotten even more morose and uncommunicative, just waiting for the day when he was "grown-up" and might be understood.

After leaving our shoes on the porch and waiting barefoot in somebody's airy, too-white living room for about thirty minutes, we were taken upstairs to an even whiter room where Ariana sat on some Indian-print pillows in a corner—an ageless, sweet-faced angel with a froth of blond curls, smiling beatifically. She took Nick first, holding his hand, reaching into his spirit, comforting him instantly. She surrounded him with light, called on her guides to watch over him, and told him the name of his guardian angel, Araul. She told Nick that Araul folded his wings over him every night and demonstrated the way his pale, gentle wings enveloped Nick as he slept. She whispered a lot of things to him that I couldn't hear and sent him back down to the blank living room while I had my reading. He seemed slightly awestruck but peaceful as he headed down the stairs. My little boy—I wanted to wipe out his problems with a twinkling Tinker Bell wand, comfort, cuddle, cleanse him, make it all better, but I just didn't know how.

I got myself comfortable on the pillows in front of her, and as Ariana held my hand and called on her guides, for a split instant I saw the inside of the universe, where all was noiseless and ecstatic. Full of vacancy—Wheeee . . . After coming back to the planet, I told her about some trouble I had been having with my right wrist, weakness, pain off and on for years. "Let's see where that came from," she said and closed her eyes again. More quiet breathing. "I see you in a large wooden structure, held against your will by a man who keeps women in this kennel, selling their services by the hour, by the night." I could see myself, seated on a small wooden bench beside a beaten old table, long, ragged dress, black straggly hair, hollow, flattened eyes. "You are required to do what the men ask of you, or you are taken out to the woodshed and severely beaten. Customers come and go, rough hands—many, many brutal encounters. One day a fine gentleman comes in and sits with you for the full hour, just talking. He elicits your opinion, welcomes your answers. Makes you smile. Gains your trust. He comes every day, requesting your company, paying for the pleasure. It seems he values greatly your answers to his many questions and finds you very clever. You start to trust the man, look forward to his visits. One afternoon the finely dressed gentleman takes your hand in his and as usual asks you a question. When you blithely answer, he snaps your index finger, breaking it . . ." Ariana seems to have a hard time carrying on, she sees the whole thing, as I do, a wide screen movie. "Aah, a sadist . . ." she says sadly. "You are required to stay with the customer, under any and all circumstances. The man continues to ask questions, and as you answer, he breaks another finger, and then another, until you answer the sixth question in dire agony, and he snaps your wrist. As you try not to weep, he gets up and bows gallantly, takes his leave and never returns."

Not exactly Cleopatra, eh?

Ariana came out of her trancelike state. "We'll see if that helps," she said sweetly, patting my hand. My right wrist throbbed, got hot, and continued to hurt for a few days, then the pain faded away and has never come back.

Nick started sleeping better knowing he was not all alone after all. He started paying more attention to his altar, the one he set up when he was about six years old. Paramahansa Yogananda, Jesus, Buddha, Krishna—they soothed his weary mind. He meditated, burned incense, and read their comforting words every night before falling asleep with the light on.

II

Nick and I were scheming over a page of math one night; I refused to let him use the calculator, and he was ticked off. In the middle of the standoff, the phone rang. "Hello, Pamela, this is Barbra Streisand." "Yeah, right," I mewled. "Ha *ha,* who is this, *really??*" Silence. "I met you at Sheri's house, remember. On Christmas Eve?" Oh God, oh Godgodgod, it really was Barbra Streisand! I sank through my own kitchen floor, red as an inflamed beet. When the phone rang, Nick made a mad dash for his Sega system, so it was me, myself, I, and Barbra Streisand hanging on the telephone. "I'm sorry," I mumbled and tried to pretend it never happened. She laughed like it happened every day and invited me to dinner at her house the following week. She and Donnie were warm and weighty getting close to hot and heavy, so she was making nice with his best pals. I thought it was smart and admirable and accepted the invitation at once.

The dinner was held in one of her magnificent pads at the beach—the one with about thirty-five Tiffany lamps and the lighting was awesome. She adored Michael, having met him with Donnie, so he was one of the guests, and everyone admired our obvious rapport. There were big Deco bowls full of all kinds of Indian food, chutneys, coconut slivers, three types of raisins. We served ourselves, chatting and chortling at a gorgeous antique round table that King Arthur probably had wild sex on hundreds of years earlier.

Barbra even showed up at my Valentine's Day party, bringing me a Godiva chocolate wrapped in a gold box, signed "With Love, Barbra." Of course, I still have it, tucked in my diary drawer along with treasured notes, loveladen mementos, and a couple of vibrators. A very safe place. The Hollywood Kids came to the heart-party, a local boy-gossip version of Hedda and Louella, and they were gaga, their double-double-take a priceless classic. Barbra hung out in the kitchen with Patti and Sheri, leaning against my wonderful Wedgwood stove, chatting busily about this and that. Amused with all our personal D.J. stories, charmed by the fact that he stayed so close with his former lovers, she seemed comfortable but had to have felt all those stolen glances. All gigantic icons are right at the front of the line for stolen glances and sometimes downright stares. Do they feel warm and good—a caress—or cold and sharp—like a stalactite crystal right through the eye?

I was a solo babe at these glittering dos but was learning to brave the cocktail chatter without expecting Michael to jump in and provide the perfect anecdote. I was nowhere near ready to have any sort of romantic entanglement; it would have been a ghastly failure. I was so confused, so swamped with dammed-up emotional chaos, Michael still attached to my hip like a Siamese twin that had been excised at birth, a phantom honey-husband, twice removed. I continued to see HIM because it was a perfect setup for me at that particular point in my life. Still, it was difficult to keep my yearning throbber at bay, because the manic passion I had with HIM felt real close to love. Something's got a hold on me, yeah, whoa—it must be love. But I knew it wasn't. My purely puritanical streak was at odds with my "purely sexual" peak, battling it out on a daily basis, and lust usually won out.

III

Speaking of lust, *Us* magazine was putting out an issue on the Seven Deadly Sins, and what better lusty femme fatale than *me,* to discuss the tantalizing topic of Lust. Ha ha. I flew to NYC, rolled around on the floor in a damp piece of muslin, goose bumps rising, while some avant photog snapped from every upside-down angle, hoping to depict damp, ardent eroticism. I had splinters in my ass and hooted inside about the zany situations I found myself in. The interview was held on my bed at Melanie's rent-a-pad in Greenwich Village. She was there filming *Working Girl,* and I stayed with her three different times in March for various career-oriented moves. She invited me to the set during one of my spare New York minutes, so I could watch her emote with Harrison Ford. She was so good, I was flabbergasted with pride.

Cree McCree, my illustrious interviewer for *Us,* turned out to be a comrade spirit, and we hit it off so well that we still hit the clubs whenever I wind up in New York. Our interview was forty-nine pages long, but the good stuff didn't make the magazine.

> **Cree:** Do you have a definition of lust?
> **Pamela:** First of all, I do not consider it a sin *at all.* It's one of the great things in life to feel lust for somebody. It makes you feel alive! In touch with your body. And since that's where you reside, why not?
> **Cree:** Why does lust happen?
> **Pamela:** It's the scent—the pheromones—the stuff that emanates

from the skin. I heard that when you make love with someone, his beard rubbing on you releases all the pheromones, and all that passion comes out.

Cree: I thought it was the rub, the burn—

Pamela: The burn! That's right. Sometimes I can see lust on someone or feel it on myself like a film over my body—kind of shimmery, sticky, an ooze. It's slurpy; you get this feeling downstairs just like fire burning.

Cree: Do you think everybody is capable of experiencing lust?

Pamela: Some turn it inward, a religious fervor that could be taken for lust. The Zen masters don't fuck, so maybe you can transcend lust. I'm happy I haven't transcended it yet!

Cree: It's a manifestation of the life force.

Pamela: It's a cross between pornography and heaven, right? It really is all in one. That's why you feel so united, in touch with your body and soul at the same time. And that's why I never saw lust as being a sin. When I lust, it oozes, dribbles, pours out into a puddle around me.

Cree: Did you ever have a purely lustful relationship?

Pamela: Keith Moon. (Ooops! I couldn't mention HIM, so I went way back). He had amazing charisma, unparalled really. He was so *there*. When he was in the room, he was in the fucking room! To be with someone with that kind of incredible passion for life—you could almost see he was going to use it up real quick, which was what he did. He was using his life force up, it was spinning around him, he was going, going! I wanted to be near that lust for life.

Cree: Were the sixties the golden age of lust?

Pamela: I'm sure there was a lot of passion going on in Rome, the Greek theater. Please, it's been going on forever and ever. I'm sure Mary Magdalene was hot for Jesus, there's no way she wasn't. If I had been around then, I'm sure I would have been hanging around with Jesus—and not just because I lusted after him.

Cree: Whose word do we have to take for the whole story, anyway? Paul's? That old tight-ass celibate?

Pamela: When He told her to keep her hands away from Him, it wasn't because she was a tainted whore, I don't think. He was trying to preserve His power. All of His power to save the world. But I don't think He meant she didn't deserve to touch him, or that she was a slovenly bitch.

> **Cree:** She was one of the women right there at the cross.
> **Pamela:** I know I would have been there too.

I could just feel my preacher grandpa Pop Miller spinning in his grave in the green, green hills of North Carolina.

Lust must have been in the air, because I soon got a call from *Playboy.* I had been writing pieces for magazines—*Cosmo, New York Woman, Rolling Stone*—and it seemed everyone was fascinated with the red-hot sixties and somehow I represented that pulsating, free-wheeling time; a wanton rock-dolly who lived to tell the tale/tail. But *Playboy*'s offer was rock-shocking. They wanted a photo layout of me—pushing forty—stark-raving naked! I was concerned about how I might have been portrayed in the piece—aging super-groupie bares ALL or something equally hideous—so after a period of hassle while they scrutinized every word I had ever written, they agreed to let me write the text myself.

I worked on the head dame, Marilyn Grabowski, to let my photographer, Randee St. Nicholas, shoot the pictures, but even after paying for some outrageous test shots, they would up using one of their own tried-true-blues. We found out later that only one woman had ever shot a layout in all those years. Oh well, we tried. It took six days of shooting with nice-guy Robert Faegli and twenty thousand photographs to get six pages in the magazine. You might think it's a sexy experience, rampant with erotic poses, but after the first day as a gymnast-contortionist, being lined up perfectly within the lighting and satin sheets, holding a bent-out-of-shape position for endless moments, walking around in a chilly room stark-raving in front of eight hunky workers, sucking in the tummy, thrusting out my midget titties until my innards ached, I realized that bare-all modeling is just a bunch of ragingly hard work. I made them play endless loops of Prince and Terence Trent D'Arby so I could at least have a steamy expression while I held a certain angle for half an hour. I tried to think lush, wicked, tangled thoughts while two different guys adjusted the hem of my frilly garment so not too much pubic hair peeked out from between my trembling thighs. No pink allowed. It was almost scientific, like a gynecological exam. The *Playboy* people see so many naked women all day, every day, they don't notice if you wear clothes or not. After a while I didn't bother to put on my robe at all, absolutely comfortable, like I was invisible.

After a tough day wearing just a gold lamé trench coat, I bumped into Jessica Hahn in the hallway and after a brief gab thought she was a tough and tender cookie snaring, entrapping her fifteen minutes of fame with a determined vengeance. Her mouth was slicked, painted-plumped-up, tossing naughty words around like X-rated conversation hearts. Proud of her new bosom, thoughtfully provided by Mr. Hefner, she was starting a new life, her Bible definitely left in the dust, under Jim Bakker's shoes. Have you ever caught Jessica's late-late-night TV show, *Love Phone?* It brings new meaning to the 900 number.

IV

Sex seemed to be the dominant theme of my working life, but on the personal side romance was ever elusive. Still, I went to parties, hoping for a cupid strike, including a bang-up basharoo thrown by Mitch Schneider, my publicist. It was held in the Coco Bowl Room at Kelbo's Restaurant—a tacky-tiki, plastic island masterpiece built in 1947 for people who wanted their drinks to arrive on fire. The black light was always on, plastic vines crawled through dusty fishing nets where long-dead puffed, stuffed blowfish seemed suspended in thick air. Some had sunglasses on, and I'm not kidding. I love the place. An old guy with a dyed black pomp played "Don't Be Cruel" like it had been recorded yesterday, while I sipped my scary glow-in-the-dark, bright blue fancy drink (it arrived on fire). I kept bumping my lip on the paper umbrella. It was perfect.

When Sandra Bernhard walked into the dim mini-ballroom, I thought to myself, Oh, there's that smarty girl with a wit like a razor-stick scabbard dipped in laughing gas. Or something like that. Her persona intimidated me, while mine still eluded me. I was proud of my accomplishment but slightly mortified at the same time, gradually adjusting. I figured this caustic, pointed comedy queen would automatically assume I was a blight on womankind for blabbing about my romances with famous men. It's sicko how these paranoid ideas dig down into our psyches and sit down like they belong there. But we all go through it, don't we? I was totally wrong, of course. She sat down next to me, and when Mitch introduced us, she couldn't have been sweeter. We sat and nibbled tidbits off the pu pu platter, shared a baked-bean sundae, cracking up about the chopped up American cheese slices on top along with a shriveled maraschino. We laughed about the sorry, seedy surroundings and actually traded phone numbers for future fun. We enjoyed a would-be exotic, goopy, rubbery yam, and it was time to split the scene.

During the drive home from Pico, I realized that Sandra gave me a strange, all-over buzzy feeling. She certainly challenged my mind, bypassing the funny bone, making my head sort of sting with the way she pushed, prodded, so accurate in her throttling assessment of humanity. I loved the way she looked, long and angular, with a big-lipped Jaggeresque pouty quality, a direct, sexy gaze. What was this feeling? Could it be? Was I aroused? Nah . . .

Mitch called to invite me to Sandra's opening off-off-Broadway, *Without You I'm Nothing,* and I was going to be in Manhattan staying with Melanie, taping a couple more TV shows, and meeting with *Rolling Stone* about the review I wanted to write of Jackie Collins's *Rock Star.* You know something's happening, but you don't know what it is, do you, Ms. Collins. So rude.

Melanie was my date for the evening, and we settled in our center seats as the lights went down. It was jam-packed, opening night. Sandra used and abused her audience. When she spotted me, she announced, "*I* have Pamela Des Barres here tonight, to see *me,* and she's definitely coming backstage later." The spotlight lingered on my blushing face while she laughed. I wore a three-piece suit and red tie that my daddy wore back in '51, and I was a nervous ruin. Why? After the finale where she stripped down to forties underwear, singing "Little Red Corvette," I did meet her backstage, where she held my hand, proudly introduced me to her band and whispered the address of the party in my ear. Melanie had to go home because she was shooting early, so I went alone and undaunted into that wild, black New York night.

The club was a frenetic madhouse, and I smacked straight into Richard Gere with two ravishing goddesses on each arm. I introduced myself and he didn't care. I got a couple of stiff drinks and knocked them back fast. I was going to tell Sandra about this unusual heat she seemed to be generating inside my skull and in other surprising areas. My heart raced, revving like a wayward engine when I spotted her lounging in an antique velvet chair with a few other people, exultant, whooping it up. She grabbed hold of me, I sat on her lap, flirted with her. Where was this coming from? She raised her eyebrows in a question. What? She enjoyed it, she was amused by it. Why not? I touched her silky curls, bent to her ear, "I find that I have a wild crush on you," I said rakishly while fireworks went off somewhere down deep where I was born female. She looked in my face, people were pulling on her, needing her attention, Sandra, Sandra, Sandra! and she said, "Why don't we have brunch tomorrow? I'll call you."

April 1, 1988—I was rummed out, so told Sandra I had a crush on her. Uh-oh. Can't tell you the incredible fantasies I've had, SO unusual and I don't know why it's happening. She touches me and I go wild. We're having brunch today and I'm a dribbling wreck. Kind of a new concept. Please, let me calm down.
April 3—I'm gone over Sandra, I feel like we share some binding karma— lovers that kept being torn apart—hundreds of years ago. I was almost asleep last night and saw her as a beautiful black-haired young man with a moustache. To have a brand-new feeling at thirty-nine is so cool. So, sweet lunch—shedding layers, pretty comfortable right away. I was telling her how all men are bums and she enlightened me that it's not a gender thing. She's so real and warm, brilliant of course, and majorly vulnerable.

That night Sandra, along with her girl drummer, met Melanie and me at Cafe Columbus, where we sat with Paul Sorvino in heated disagreement with just about everything he blustered about. He was mightily pissed off that night. Robert De Niro was at the next table and when Melanie introduced us, he raised his head slightly and mumbled, "Uh . . . hello." I guess he didn't remember me from the time Chuck Wein tried to offer him the two-bit second lead in that A+ movie, *Arizonaslim*—in which one of his lines would have been "A stiff dick has no brains." After half a drink at the Beekman Tower bar, he told Chuck he would think it over, then went on to do *Godfather II*. I didn't really expect him to remember me.

The table was full, it was a tight squeeze, so Sandra pulled her chair in next to me and I could feel her thigh pushing against mine. The busy, dizzy hubbub went on around me, Mr. Sorvino's action-packed monologue continued unabated, lots of witty, gritty girl rapping at the table, and I shook. Nobody noticed except Sandra. "Is something the matter, baby?" she asked, searching my trapped eyes. Baby. Baby? Does she call everybody that? I told her I was feeling a little strange and gave her a long, searing gaze. What was coming over me? I could tell her drummer was trying to figure me out. My crush was that apparent—nothing but a clear picture window in front of me, with no shades or curtains. Even Melanie gave me a quizzical look.

We all shared a cab home, and when Melanie and I got out, Sandra embraced me briefly, tightly, grazing my lips with her own.

April 4—. . . I gave her my book, inscribed "To Sandra—the only girl I've ever had a crush on," she was almost speechless. I'm so blatantly hetero, but I kept wanting to get close to her. We had a major hug and kiss, just a heartbeat longer than it should have been. What a turn of events. I just had a naughty, steamy session with myself, thinking about her. I'm wild.

I called her the next day, needing to let her know I had been walking around in a daze with her name on it. It seemed to make her feel good, but she replied, "I don't know what to say," then asked me, "Why now?," meaning *why* all of sudden was I attracted to a woman? I said it was because of *her,* and I had no idea how or why myself, it was just *there.* My imagination was running rampant and I was determined to pull in the reins, knowing I had said too much, but I was almost functionless. She told me she had written me a letter but then torn it up. My frightening, instantaneous super-crush was clearly mightily confusing—to both of us.

V

Back in L.A. boys wanted to take me out, especially guys in their twenties who were intrigued with the "older woman" who still dressed and acted like a bohemian freak, the older woman who had written "that book." Was I actually "dating"? I hadn't been on a real date since 1965, when Bob Martine took me to the Teen Center to do the slauson and the frug. What we did in the sixties wasn't dating. It was meeting at love-ins, clubs, concerts, and hanging out, rocking out, grooving with each other. There were very few rules, and nobody knew what time it was. The formality of knocking on the door at eight was nonexistent. But here I was, straddling the big 4-0, being taken to restaurants and movies by guys who were in their cradles when I was sweating a stream on the Whisky dance floor. I went out with a twenty-one-year-old guy who ran a club in Venice, but I realized all his moody silence was a cover-up for being boring; had a couple sushi encounters with an ex–coke dealer, twice reformed, all his dirty money invested in some sort of self-help lecture series. I let the machine pick up, sorry. Then I got all hot and bothered over a greasy-haired former skateboard champion, dangerous punk, bad boy who took me to his brother's wedding on our second "date."

The theme of the wedding was a fifties kind of thing, and my bad boy was the only one there who was totally comfortable in his attire: rolled-up blue jeans, white T-shirt, black leather jacket. But he stood me up one too many times. How about *that* concept? Being stood up. What a nightmare! Standing around the house, all dressed up, while the baby-sitter keeps checking the clock for me at seven bucks an hour. Nick saying, "Mom, I thought you were going out?"

This prompted me to take a look at my age-old penchant for punky, perilous troublemakers with the kind of cocksure attitude that could set off smoke detectors. I know it started with James Dean, that rebel of all rebels, the very first one without a cause. When I was growing up he represented all that was brave, rebellious, and true. He slouched, he suffered, he gazed out of his squint from a place of potent pain that I couldn't even fathom. If I couldn't fathom it, maybe I could fix it? Uh-uh. Not anymore. There is nothing worse than cocky pain for a woman who feels the need to fix it all up. I had to be strong. In a burst of growth, I stopped seeing this particular dangerous punk, but still saw HIM on occasion and tried not to dwell on Sandra Bernhard.

But eventually I had to return to New York on beeswax, and Sandra and I went out for a drink after her show, and in the bar I boldly tampered with her hair, stroked her fingertips, asked questions about her childhood, her family, her lovers. Still not knowing what to do with me, she rested her head on my shoulder and sighed. We walked back to her temporary Village pad, arm in arm, laughing, intimate, nervous. Her place was bright and blank; she hadn't been there long. A bare bulb blazed into my flushed face as I sat down on the couch with her, awkward, clumsy, junior high school revisited. The melee of feelings I was having were big news to me, and I told her so. I nuzzled her in the glare of that blasted bulb, heart wrenching. If the lighting had been more pleasant and gentle the whole thing might have been different. I wanted to kiss her but couldn't do it. She sat there stroking my leg, sort of humming to herself. Why didn't she kiss me? I was a mass of thunderous heartbeats, momentarily deaf, dumb, and sightless. She got up to make tea and I followed her blindly, attempting to hold her to me, and she sweetly pushed away, held me at arm's length against the stove, looking at me, leveling. "You love men! I know because I read your book! Remember how much you love men." She was smiling at me. What could I say? I smiled back at her, silent, wanting to say so much, realizing I was right near the door—escape from rejection—so told her I'd better get going. As I slid back the lock, she held me from behind, kissed me on the neck, and told me how sweet I was. Breath caught in my throat, a panicky surge of desire moving through like a wagonload of spun glass. "See you soon, honey." Honey. Did she call everybody that?

I wandered around the Village very confused. It was late, my feet hurt in the high heels, I was chilled, I was cross-eyed. I went back to Melanie's and everyone was in bed. I made a hot, hot cup of tea and contemplated, questioned, attempted to turn inward. I had been tied down for so long, a very married woman, out of commission, and now untethered, I floundered—bewildered, green, groping around on a constant blind date. I felt like my nerve endings were raw, on display. As I wrote when I was seventeen, about some wild Sunset Strip boy who wouldn't give me the time of night, "Unrequited lust is worse, by far, by far, than unrequited love." Even though that's not exactly true, it sure feels savage when you're going through it. And Sandra was right; I do love men. She is the only girl I ever really wanted. Of course, I'm not dead yet. Ha ha.

So I took Sandra's rejection on the chin. I took it like a woman. The next day I scoured thrift stores, antique markets, and lamp shops looking for a very special item for Sandra, finally finding exactly what I wanted from an old man going out of business on Christopher Street. On my way to the airport I dropped the present at the door to her apartment—half fearing, half hoping that she'd burst out and see me, bumbling and mumbling with my gaily wrapped gift, ribbons and bows in profusion. There was no word from her when I got back to L.A. so I had to bust down and call her. "So, did you get the present I left you?" "Oh, yes," she said. "Thank you so much for that sweet little lampshade. It makes such a pretty glow in the room."

CHAPTER SIXTEEN

I

The first thing I did when I got back to L.A. was to cash my very first—big!—royalty check and buy two tickets to Japan. Nick had always dreamed of going to Japan, his extreme fascination for everything Japanese having continued unabated. He was so excited, genuine joy spread across his face when I handed him the tickets, and it was worth all the tea in Kyoto. The day school let out (much to Nick's relief), we boarded a bird for Tokyo, a twelve-hour flight, and Nick was the perfect child. No complaining, no demands—actual happiness! We put on our Japanese slippers, played cards, ate white rice with chopsticks, watched dumb movies, and tried in vain to sleep a little. He was so electrified by the time we arrived, I thought he would pass out with exhilarated expectation. Instantly at home, he seemed entirely comfortable on the wide, crowded streets. A serenity enveloped him that I had never seen before, a feeling of "fitting in" at last. The massive hustle-bustle madness of Tokyo somehow calmed him down.

It was Nick's holiday, so besides all the wonderful meditative times spent at Buddhist temples and calming moments in immaculate gardens, with white deer all around us, we spent tons of hours in modern techno malls, perusing the latest in video systems. He wound up getting the newest version of Famicom, the Japanese Nintendo, and several nutty games, all in Japanese, of course. He was already teaching himself the Japanese language and today is almost fluent. Pretty good timing.

June 22—*Mommy and Nicky are in Tokyo! Nick gets up every morning and makes me a cup of coffee in the little pot provided in our hotel room. We went to see the long row of rock bands today—all so loud, each clashing with the other—miles of giant James Dean pompadours, Kiss clones. Nick was especially curious about a punk band called Burst Head. Spent hours in Kiddieland, the biggest toy store in Japan. I just had a shrimp burger and a delicious, cheap cappuccino. It's true that picture-perfect melons are a hundred dollars, but if you don't hang out in touristland, prices aren't bad. Yesterday Nick crawled through the nostril of the world's biggest Buddha and is supposed to get tons of good luck. Maybe we'll find the perfect school in the fall. We're having a ball. My little boy and me buying sugary canned drinks out of vending machines—Milky Tea and Pocari Sweat—walking down ancient streets, finding real antiques! Quiet times, eyes closed, at glorious temples, and we took a whizzy trip to Kyoto on the bullet train. We wrote the Des Barres name on a stone that will be embedded in the wall of the Todai-Ji Temple for all time. They have James Dean and Mickey Mouse on everything! I got a pair of James Dean boxer shorts, wearing them right now!*

At one of the temples, as we silently peered into a thousand-year-old prayer room, Nick pulled one of the blessed good luck charms from his pocket and gazed at it, rapt. When he looked up at me, his eyes were misty. "Do you really think this will help me feel like a regular person?" It seemed like no matter how hard I tried, Mommy couldn't make the boo-boo better.

We were in Japan for two weeks and Nick flourished. I think the clean, severe feeling there gave him a sense of purpose, and he felt important when we stopped over and over again to pose for pictures with the Japanese people—the long-haired blond boy and his flaming redheaded mother. But when we got back to L.A., his customary culture shock set in. We had reserved him a spot at Cottonwood Camp up in the beautiful hills of Santa Monica. The little blue bus would pick him up every morning, but whenever the phone rang, I had to brace myself for another complaint from a squeaky-clean Cottonwood camp counselor, telling me how Nick wasn't making an effort to fit in, play sports, or jump through any of the hoops provided. Two weeks in and he was out.

I was left with the task of keeping him amused for the rest of the summer, dropping him off and picking him up at his dad's (since Michael still wasn't driving), taking him for little visits to my mom, down to Little Tokyo, to the Self-Realization Lake Shrine, for overnight stays in Santa Barbara, to San Diego, and to Ojai to visit the Begleys. He now saw Laurance, his psychologist, twice a week, but was no happier with himself or anybody else. I prayed a lot and continued the lengthy process with the Office of Counseling and Psychological Services and Santa Monica Unified Schools to find a place where the teachers might understand what my little boy needed. It would take until the end of November for the officials to secure "placement," and until then, Nick was home—bored, needing distraction, attention. In September an old, tired tutor arrived. Nick roasted her on the spit. She left her post without warning and probably retired soon afterward.

II

I was so over-worried about Nick—really tormented, finally coming to the painful conclusion I had zero control over the situation. Right on cosmic cue my new friend Ron Zimmerman raved to me about this psychiatrist, Dr. Frederick Silvers, a Jungian, and recommended I start therapy with him right away. Ron saw that I had a whole lot on my plate—it was dribbling onto the table, messing up the floor, and I hadn't even noticed—and he thought I could use some professional help sorting it all out. Nobody had ever been more correct. After spending a relaxing Fourth of July under a billowing tent with good old Donnie on his massive new chunk of property in Aspen, I went for my first session with Dr. Silvers. Soul excavation with a fearless, probing pickax.

I climbed Frederick's stairs, sat across from him while he smoked his pipe, and expected all the answers to drop out of the skylight onto my lap. After my third session I realized it didn't work that way. It was laborious toiling. Mistakes, errors, blunders, and botchups are hard to see at first, much less admit to, accept, and understand. Therapy is like walking around in a dim, comfortable fog then coming up against a blinding light. At first you shield your eyes, then you take a peek at the light, finally getting the guts to stare at it, allowing yourself to see all the imperfections and cracks in the foundation, some of which you created. Oops. Uh-oh. Excuse me. I'm sorry. Who do you apologize to? Stop the world, I want to get off, please.

One rainy day I had what is called a "breakthrough," which is just another of those twelve-letter words until it happens to you. I was telling Frederick how I used to drag Michael to Disneyland and force the mouse down his throat. Make him feel guilty if he didn't accompany me to Science of Mind spectaculars. Frederick sat across from me, doing his job, puffing his pipe, nodding. I was laughing as I remembered waiting in the longest, winding line for Peter Pan one long-ago day when Michael still had streaks of silver running through his hair—when I suddenly stopped in mid-sentence. A gush of tears—unexpected—burst from a place that had been shut off for eons. Bright, clear anguish and the stunning realization that I owed Michael a sincere apology. I had tried to alter the man I was married to as if he wasn't good enough in the first place. Mold and squash him into a heart-shaped cookie cutter, so out of the oven would pop my perfect man, complete with an inner-peace happy face. Nothin' says lovin' like something from the oven. He rebelled. He slept with other women. Maybe they thought he was A-OK just the way he was.

I came home and called Michael to apologize. "Forgive me, Mikie, forgive me!" I blurted. "I dragged you to Disneyland, you didn't even *want* to GO! I forced you to go, over and *over*!" As I ranted with sorrow and relief, he was gracious, loving, and a bit surprised. "You didn't mean it, darling," he said gently. "I actually came to enjoy the little rat bastard. Besides, I'm sure you thought it was all for my own good." I hung up the phone and felt like flying out the kitchen window, a burden I didn't even know I possessed two hours earlier had lifted, and my slaphappy, unshackled soul flew on light-as-feather wings.

There were, of course, more mistakes to plow through, peek at, and mourn. By not wanting to flatten Nick's spirit, hoping he might remain a free, unencumbered human being, I had not provided the all-important boundaries, guidelines, structure—whatever you want to call parental discipline. Since Michael had been raised with only a bohemian smidgen of parental supervision, the task had been left to me, the "yes" woman. Nick slept enough hours, ate enough food, wore cool clothes, had acres of spiritual and psychological input, lots and lots of love, but it wasn't enough. Who knew? Nick especially needed to know how far he could go within his world, because his giant mind let in too many things. He didn't know where he stood. The vast, full dark scared him. Too many options.

I cursed myself for being Miss Goody-Blue-Bonnet, the perpetual Snow White. After I had been in therapy for a few months, Patti started calling me "Snow Black." I actually allowed myself to scowl and bluster once in a while. I started telling people off, and they said, "Why, Pamela, that behavior is *so* out of character!" At last! Was that a sparkler down there at the end of the tunnel?

III

My Jane Fonda fitness trainer had started making treks down the coast to work out a few lucky people. Just in time too, because I was getting tired of doing listless leg lifts to "Erotic City" at the Sports Connection, next to sweating strutters who were only hearing the thud-beat instead of Prince crooning, "We can fuck until the dawn, making love 'til cherry's gone," over and over again. Four times a week for an hour and fifteen, Kathy and I high-impacted, toned, pumped, stretched, and stepped our way to blood-boiling queen-machines. She even gave me a series of exercises using a hot-pink rubber band that I could do out on the road and they were about to come in handy-dandy.

Berkley had bought the paperback rights to *I'm with the Band* and sent me back on the road to sing for my supper. I dished with Sally Jessy Raphaël somewhere in Connecticut, filled a sweetheart half hour with Bob Costas, got through the intensity of Geraldo one more time, and met Joan Rivers—finally—and she talked to me like we were sipping martinis on her patio. One of the girls. I was getting oh-so-comfy on the chat shows, no more butterflies. All kinds of fun.

I was on the Miami stop of the tour when I got a call from Berkley. I had just hit the *New York Times* Best Sellers list. The call came directly to a radio station where I had an hour to kill on the air. I was one happy former groupie, let me tell you, and that particular interview was a giddy smash. But right at the end of the peppy hour, the DJ said to me, "So what do you think about Jimmy Page calling you a bimbo?"

A few months earlier, Jimmy had attempted to snub me at the Atlantic Records reunion bash, where Zeppelin played together for the first time in many years. With John Bonham's son Jason playing drums, John Paul Jones in top form, and Robert wailing with memories of a ripe, rip-roaring time, long, long gone, it had been a magical night. Backstage hanging with Robert, I greeted Jimmy warmly, and when he kept walking, I called his name so loud that everyone turned around. "Jimmy *Page*!!" He stopped in his tracks, slowly turned to face me, and said, "Why, Pamela, dear. How are you?" But his eyes weren't kind, and it was clear he didn't care how I was. I had heard it through the grapeslime that Jimmy had been angry about the way he was portrayed in my book. I guess I didn't kiss his skinny ass quite hard enough.

Still, I told the DJ that I was sure Jimmy didn't even have such an antiquated, lamebrained word in his vocabulary. The DJ then proceeded to play an interview he had done with Jimmy a mere few hours earlier, and if I hadn't heard it with my own be-jangled ears, I wouldn't have believed it in a million years. When asked what he thought of my book, Jimmy replied in his soft, sweet voice, "Oh, I've met a lot of bimbos out there. You know how *girls* like to exaggerate." Period. Since I was on the air, I professed sadness that Mr. Page would stoop so low as to drag out that worn-out, pathetic antifemale name tag, reminding Mr. DJ that I had all the facts in my diaries, nothing but the truth, so help me God.

After the interview was over the DJ ran the rest of the tape so I could hear what Jimmy had to say *off* the air. "You say Pamela is in town today? I wouldn't mind if you brought good old Miss P. down to the Firm [his new group] show tonight." Good old Miss P.—the bimbo. No thanks, doll, former *amore,* back stabber with a violin bow. But even Jimmy's two-faced hostility couldn't shake my glorious best-seller mood.

That evening I met Donnie on the set of *Miami Vice,* and he took me to celebrate at his favorite Italian restaurant. Danny Sullivan, the handsome big-shot race-car driver came with us, along with a few other doting tagalongs, and glasses were raised high to the best-selling author. It was fascinating to see how Donnie maneuvered around Miami. He was like Elvis in Memphis. They ushered us into the fancy back room of the restaurant like the Godfather had swept into the building, while hushed onlookers tried not to bore holes through the famous man in mauve. And later that night as we raced back to Star Island in his new Ferrari—like the wind—a hundred miles an hour, sirens wailed behind us, and Don drove even faster, flying. He finally allowed the infuriated cop to pull us over, and when the boy in blue saw Donnie's grinning mug, Sonny Crockett himself, he laughed like a good-natured, jovial extra on the set of *Miami Vice* and let us continue on our way. My dear friend Donnie was at the peak of his roll. D.J. was still enthralled with Barbra Streisand, even to the point of singing a duet with the grand dame songbird that was to be featured on both of their albums.

When I swung through New York I popped in on him and Barbra in the penthouse sweet suite of some ultra-fashionable, snobby-posh hotel. There was a lot of laughter and caviar. The head of Warner Bros., Mo Ostin, and his nice-as-pie wife dropped by for a small drink, and my mind started to whir. Since I was going to be in Minneapolis at the exact right time, I had been trying—in vain—to get an invite to Prince's party at Paisley Park after his show. As we wittily threw nice words around, I tossed my caviar-cool out the penthouse window and casually told Mr. Ostin of my predicament. "No problem, Pamela," he said, as pretty as you please, "I'll arrange for you to see the show and attend the party." He then got all my Minneapolis hotel info, and when I arrived, the entire Prince package was waiting at the front desk. That's the way to do it.

They were passing out heart-shaped mirror armbands as you entered the Paisley Park tent, and after grabbing one, I wormed my way through the decked-out crowd to the front-front of the stage, and leaned on it, staking out my space. I waited there, pooped out and exhilarated until two-thirty in the morning when I got to gaze up at Prince's crotch for the next three hours. I could have touched his five-inch stiletto boot, but remained calm. The show was entirely different from the usual Lovesexy stage romp—lots of soul ballads, gospel glory, and duets with Mavis Staples. I was receiving manna, he was heaven-sent. Later on, the crack of dawn, I saw Prince in a corner by himself but left him alone. He's definitely the Greta Garbo of rock. At least I could woman-handle him in my dreams.

IV

The second to last stop was Seattle, and I was on one of those afternoon TV shows where I had to fill an entire hour. "And then Mick Jagger said . . . Ha ha! Isn't that amazing!? Keith Moon really did try to squeeze into my spike heels. . . . I was *in love* with these guys. . . . No, Nicky's too young to care about the subject matter. . . . The book didn't really have anything to do with my separation from Michael. . . . You know I never knew what controversy those two words—'huge -----'—would cause. . . . No, Donnie doesn't seem to mind at all! . . . Har-de-har. . . ." And so on.

As I signed a few books and posed for a couple photos, a deep, long-ago familiar voice behind me said, "Hello, Pamela." I knew instantly who it was. Victor Hayden. One of the very few people who drastically altered the course of my life. I spun around and there was my intrepid friend from high school, Captain Beefheart's cousin, the guy who carried Kant and Freud through the corny corridors of Cleveland High, hiding joints, running from the vice principal because he dared to defy almighty authority by growing his hair a half inch below his ears. I had first seen the Rolling Stones with him in 1965, I listened to jazz at a downtown club, Mother Neptune's, just to impress him with my pretend, fumbling hipness. His influence forced me to comb through my flippy bouffant and part my hair down the middle, rub off the blue eye shadow, cast aside the rah-rah cheerleader concept. I probably would have married bitchen Bob Martine and still be living in the flat heat of Reseda if not for Victor Hayden. He turned me on to Bob Dylan, Allen Ginsberg, Ferlinghetti, Kerouac, Kafka, Coltrane, Captain Beefheart, he made me dare to look within, to question *everything.*

It had been nineteen years since I last saw Victor. The man who smoked black widow spider-webs for pleasure. He had slowly disappeared into the wilderness, too sensitive to deal with the brain-breaking world. The last time I heard from him was way back in '75 when he wrote one lone letter advising me to check out the Vedanta Society. After residing for a few years with silent monks on a still retreat, he had been living in the hollow of a giant redwood tree with no electricity, no running water. It seemed Victor had finally dropped out entirely. But here he was, looking much like he had the day he decided not to attend the graduation ceremony at Cleveland High. Dressed all in black, his hair was clipped severely, and he seemed fairly normal except for the look in his eye behind the Mr. Middle Class eyeglasses. He was incognito.

"Victor! I'm so thrilled to see you!!" I hugged him hard. "What do you mean, Pamela? We've been communicating for sixty minutes." He had been in the back row of the audience assuming we had been making a connection throughout the entire show. I reminded him how near-sighted I was, and he nodded gravely. Hmm. Sense of humor missing? My Seattle author-caretaker gave me half an hour for lunch, so while she waited outside in her nondistinct car, checking her stopwatch, Vic and I sat in his fave place, the Thirteen Coins, a dimly lit seventies-style coffee shop, trying to fill each other in. He was nervous, and I couldn't imagine why. He confessed to me that he had been considering suicide the day before, but then my face flashed on the TV screen, so he came down to the studio and sat in the audience instead. A bit extreme, but that was Victor. Every sentence out of him was unique, his carefully chosen words almost poetic with an off-center touch of the absurd. He had been managing thrash-metal bands, had his own underground record label, and was still painting. Why Seattle, I wondered? He was trying to make a slow comeback to humanity, a gradual return to mainstream mania. I invited him to Los Angeles for a visit, grateful that I could finally feel on Victor's level rather than several rungs below. What he said

In bed with Stallone—emoting for the cameras

The Face Pack —Donnie, Melanie, Michael, and me DIANE SILLAN

Me and my precious, serious son in front of Victor's artwork
RICHARD CREAMER

Nicholas Dean Des Barres— such an intense gaze for such a little guy
RANDEE ST. NICHOLAS

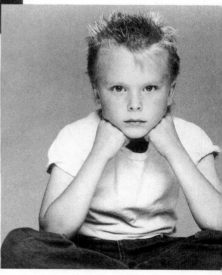

Seven years later—my little boy wears a size nine and a half shoe. It was Nick's clever idea to repeat the same pose. RANDEE ST. NICHOLAS

Patti, Melanie, and me. Patti sees too much, Melanie talks too much, and I don't hear a thing. RANDEE ST. NICHOLAS

Cozying up with Warren on a warm Hollywood night— Patti's birthday at a trendy dive PATTI D'ARBANVILLE

And then Bob Dylan said to me, "Pam, I missed you on Oprah." It was almost too much. PATTI D'ARBANVILLE

The twenty-seven years were up—and I finally met Dion. MICHAEL FRIEDMAN

The man who altered my brain cells —Victor Hayden   ALLEE WILLIS

"Sweetheart." Hmmmm, does Sandra Bernhard call everybody that?
RICHARD CREAMER

The good new days—
Nick and his dad
STEVE SCHAPIRO

Patti and I at the "Imagine" premiere. Two
hot-to-trot babes on the town JILL JARRETT

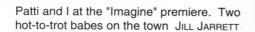

Ariana, Jimmy, and me—thinking good thoughts VICTOR HAYDEN

I got Ozzy Osbourne
and Annette Funicello
to interview each other.
Brilliant idea, huh?
RANDEE ST. NICHOLAS

Nick and his devoted
parental figures
RANDEE ST. NICHOLAS

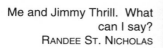

Me and Jimmy Thrill. What
can I say?
RANDEE ST. NICHOLAS

didn't elude me anymore; I understood him. Maybe I could return the high school favor by helping him back to earth.

A few weeks later he not only came to visit but bought an antique teardrop trailer from a tightrope-walking circus troupe, set it up in my backyard, and painted it forest green. He took out the trash, ate my home-cooked meals, and we had side-winding, searing conversations until late at night. He called himself "the purgemaster," and attempted to keep the house spot-free. "The only way to really clean a house," Vic announced, "is with a microscope." He gave it the old Cleveland High try, he really did, but after a few weeks he realized that I live a messy (but mostly clean) life, and had to drop the subject. Victor became sort of a guardian angel for Nick, just as I suspected he would. They were from the same planet, so Nick no longer felt quite so isolated. He became a constant, cosmic, mind-bending companion.

V

I started hearing from all kinds of people out of my past. Trip Webster, the '66 class president at Cleveland High, wrote and praised my book, telling me how I had recalled all sorts of tidbits from his glory days. He had never spoken to me in the halls; his letter-sweater heyday had zero to do with the freaky chick with the Beefheart sticker on her notebook, but he said he rememberd me fondly. I recall his flattop without much fondness, to tell you the truth. He's some judicial bigwig downtown now, and he told me to call on him anytime for assistance. What kind, I wonder?

My favorite letter came from Polly Parsons, Gram's only daughter, the precious tot I used to babysit in 1969 while swoony-mooning over Chris Hillman. Her note said that reading about her dad in my book made her feel who he really was for the first time. I was ecstatic, called her up, and we met for lunch at Farmer's Market. She was so sweet; her beautiful smile was all Gram. She wanted to know every little thing about her untamed pioneer daddy, and I lovingly recounted my long-lost moments with GP.

Chris was playing with the Desert Rose Band at a club on the beach, so I took Polly to re-meet her dad's best friend and closest musical partner. He dedicated a song to her as we swayed in the front row, and she cried, big old tears rolling down her cheeks. The music sent me straight out of my body and onto the wide, open plains, driftin' along with the tumblin' tumbleweeds. Chris also played a song for me that night called "The One That Got Away." He said he had written it for me after our last sweet lunch— ". . . Her dancing eyes are laughing so bright . . . if she gets away from me again, I'll miss her 'til the end . . . if I'm right, I should go home tonight . . ." And he did, but not before I had a timeless moment with him—his eyes into mine, over and over, over and over like a camera shutter, I could see our many different lifetimes together way down inside his bright blue eyes. The instant seemed to go on for eternity, but sounds started to come back—Polly's laughter, clinking glasses, jukebox howling, and I realized I had been lost in another realm of possibility. I knew without an inkling of a doubt that Chris and I were connected, bonded tight by the big picture, the never-ending round and round of soul life. It's not over yet. It's never over. And I finally had a song written about me. That sent me for a triple loop.

I had one reeling reunion after another, but the one person I was surprised I hadn't heard from was Bobby Martine, my first teen squeeze, especially since there were photos of him in the book looking all sulky and hot-stuff. I had last seen him on the big screen, playing a greaser bartender in *Saturday Night Fever*, but in person it had been twenty-three years. I had scoured New York directories, wondering if he had gone back to his roots, checked all the Martines in the San Fernando Valley to no avail. And one afternoon Mom called to tell me that Bob had somehow gotten ahold of her number and she had just spoken to him! I called Bob immediately. After having an old-times chatathon, we made a dinner date for the following evening, and I was sure curious to see how the years had treated him. When I opened the door, there was the same old Bobby—less grease in his hair, minus the sharkskin suit, same grin, same great big brown eyes. He took me to a quasi-fancy Italian place in the North Valley, where we got over our jitters by getting slightly tipsy, then came back to my house and rooted through paper sacks full of old love letters we wrote to each other when I was still a virgin. Some of the fading mush-novellas still had a faint scent of Jade East, Bob's sexy teen scent that drove the young me into preorgasmic spasms. In those aching high school days, when we finally got into spicy foreplay, Bob always wanted *more*. His penis was called "Mick," and my vagina's name was "Cher." So scary.

Love-bunny Bob,

I'm laying here on the beach, thinking of you and what we almost did yesterday. It makes me cry. Even those little things I did with you made me feel bad. Of course, I enjoy doing it . . . I'm only human too! I love it!! But I just can't do it. Maybe I'm different— no, a lot of girls feel just like I do, they just give in too easy. You know I love you so much, *so much*! and you love me, I'm so glad you understand me. No other boy would do what you're doing for me—but I promise you'll be glad later . . . I promise.

Hi Lover-dover,

Is everything OK with you? Pam worries about her li'l one. I hope your dad doesn't stick you in the service. Jeepers creepers, it's too bad you can't get better grades. Please get them for me. My Cher is still very sick, if you really want to know the reason I don't want sex—it's because I'm very worried about her. So, please stop asking for it, Bob. You know one day I'll do it for you.

What would Cher think about someone naming her pussy after her? So very scary.

Bob's parents dragged him to New York for a few months, and when he returned, much to his dire dismay, I had altered entirely. He so much wanted the old Pam to come back, but I had squirmed out of the cocoon as Pamela, so look out.

Hi, Bob, Honey,

I am changing. I am the weirdest thing in the world. I love all black, bell-bottom capri pants, bare feet, sweatshirts, and straight hair on girls! (me!) I'm starting to go around with some new, weird kids. I love you. I like tight corduroy pants on guys, suede shoes, and *long* hair. I got my Rolling Stones tickets. Seven rows from the front! Honey, please tell me if you have stopped smoking. I've stopped ratting my hair. Write soon, you are mine.

Pamela.

Hi Pam, Honey

I started smoking again, but please don't be mad at me, my dearest darling, I only have about four or five a day. I guess I'll start by saying I love you, and the reason I am so, so, so, so, so, so, so sad is I know how you feel about Victor Hayden, and it's driving me right out of my mind and is making me so, so, so, so, so, so sick. Also, I know how you feel about Mick Jagger, and if you had

the chance, you would go out with him, the way you feel about
Mick is like you want to fuck with him. I'M NOT SAYING YOU
WOULD. That's just how I feel. I don't like you going to Hollywood without me and seeing all those long-haired boys. I don't
want you to see the Stones without me either. It makes me so, so,
so, so, so, so sad. I love you.

Your Boy Bob.

It took us hours to go through the yellowing stuff while Bob and
I cracked up and cried over the sad fate of Pam and Bobby. I think
he would have liked to rekindle the ancient, fractured romance, but
it felt better just to be friends. He just had another daughter with
some sweet young thing and seems pretty happy. I hope he is.

CHAPTER SEVENTEEN

Little by little—through my book, the reunions with long-lost loves, and the scathing revelations of therapy—I was making peace and love with my past, if not my present. Michael had accepted my loopy apology, and we were getting along pretty well, considering all that had gone before. We never went too deep because of the untapped emotional danger below the sheen, but had reached a common point where we could laugh and have fun because we knew each other so damn well. No grudges, that's one of my main mottos. We also needed each other because our son was stuck in his own pit of despair, and we could at least commiserate. No one else could have possibly understood. Communication with Nick was hard. He was insecure about what he felt and locked his fearsome thoughts into an airtight double knot. And, unfortunately, Houdini was long dead.

We had many redundant, repetitive, painful meetings with overly educated authority figures whose eyes darted all over the room, hoping to land anywhere but on our beseeching faces. They *wanted* to help. I suppose there are a lot of sensitive children who have an impossible time fitting into this bombastic place. When Victor Hayden was a child, he put aluminum foil over all the windows in his house to keep out unwanted invading energy. What did *his* parents think? What did *they* go through? God love them.

These overworked, overwrought officials finally placed Nick in a new program at a Santa Monica hospital, luckily real local. At least it seemed lucky at the beginning. We needed help with our son *so* badly that we naively assumed these "specialists" knew what they were doing.

Finally the paperwork was completed, all the meetings taken, and Nick started "special" school and therapy sessions the following week with a furrowed brow whom I'm going to call Adolf. He instantly hated the place, equating "special" with "crazy," and tantrums erupted in bitter protest at having to sit in a room all day with six other boys (no girls) whose problems ranged from Tourette's syndrome (constant cursing and twitching) to extreme goofballism. One uncontrollable boy became the enemy right away. He physically abused Nick when no one was looking, and his vocabulary was severely limited. All day long he repeated over and over, "The copper cat is *too* long, you are *too* long, the copper cat is *too* long . . ." At first Nick found this litany humorous but soon had to hold his ears, and create his own incantations to escape the incessant jagged jibberish.

Many sessions ensued with stern-burn Adolf, the ever-changing teachers who couldn't seem to cope, and astringent, bespectacled know-it-alls who tried to figure out why Nick couldn't fit into the big, bad world—why he *refused* to make the attempt to fit into any type of program. Adolf soon became the devil, and Nick would cross himself before entering the therapy room. Sometimes he had to be dragged in and held down. The heavy-handed psychologist was so sour-faced and deadly serious that even though I was supposed to meet with him weekly, I found it very difficult to open up to him. He made me cry one despairing afternoon in a rush of release, and the self-satisfied look on his face (one of the only times he smiled) ate up the moment and spat it out in a glob. He sat in cheerless judgment of the Des Barres psyche, and I wondered how it had come to this. How had I created this poker-faced goblin into my life? What lesson could he possibly teach me? Or Nick? Sometimes Nick would absolutely refuse to enter Adolf's therapy room and wound up being "restrained" by big burly men in white overalls whom he kicked in the nuts, then being put into a carpeted closet called the "time-out room." Some days he spent three or four hours alone in the tiny space. They said it was good for him, it gave him time to figure out what he had done wrong. I asked why he had to be in there so long. Because he refused to apologize for his mistakes, of course, they said. Nick's sense of fair play was highly refined, and if he thought he was in the right, *nothing* could get him to say he was sorry. Nothing.

I was constantly aching inside for my darling son who couldn't figure out why he was alive. "Why am I back here, Mom?" he said to me after a particularly hard, hard day. "I thought I had finished on this planet." How, how, *how* was I supposed to answer a question like that? There must be something real important for you to do this time around, little boy. Something special. (Oops, that word again.) Something to help all of humanity. So much blah, blah, blah, I felt like my hands were tied with barbed wire and on fire.

I begged for a name, a title to hang on Nick's supposed illness. After Adolf could no longer avoid telling me *something,* he looked at me grimly and said Nick had a "personality disorder." A vague term for "We don't have any fucking idea." Only long-long-term therapy could put a dent in his pain. "We have a long road ahead of us," Adolf was fond of saying. It got to where I could hardly look at him, the man who was supposed to be helping my son.

II

To give Nick a break, I took him on a little trip to Vancouver, where I was taping a dumb rock show. I had recently heard from another long-lost—one of my Beatlefriends, Linda, who now lived in Oregon. She and her daughter, Aura, would take the train to Vancouver, and Victor would drive up to join the reunion. It should have been a lot of fun. It should have been. Anybody who called their kid Aura should have had some sort of clue, right?

The first day started out fine. We went shopping, we ordered room service. Aura and Nick seemed to hit it off. Then I noticed how Linda was looking at me—kind of off-kilter. She spoke sharply to me; I wasn't living up to her expectations, I could feel it, but what could I do? She had had a crush on Victor in high school, but now— apparently in her estimation—he didn't make the grade either. She seemed to want to feel a part of things, but wouldn't let herself. Aura, on the other hand, was twelve and a half pushing twenty-six and was trying to have some fun. I attempted to keep a happy face, as usual.

Nick got hellishly sick on the second night, high-fever hallucinations. I couldn't keep him in bed; he was on some kind of dangerous mission, so hot, crawling around the room, calling out to some wizard who kept evading him. I put cold washcloths on his head, I fed him medicine, I tried to keep him prone. Linda and Aura were in sleeping bags on the floor, trying not to notice the foreign language Nick was speaking. You can't even imagine what it was like. Thank God Victor was there with us.

January 30, 1989—Back from Vancouver, a nightmare trip—mainly in retrospect—I tend to drizzle honey over the facts as they happen. Nicky got that horrid flu, and I wasn't what Linda was expecting, or projecting, I should say. Aura is very grown-up and pushing it to the max, and Linda can't seem to fit in. I recognize that paranoia, having been there myself, but not so constantly. Aura called today and told me her mom said I had let success go to my head and I was living in a phony world of my own creation. I really tried. I know I have moments of pride, but it's harmless, isn't it? I could have been more generous, I suppose. Where is my lesson?

Try as I might, I couldn't find one in that situation. Should I have paid for everybody's pancakes? Grilled cheese and fries? Brought colorful gifts and balloons to make up for the hours spent wrestling with my delirious, sweating son? Victor told me to forget about it, I had a lot of other stuff to deal with. He was right. Maybe my lesson—though it broke my heart—is that not every single closed door should be opened.

One more flash from the past, Darryl DeLoach the first Iron Butterfly singer that had unleashed a primitive personal series of events back in '67, came back into my life for a tiny while.

L.A. Weekly had the idea of teaming Darryl and me together, piling us into a convertible, and driving down the Sunset Strip to gab about the good old days one more time. It was silly-nilly fun, and the fact that Darryl had as many memories of me as I had about him, boosted my question-mark self-esteem a notch or two.

Darryl lived in San Diego with his longtime girlfriend and invited Nick and me on a weekend visit to Tijuana. The four of us cruised the colorful, noisy streets eating borderline food, buying trinkets. Darryl, the former rock maniac, seemed to understand Nick, which helped make up for our boo-boo visit to Vancouver. "You know, Nick," Darryl surmised, slapping a giant sombrero on Nick's blond head, "with a brain like yours, you could take over the world some day!" Nick grinned and bent down to a cross-legged, brightly bundled lady, inspecting her merchandise. Darryl bought a giant pile of her cheerful handmade friendship bracelets, draping them over Nick's arm. You're supposed to give them away, but Nick still has every single one of them.

III

The spring of '89 I entered a lengthy introspective phase. I was still in therapy with Frederick, seeing Adolf on a weekly basis regarding Nick and his frustrating lack of progress at school, and since I felt like I hadn't done shit to help humanity, I started lending my time to an over-sixty-five free lunch program at Virginia Park. I poured milk and passed out easy-to-chew slabs of protein and different shades of wobbly Jell-O. I felt the trapped young hearts of the senior citizens as they told oft-repeated stories as if for the very first time. Some of the old guys gave me a nudge, nudge, wink, wink, and commented on how red my hair was, how tight my skirt.

That was the extent of my erotic life. I had gotten over my sweet, unrequited crush on Sandra, and stopped seeing HIM because it had gone as far as it could go and had started to backfire a bit. I got a call from one of the rags right in the middle of a high-impact workout with Kathy, a clipped British voice saying, "We have it on good authority that you are having an affair wth HIM." Oh, no, you don't, you slimecreeps. I gave an unheralded Academy Award performance on the phone that day, and nothing ever came out in print. So ha, ha, HA! Kathy was really impressed. I told her I had studied acting for many years and still had my SAG card.

But the gnawing sexual impulse demands expression. I started a rock novel, hoping to continue the career I had sliced out for myself. It was going to be about an aging groupie named Blush—someone *unlike* myself, in that she just couldn't stop flinging herself at the tempting rock gods.

BLUSH
By Pamela Des Barres

I'm alive.

Isn't that something? Surprise, surprise, surprise.

I must be in a hospital, because the air smells like serious medicine, cloying chemicals. It makes me gag. When I try to check it out, I can't open my eyes and I can't move. I feel like someone has shot me up with ice cubes full of razor blades. Bandages across my eyes, I obviously can't see anything. When I try to move my arms, I realize they are strapped down, tubes and needles in profusion. I am reeling, dizzy, stoned on painkillers. Even so, the deep, pulsating agony throb in my pussy is profound. The filthy ache of too many cocks where I didn't want them. I have been raped. One of those things that could never happen to *me* has happened big time. But how?? My thoughts are too pure. I surround myself with white light every morning so the boogeyman can't get in. Had I forgotten this morning? Had I been in too much of a hurry to imagine that big hand holding the shimmering sparkler, moving over me, up and down, round and round? Protection from the shiny, sticky, red unknown. I have been mortally invaded.

What day is it? The next day, or many days later? How bad is it? How damaged are the goods? Rip, tear, bleed. Beg, plead, bleed. Where is my son? I left him at home with the baby-sitter; he was playing his newest Nintendo game, he hardly even noticed when I left for the concert. The mother-fucking concert. Why are Jim Morrison's lyrics pounding through my temples? Pounding, beating, begging for some of that bloody, motherfucking mercy; we want the world and we want it now. . . . Mother, I want to . . . when the music's over . . . turn out the lights, turn out the . . . cancel my subscription to . . . the . . . res—ur—ec—tion. . . .

It's my second day in the hospital. The bandages have been removed, and I can see. The metaphor here is too obvious. I can see clearly now, the rain is gone. Let us not talk softly now, the hour is getting late. My head hurts. I have been pondering my fate and my faith as my private parts heal. No permanent damage unless you consider that my soul has been charred and shredded. I have been humbled before the Lord. I have crawled on my belly, repentant, to the dungeon where sluts are bound and gagged. I have acquiesced and apologized for being raped by rock and roll. My life-style preceded me, and I got what I deserved.

What a crock of shit! I didn't deserve to be split apart by an entire rock band and two roadies. I didn't ASK FOR IT. I was skewered by fate and then decided to poke more holes in myself for good measure. Lots of groggy time to think and rethink, spin around in raw sewage, float undamaged in crystal-clear waters where it never happened at all. Take me down to Paradise City, where the grass is green and the girls are pretty.

I'll never forget the look in the drummer's bleary eyes when the blood started pouring out all over his stubby hands. I don't think he'll ever get over it. He climbed off me and started bawling, trying in vain to zip his jeans and wipe the blood across the wall like he'd been contaminated with it. I had seen his face so many times on MTV, grinning maliciously at his many devotees. Is he afraid of me now? Will he try to make up for it the rest of his fucking life? Play gigs for charity? Give all his royalties to Mother Teresa? God, I hope so, but I'm probably giving his cum-stained conscience way too much credit.

After the final insult of the sweaty, stinking roadies taking turns on me, I was dragged, mewling, into a janitor's closet that reeked of ammonia and sour rags and left there to rot. I lost my mind and wandered around on another plane—one where lilies bloomed in slow-motion synchronicity, and cocker spaniel puppies frolicked in perfect pastures. And I woke up here at Cedars Sinai, where many movie stars have cleansed insulted veins and dried out gin-soaked livers. I believe Zsa Zsa had her skin tightened one too many times right here within these walls. I recuperate among the glorified, and a misguided part of me glides painfully and silently down the cool corridors at night. I peek into the closed doors where the mighty have fallen, at least temporarily. We are all one.

Raped by an entire rock band and not one, but *two* roadies! What was up with me? This was just the first few pages out of a hundred or so that I had completed. The entire book was going to take place with Blush in her hospital bed as she thinks back over her wild-child life, and tries to make some sense out of it. I should have shown this stuff to Frederick, but I sent it off to my publishers instead, just knowing I would be the new queen of rock novels.

Then I flew off to Aspen to don a wedding frock.

IV

Melanie had had yet another bout with cocaine—her final one. I had been worried about her in New York, but she always half-assedly hid her addiction from me, so it was difficult to help. After *Working Girl* wrapped, she checked herself into rehab and called her first husband, Donnie, Mr. Clean and Sober, for moral support. They spent hours and hours on the phone while she fought her scary battle, rediscovering each other, and ah, romantic corn—surprise! surprise!—falling back in love. I felt real bad for Barbra, because I knew from experience that Donnie was addictive, but it was obviously the right heartfelt move. And now Melanie was pregnant, and I would be her matron of honor.

People didn't understand, but Don adored the idea of keeping company with his former gal-pals. There was a definite harem feel to the situation that he reveled in, but it was really more like an extended family. We just loved each other.

Donnie flew Patti, Michael, and me to the ranch in Aspen a couple days in advance to prepare for the divine wedding festivities. Everything was blooming and blossoming, wildflowers in abundance covering the glorious green mountains. Lots of birds were chirping, horses braying, doggies yapping, blond children romping; it was almost too delightful. Melanie needed Patti and me to tend to her excited, emotional state, and we did so with love, giggles, and aplomb.

When her dress arrived, we oohed, aahed and got teary-faced, huggy-huggy. It was Romeo/Juliet empire style to make room for her burgeoning baby tummy and looked so frothy and exquisite. Oh boy, you're getting married tomorrow! Baby's breath for her hair, a luscious bouquet to toss. Who would be the lucky bitch to grab it out of the air?

Patti brought a certain lovely dress to wear but wasn't satisfied, so we tromped through the cobbled streets of Aspen on a search for something billowing and blue at almost the last minute. My dress was très flowery and colorful, matching the hills that were alive with the sound of wedding bells.

Dismayingly, the rags got wind of the wedding day and started circling the ranch, their rot-rag helicopters sput-sput-sputtering throughout the morning. Don's temples pounded. Enraged, he called all the proper authorities, and they tried to intervene, but it was too late. Then Donnie changed the time of the actual ceremony, and the worms just missed it—hooray—but not before shooting photos of Michael, Patti, and me cavorting up on the balcony. Patti, flirtatious nymph that she is, raised her white cotton nightie, flashing the attractive gardeners hoeing below, and the rags erroneously reported that it was Melanie flashing Don before the wedding. They never get it right. D.J., Patti, and a few other enterprising souls decided a little skeet shooting might be just the thing, and the flustered helicopters were kept at bay like squalling goblins, returning only after the vows were taken. Patti looked real cute taking aim with that gigantic rifle in her shiny satin ball gown. At least nobody drifted down from the skies with a camera in their helmet like they did at Liz and Larry's wedding. There's always something to be grateful for.

Michael spent the moments before the wedding with Donnie, putting the flower in his lapel, communing Iron John–style. I wish I could have been in on their husband-to-be, husband-that-was conversation. Mmm-mmm. All of our strange, healed love-triangles somehow lifted us up, made us happy together.

A beautiful, woodsy spot behind the main house, under big, hanging trees had been chosen. I followed Jesse and little Alexander, carrying the rings, down the pathway and stood next to Melanie, all trembly-chinned. I was so happy to be maid (matron?) of honor, since I had been there from the sizzling second they met even though it had been ferocious for me. Short and sweet, man and wife one more time. Tears, laughter, joy, a three-tiered yummy cake, all the stunning trimmings when two become one (for the second time, with a third on the way). There was a massive festive gala following the nuptials and there was a free-for-all when Melanie tossed the wedding bouquet—a lace-and-satin wrestling match with Patti tumbling around in the grass with another sprightly girl. It was Patti, of course, who snatched up the shredded prize, raising the crushed bunch of flowers over her head like gold-plated ill-gotten gains. The next bride! The bouquet charm would take a little while to work, but now she's about to strut down the aisle again herself. So I guess the tumble was worth it.

V

I came back home to the godsend good news that Ariana, the psychic healer who mended my wrist, was planning a trip to California. Ariana lives in Las Vegas, surrounded by slot machines and big-buck losers, arid desert all around. She's past fifty, living mostly under the stars with her flower-fairy backpacking, gnomelike boyfriend with endless eyes. They have the same dreams at night, meet there on purpose, and discuss it in the morning. Her tempest-tossed life has been very hard. Married off at thirteen by her Southern parents, she has experienced all kinds of horrendous physical and mental abuse. Her first husband won't let her see her only son and has turned him against her for fictitious reasons. She takes care of her ailing religious mother, who believes Ariana has sided with the red guy and his pitchfork. So, even though her gift is otherworldly, she very much understands the ways of *this* seemingly cruel and orderless world. She sees everyone as being in their perfect place, learning their needed lessons. People put themselves in our lives, we put ourselves in theirs *on purpose,* as Ariana says, "to see the unfinished part of ourselves," the stuff we need to work on. In her sessions with people, part of what she does is to help speed up their karma by taking them back to previous lives at the point where a belief system was formed, where something got stuck, a negative pattern that keeps being repeated over and over. By freeing up all this old crap, we can move forward on our ever-expanding, never-ending journey. Whew! It's a lot to take in.

I offered her my bedroom for her readings, and she accepted. I thought it would be great for Nick, who was feeling increasingly distraught, and I so hoped Ariana's presence in the house might help him see his true, blameless spirit. All my openhearted friends poured through the bedroom door, needy and ready for info. The vibe in my house shook the bed at night.

Several of my friends glommed onto Ariana like she was a life raft and still see her whenever she comes to town. Others took what they needed, or what they could stand, and kept going. I have sessions with her whenever I can. I get them down on tape, but I haven't forgotten any of them. Ariana no longer has to tell me what she sees. I see it *all* myself with her guidance. It's just like going to a soul-movie, and sometimes the scenes hurt real bad.

"I'm an old, graying man, ragged, in a damp stone cell. One window very high, out of reach. My eyes always have tears, my face haunted, I hold my ears as not to hear the screams." Ariana had me go back. How did I wind up in the cell? "I did something against the king. I betrayed him, and now I will forever have to hear the screams." Go back, go back. "The king had me round up little boys, telling them about a carnival or party, bring them to the castle, where he took them down dark stairs, never to be seen again. I didn't question this. I worked for my king. One night I heard stifled screams and stealthily made my way down the stairs to witness the horror of my king assaulting a young boy, sodomizing him, killing him. My guilt became my hell. I had brought these children to this madman. The trusting face of a small boy constantly haunts me, his eyes looking into mine. He smiles at me as he goes down the stairs to his torture and death. A sweet smile with just a hint of a question forming. Why are we being taken down these stairs? Where's the party? I did not know! I did not know!!!"

I could feel tears pouring out of me, Ariana comforting me. I was shaking; she held me. "When the king asked me to gather some more small boys for a festive occasion, I went off as I usually did to bring the boys back to him but hid myself instead, unable to do what he asked. I, of course, was found and put into this cell. The cell is under the castle, down those same stairs. I am forced to listen to the agonized screams of young boys as they die. I cannot live any longer." At this point I was uncontrollable, seeing myself as this old tortured man, banging my head to a bloody pulp on the dirty iron bars as high-pitched screams pierced the dank air until I was no longer there. I was a dead thing on a cold foor. Ariana held me until I came back to myself, confused, sobbed-out, and sad.

At the end of a session Ariana asks if we recognize any of the people we saw in the former lifetime and what we learned that we will never have to repeat. I thought and thought about the castle vision, but no one came to my weary mind. Ariana gently suggested that perhaps Nicky had been there with me. In a scary flash of recognition, I saw my son in the trusting face of that doomed boy and felt the guilt still set in my bone-structure but not set in stone. Here, Nicky, honey, here's more, more, more! Take it, take another little piece of my heart and another Sega game—maybe it will ease my ancient guilt. I've been working on getting rid of it ever since. Who knows how many hundreds of years I've been dragging that around?

Insights were blasting me from every direction. Around this time I also had a painful experience with a man that taught me a lot, even though it seemed to be just another boy-girl mistake. It's way too easy to say, "Oh, come on, everyone makes mistakes." There are no mistakes. I let this guy in too fast. I opened up too far. I emptied my entire bag of delights, leaving nothing new and exciting under wraps for him to discover later. Too much too soon. He got petrified of the sweet, pink flood, turned around, and fled. It was only a six-week situation, and even though I exposed myself like I was under an X-ray machine, I forced myself to look at the cringing behavior, becoming the "observer" and the "observed" all at once, like Krishnamurti had taught me. While I flopped around in that bluesy unrequited fog, I watched myself, and learned.

August 10—*Agony and ecstasy, why can't I grow up? What does it mean? What kind of importance could this incident inspire? I'm still a romantic slave, but it all feels like an illusion to me. I went to church, and it gives me strength. My emotions are rampant, and I am working on dealing with them—ordering them. It's all just a flash—an instant of life—a split-flaming second. I watched myself flounder, so interesting if you can detach. I had an insightful talk with Frederick. It's all a big learn-o-rama. It appears that men can just hack the heart out of the process, and as Alice Cooper once said, "only women bleed"—continuously and profusely, or so it seems. But I learned two big lessons in a short period of time: Don't hand myself over to the first bidder in the blinding glaze of infatuation, and don't allow myself to wallow in the torpid drop-dead aftermath. We are each on our path, doing exactly what we are supposed to do, and I have to learn to let go. I've been of two minds lately: the standing-up-for-myself-proud woman versus The-cosmic-acceptance-of-everything-in-its-proper-place. I know I can no longer present myself on a silver platter to anybody, but I refuse to play the fucking game, and I'm interested in drawing someone to me who has no interest in playing it either.*

I was going to have to wait awhile on that one.

CHAPTER EIGHTEEN

Growth spurt aside, I got a bitter-blow phone call from my agent Mel in NYC. It had been awhile since I had turned in the beginning of my novel, but I was keeping paranoia at bay, praying Jane and Jim had been too backed up with loads of work to read it. I was hanging on the meat hook but trying not to notice. I could tell from Mel's tone of voice that all was not well in Fantasyland. He didn't sugarcoat the facts or spare the rod. "Jane and Jim had a lot of trouble with the manuscript," he said sadly. "They thought it was full of gratuitous sex and wasn't going anywhere. To be honest with you, they hated it." *Hated* it? Jane was a wee bit gentler. "It's a whole different experience to write a novel," Jane said. "You made a valiant first effort. It's a very difficult thing to undertake." Until Nick's bus dropped him off from school, I sat in a fog of black despair, where he found me, almost stiff on the couch. "Mom! What's wrong?" He sat down next to me, and I uttered the rotten truth. Nick had watched me slave over the computer; we often took turns with it, since he had recently jumped up a step to the world of IBM role-playing games. "Oh, Mom, I'm so sorry." He put his head on my shoulder and told me it would all work out—things happen for a reason, etc. All the sincere platitudes I had presented to him during his own spates of difficulty. My caring, wonderful son. I fixed him a grilled cheese and pulled out some pages from *Blush,* reading a chunk at random:

On the way back to our room, Davy and I ran into the bass player, Ian Stone, with a beautiful sobbing girl in the hallway. "Sweetheart, the fact is, I got married when I was eighteen," I heard him croon to the anguished, trembling temporary replacement. He was giving her the wedding-band brush-off. While Davy unlocked our door, I imagined Ian's dumpy little British wife folding diapers in Brighton while he caressed this stunning doll-girl in Dallas. Did wifey wonder if hubby was faithful to her? Before I could ponder this too hard, Davy tied my hands behind my back, pushed me down to the bed, and straddled me. Unzipping his corduroy trousers, he caressed his stiff cock, stroking my cheek with it and rubbing the tip across my lips. I gobbled at it like a starving alley cat, watching it sway above me, getting Real Real Red with my Revlon lipstick. He rolled me over onto my stomach and spanked me, "You've been extremely naughty, Blush, and a bad, bad girl like you needs to be severely punished." My hands were tied, I couldn't see him, I was trapped like an endangered species, loving it, but so scared—smack, smack, smack, stinging my bare ass. "I'm so hot for you, darlin', I wish I could suck my own dick."

What did they mean, gratuitous sex? Ha ha. I was all alone with nobody to cuddle my cares away, and my novel had been tossed in the dumpster. Woe woe.

After a brief period of mourning I reread a whole lot of Science of Mind reminders, re-remembering how I was supposed to face a seeming nightmare head-on, and see it as a challenge—another good old learning experience. I had just turned forty-one. Could I actually be growing up? One suspenseful night, I even wiggled out of my body to work things out:

February 21, 1990—I floated downstream, and these words came to me: "I don't have to sacrifice my genius—my genius is my God." I felt it all so deeply that we are all out of touch with our center, and our center (God) is our genius. It was all so clear, but what can I do with this snippet of knowledge, and I hang onto it? "Lives full of challenges met, to be channeled into this one." I came out the top of my head, swirly-twirly, I can leave if I want to, oh yes.

II

I had flubbed my first attempt at fiction, but my questionable notoriety was getting me some interesting writing jobs. I was doing the music news on a cornball Playboy Channel show called *The Hot*

List, reading teen poetry and passages from the book at Michael's eclectic "poetry nights" at various local haunts, and writing a column called "Yakety Yak" for a rock mag. I found myself in small conference rooms with L.A. Guns, Mary's Danish, Dramarama; eating handfuls of sushi with XYZ, plates of pasta with Lions and Ghosts, the Sea Hags, sipping frothy cups of cappucino with the dashing Adam Ant, Zakk Wylde, Bryan Adams; hanging on the telephone with various members of Faith No More, Bad English, Corey Hart, Dave Edmunds, the exquisite rock grande dame Marianne Faithful. But I think my fave interview was the one I did with Dwight Yoakam, that lanky golden-throated cow-punk with the billion-word vocabulary. I had to wait in the lobby while he finished up a conversation, and I discovered I had actual nerves. Dwight had been one of my pet faves for a long time because he had the guts to tackle the stiff country music scene and speak his prolific mind. Not to mention his incredibly long, lean legs and tight little butt. Finally ushered into his office, I got into such a turbulent conversation with Dwight about the insensitive treatment he'd received from the L.A. press and the backwards goons in Nashville, that the phone was ringing back home as I walked through my door.

"One more thing," Dwight launched into a thought he hadn't been able to finish at the office as I scribbled wildly. "Remember, I grew up watching Elvis and Mick Jagger, so what I do with country music isn't calculated. For them to say it's inappropriate is a blatant example of cultural prejudice, trying to keep me down on the farm with some straw in my mouth going, 'Aw shucks.' It destroys their comfortable perception of what is tolerable from a country artist—figuratively asking the country musician to perform in blackface in a colloquial sense. I engage in it because of my love for the form, and I'll do as much or as little of it as I see fit." Go on, Dwight. Gosh, I was starting to feel like a real journalist, and I was about to be proven right.

I met a true mentor at my dear friend Allee Willis's famous fifties pajama party, Annie Flanders, the inimitable founder of *Details* magazine. While Annie and I rambled on, Joni Mitchell sat by the pool in her fuzzy robe, dourly surveying the other nightie-clad ladies. Teri Garr had on a shortie fluff-job, Cyndi Lauper had on an indescribable sweeping sleepy number, Sandra Bernhard wore a leopard-print getup. I waved to her, blushing, and she called out, "Hello, sweetheart, how have you been?" Sweetheart. Did she call everybody that? Girl games went on all night. The best prize was a date with fifties-throbber, Fabian. Boo-hoo, I didn't win.

Annie Flanders had an instant, unswerving faith in me, and I promised to confirm her good taste. She wanted me to do articles on
anybody I thought was cool enough. She even wanted me to appear
in photographs with my pet subjects. Wow! My first piece was on
Hunt and Tony Sales, my old pals and new members of David Bowie's
Tin Machine, and I got Randee St. Nicholas to take the arty, charcoal-
and-chalk shots with me in the middle. What fun! Then Annie flew
me to New York for a piece on Michael Hutchence from INXS,
and I spent an entire, brilliant fall day with him in Manhattan, discussing the Higher Power and posing for hours of hands-on photos
in a vast, vacant loft. This was the perfect job for me! I could flirt
like a she-devil, but having to remain a professional journalist,
couldn't get into any trouble. "I believe you and I are kindred spirits,
darling," Michael said to me, so I called the article "Kindred Spirits."
I did my first cover story on the legendary Iggy Pop, photographs
taken by bigshot Greg Gorman, and I really felt on my way! Annie
let me write about my favorite unknowns, review hip movies, and
travel around the country with my trusty tape recorder. She even
shipped me off to London for tea with one of my ultimate inspirations
and old-days crushes, Ray Davies, founder of the Kinks. Diary jot-
tings:

> So grand! A lovely time spent with Ray—equality—which means personal
> growth. I was still in awe but fully able to do my job. We reminisced sweetly.
> "Remember that time you came to my hotel room door with two cheap bottles
> of fruit-flavored wine and we drank it all down?"

La-di-da, la-di-da.

After the flawless meeting with Ray, tea and scones, an hysterical
come-clean interview, I arrived home to the horrendous news that
Annie had been fired! How could she have been fired from her own
magazine? It turned out she had put half the ownership and all her
trust in the wrong soulless giant-shots. Annie had stapled together
the very first copy of *Details,* and there ought to be some kind of
law protecting creative individual rights. You can bet your nine lives
that it will all come out in the cosmic wash. Don't even worry
about it.

III

Speaking of the celestial laundromat, I had another awesome,
cleansing session with Ariana:

March 26—I went way down/out/in—got warm all over, realized I was underwater, in a flowing Greek-type garment, on my way to complete an important task for my "teacher." I was one of twenty people trained to go into this large city, reach the powerful leaders, and alter their consciousness for the better. Sounds simple, eh? I got into this massive hall—a long table full of men in political power having an all-important meeting—by posing as a servant girl. As I poured their wine from a stone pitcher, I caught their eye and zapped them. It was supposed to snap their consciousness gradually to include more universal ideas, make them more accepting, not so set in their selfish, rigid ways, opening them up to a whole new way of thinking, slowly changing the world as it was. On my way back to my teacher, a powerful sense of peace came over me. It was my mission, and I accomplished it just by sticking my soul into their eyes.

As I came out of this creamy, turquoise trance state, I could see Ariana grinning like mad, she was so excited for me, her face was glowing. "Do you see how powerful you were in that lifetime? You can access that power any time you want to. It's yours. Remember that." Powerful. Not a word I used about myself too often. And why not? The power of God is right in the center of all of us, smack dab in the middle.

I needed all my Godly power to deal with the authorities at the "special" school. It's true that math, science, and English were taking a backseat to the so-called emotional counseling Nick was supposed to be receiving, but Nick was bringing home the same stupid printed-page homework assignment eight or ten times and, of course, refusing to do it over and over again, then getting in trouble for not handing it in. I was concerned that when he got back into "regular" school he would be way behind academically, which was a sin because he's sooooo damn bright. The teachers kept leaving—endless substitutes brought in only to be run ragged by the mutinous boys. When a teacher came in that Nick finally related to, promising to stay the entire school year, things got a little better then got hellishly worse when the guy couldn't handle it either and left with no notice. Nick rebelled riotously, with good reason, and wound up in their damn time-out isolation room one too many times. "It smells bad, Mom. Kids pee in there," Nick told me, and I stormed into the school, demanding to see the punishment chamber for myself. I was told that the proper authorities had to be consulted first. Fierce, fangs-bared, mama-lion madness erupted from inside me. I had to find out what was going on.

I had always had a very hard time with Nick's therapist, Adolf, who refused to put any credence in Nick's spiritual nature and saw his reliance on meditation and prayer as an escape from his problems—the same problems that nobody at the "special" school could ever seem to name or fathom. When I wanted some answers, they spoke in smart-ass psychiatric circles, such a pile of Freudian crap, I was inflamed with despair. After throwing a fit in the main office, I was finally taken down to the time-out room for a look-see. A look-smell. Nick had been so right. The closet-sized, carpeted space smelled like a urinal, smeary spots spread across the walls. This horrendous, fetid isolation even for a few minutes must have been so wretched. Such a hopeless, ensnared feeling wafted out at me. I begged silent forgiveness for unknowingly allowing Nick to spend one single second in there. After speaking my mind loudly, threatening to tell the school system about this squalid hole, I went straight to the classroom, took Nick by the hand, and removed him from the premises forever, having no idea what I was going to do next. Nick told me later that kids pee in the time-out room because they were pissed off. It made a whole lot of sense.

Nick's next "placement" was in "special education" at our local junior high. At first he was so quiet—almost invisible despite his ever-lengthening mop of hair—that he was pretty much left alone. But once he started speaking up, he got the usual cruel taunts about being "weird" and finally blew up one day in class. I was called in, a therapist assigned, and I felt like a hamster, caught on an endless, rusted, squeaky loop. What did Nick feel like? Since his art skills were off the map, Nick was sent to an advanced art class but immediately had a run-in with the teacher. She told the pupils to put ten things in their picture, and Nick asked why. She told him it was the rule. Nick said, "Art has no rules." How could anyone argue with that? I had long talks with him about authority figures and how teachers should be obeyed, that's why they're in charge. Respect your elders, yada-yada. "But art has no rules, Mom," he said to me. Nick told the prim, grinny-faced school psychologist that she was "plastic," and I started looking around for yet another school setting.

I even tried our local Catholic school, remembering what dear Shelly had told me about the high-level academic expectations and the very strict rules that had to be obeyed *or else*. Michael came with me, and as we sat across from the dignified nun with a severe bun, nodding quietly as we told our tale once again, I realized this wasn't the right place either. Our Lord hung forever suffering on His cross directly behind the headmistress and in several other places throughout the school grounds, while the Holy Mother Mary bared her raw, flaming heart for the students to witness in every single hall. Nick was forming his own wide, open-minded religious beliefs, and he was having enough of a difficult time without being thrown a humongous trowel full of guilt. I thought about the time at Jesus day camp when the person in charge told Nick to cast his eyes away from the statue of Buddha, lest he be contaminated by the devil, and I thanked the bunned nun for her time. Michael and I hung our heads and held hands through the echoing Catholic halls, heading back to the real world. We were at a loss.

IV

Despite my increasing search for potent inner discovery and some much-needed assistance in the blindfolded mystery of parenthood, I was still having a good time on the planet. My book had come out in England, and I flew over for a two-week blast into the British public eye. The scathing *Sun* had crammed my life into their centerfold, complete with some rip-off hot shots from the *Playboy* layout, rewriting my personal history so it seemed even more salacious and hornified. Thank God I had gotten the hang of self-defense, because no one else was going to defend my blemished honor. I did a Johnny Carson—type talk show, and the other guest happened to be Dion. He and Runaround Sue hadn't liked an article I'd written about them, but the former Mr. Slippery-Suave was sweet to me. Zach, his manager, told me he had finally reconciled it with the Lord, so I guess I was forgiven.

Then I packed up all my cares and woes and pitched them out the window of a 747 on my way to Berlin. I spent a week in that severe, stifled, elegant, buzz-cut city where *Band* had just been published under the title *Light My Fire*. There was no such phrase as "I'm with the band" in German. What did the girls hanging off drummers' arms *say* in that country? "Let me in, I'm next to the band?" Close to the band? Near the band? Under the band? The big Berlin newspaper had run a tawdry spread on the naughty, wicked girl who slept with all the bad boys of rock. They paid me many thousands, and nobody in America ever saw it. Should I care? Isn't it the same as Woody Allen selling whiskey in Japan?

Every street corner seemed haunted. I went to a radio station down in the dungeon of a former Nazi headquarters, which was cold and dismal with the highest ceilings I've ever seen. I wanted out of there fast. The people who published my book in Berlin were brave souls doing a daring deed. Freaks among soldiers. We went out to macabre bars until almost dawn, downing deep blue drinks and laughing loudly about things American. The oddkins in Germany stand out strong: They have to push a lot of buttons to find the one that plays the right music. I was proud to be with those people. They were undaunted, genteel, and belligerent. They appreciated Gram Parsons and Frank Zappa. I loved my spartan hotel in Berlin—the scratchy, stiff, white bedclothes. I adored the smelly food, and I found a couple pairs of very fabulous, bizarre shoes that my friends didn't understand.

After a short stop in Hamburg (I went to the spot where the former Cavern Club had been, where the Silver Beatles once played . . . aah, now just a squat vibeless building), I spent four days in Dublin, staying with my friend, Rona, and her three Irish flat-mates—all lovely, swinging girls with Irish eyes that cracked up constantly. I was on the front page of the Dublin paper, an old shot of me with Noel Redding, who happened to live in Cork, not too far away, with passages from my book all about our young, hot fling when he had been the bass player with the Jimi Hendrix Experience. The local trendy pub was throwing me an afternoon book bash, and Noel was coming on the train to attend the proceedings. Although we had written intermittently, I hadn't had my eyes on Noel for almost twenty years, and when he walked into the full-house, cacophonous, ale-swilling pub crowd, everything seemed to get quiet as we looked at each other from across the crowded room. Ha! My second lover— the very first guy I had an orgasm with. There's something to be said for that. Noel and I spent that entire day and evening together, having loads of photos taken, answering moss-grown questions like the rock-and-roll antiquities that we were. We talked about all our dead friends and counted our blessings. "Pamela, me old lovey," Noel whispered at the end of our exhilarating reunion, "how about a night together for very old time's sake?" I was touched—but not by dear Noel. He had a long-time ladylove, and I'd long since learned you just can't go back.

Back home I gave Melanie her baby shower, my house full of elite, wealthy females who brought Melanie so much incredible baby stuff it was almost embarrassing. I found an old thirties baby book at a swap meet and planned some superdumb games, the best of which was called Draw the Baby. I went around the room, blindfolding all the dames, having them scribble their rendition of a baby on a big white piece of paper. I took a photo of her mom, Tippi, her head all wrapped up in a flowered scarf, the pencil in midflight. It's really hysterical, but I guess you'd have to see it to get the full zany benefit. The drawings were so goofy and outrageous, we all became One with laughter. Melanie was the judge, awarding the richest woman in the room (I'm talking approaching ten figures) a fabulous prize I purchased at Pic 'N' Save. I've got to hand it to her; she was gracious as pie, as if she'd received a precious jewel from Tiffany. I brought out a ball of yarn and everybody had to guess the size of Melanie's stomach. Tatum O'Neal won. Most of the girls' yarn strands were two or three feet too long. Melanie said, "I'm not *that* fat!!" And all the women went ha-ha-ha. We ate cake and drank punch. A lot of fun was had by all, and then it took Melanie almost an hour to cart all the exquisite baby loot out to her car. Even with some of the girls helping her.

V

Right on cosmic cue, the gigantic century cactus was putting forth a massive phallus, shooting high into the Santa Monica sky like King Kong in heat. Supposedly it's a rare occurrence that only takes place every one hundred years, but the unfortunate thing is, the poor plant drops dead after consummating with the atmosphere. Sort of like when the female black widow puts the make on her male counterpart. *Adios,* arachnid. Anyway, it was a truly remarkable sight, and the least I could do was to share it with a few dozen of my closest friends by honoring it with a barbecue. Turkey dogs for everyone!

One of the people I called to invite was Jaid Barrymore, and since we hadn't spoken in awhile I asked all about life with daughter Drew. She told me that a miracle had taken place in their lives, their relationship was turning around, Drew was totally off abusive substances, and things were on a major upswing. All because of a program she had checked Drew into called ASAP, a live-in situation for adolescents with all types of drug/alcohol abuse and/or family problems. Since she had been so open with me, I blathered my mom-angst to her concerning Nick. She told me all about how lax she had been with Drew in the name of love, overly accepting about her way-too-early grown-up behavior. She admitted she had been floundering rampantly when she discovered ASAP, and told me to call my insurance company *right now* to see if we were covered for the program. "It'll change your lives, baby," Jaid assured me. She's definitely a hep chick, and I trusted her, but the thought of sending my so-young son somewhere, *any*where, away from me could not even be considered. No siree Bob. We would work it out. I thanked her for the info, told her I would ponder it hard. "See you at the barbecue, doll."

I bought a poppy-strewn, sheer antique dress for the occasion, because I had recently lost that nightmarish ten pounds that creeps up on all of us while we pretend not to notice. I was tending to the baked beans as Miss Mercy regaled me once again with her spectacular Stax stories and bawdy tales of hanging out with Al Green in Memphis long before he took sides with the Lord. Mercy hasn't changed much since the GTO days. All the drugs she ingested have left little tiny holes in her mind that the sixties poke through. Her synapses are shot, so once she gets stuck on a subject, your mind spins, your mind spins, your mind spins. The soft spot I have in my heart for her, however, has remained entirely intact. In between chopping vegetables, she punctuated her anecdotes with sharp, bellowing snatches of song.

Nick had invited two friends to the bash, and I was keeping an eye on him while whipping up onion dip and concocting Mom's famous coleslaw. He was agitated and lethargic all at once and seemed ready to blow at the least little slight. I cast my eyes heavenward. Keep him happy today, you guys. I'm beggin' this time.

As each new guest arrived, I introduced them to my magnificent century cactus and they were appropriately awestruck. Danny Sugerman arrived with his new love, Fawn Hall, which I thought was a curious combo. He told me she never attended dinners with him and Oliver Stone (he was directing *The Doors,* and Danny had written the definitive Jim book) because she was so dedicated to Oliver North, who thought Ollie S. was a left-wing maniac. Personally, I would love to be a bug on the wall if the two Ollies ever met up. Fawn and Danny are still very much together, so I try to never judge a romantic relationship, just let it alone. Ariana drove in from Las Vegas, Chuck Wein was there, Moon and Dweezil, who brought his hug of the moment, Winona Ryder, Hunt and Tony Sales, Patti, Sheena Easton, Gene Simmons, who brought Paul Stanley, new friend Christina Applegate and old friend Katey Sagal, who were both flying high on *Married with Children,* and dear Michael, who tended to the sizzling dogs all day long. Oh, all kinds of fabulous people were scattered around the century plant, oohing and aahing, eating all-American health (sort of) food and swilling gallons of sparkling water in the S.M. sunshine.

I was feeling free, festive, and flirtatious. You know how sometimes the cloak of cool descends and nothing can get in your way? Maybe it was because I was packing ten fewer pounds and wearing that see-through dress. And a new friend, Lynn, had offered to invite some "cute boys" to the bash. Now, I have nothing against cute boys, and I never will, but having been pretty much alone since Michael and I shattered apart, I figured the one thing I didn't need in my new, successful, grown-up life was a cute boy. What I needed was a fortyish, established but hip, well-heeled, well-rounded, well-read, spiritually elevated Mr. Somebody With His Head On Straight. Actually he would have to be beyond hip to deal with the "former-groupie" crap that would inevitably flail around his ears. Still, I considered Lynn's proposal. She is a video stylist, constantly inundated with young, newly signed rock boys. Why not have my yard dotted with them like pretty flowers? What could it hurt? Sure, Lynn, bring on the cute boys.

By the time Lynn arrived I was a little tipsy on the delightful spiked fruit punch, and true to her word, she had dragged along some *very* cute boys. When she introduced me to the sweet, long-haired blond with the big lips, I was nice and polite but tried not to pay too much attention because I thought he was too young. Dusk brought us all into the house, where I propped my bare feet up on the bamboo coffee table and railed against Mark David Chapman, Dr. Nichopoulos, Donald Turnipseed, and all the various and sundry drugs that had ripped off my heroes, snatching them from the planet in their prime. Ariana said they had done what they came to do and got out when they were supposed to. Mercy said it was all one big political conspiracy. Or maybe it had something to do with Warner Bros.? I was deep into the story about how James Dean plowed into Mr. Turnipseed's flatbed and the slimy rumor that his mechanic (who was in the car at the time and escaped injury) had been giving him head at the time of impact, when I looked up to see the beautiful blond boy watching me through his streaked hair. His eyes were this dusty, opaque hazel, kind of endless and clean. Mysterious and wild. Come-hither but shy. Uh-oh.

Nick chose that moment to roar at his two pals over a supposed slight, the wrong kind of glance from one boy to the other. He accused them of complicity, ganging up on him. He was yelling, cursing, tears spurting, his face red. One boy went home and left Nick and T.J. alone, and it got a little better, but not before Jaid Barrymore caught a glimpse of the edgy situation. She pulled a piece of paper out of her purse and jotted down a number. "Call these ASAP guys, I'm telling you." I saw Ariana out of the corner of my eye, watching, listening. Smiling.

CHAPTER NINETEEN

I

The very next night Lynn took me to a sixties throwback club called English Acid. It had been awhile since I penciled in red lips to wade through a steamy, sweaty rock-and-roll jungle. The thick atmosphere was exhilarating; I felt skin-prickling alive and verging on dangerous. We were there, Lynn had told me, to see "Jimmy." "Jimmy?" I asked. "Who's Jimmy?" Lynn sighed, exasperated by my obvious ignorance. "Jimmy Thrill, the lead singer in Rattlesnake Shake. The cute blond boy I brought yesterday." Oh, him! The gaze I was getting when Nick erupted into flames. In a flash I remembered those dusty, come-hither hazel eyes.

Walking into English Acid was sort of like a ride Nicky and I went on at Knott's Berry Farm—Timothy E. Leery's Time Tunnel—all black light and trippy-hippie. The kid and I had gone to see our friend Elvira strut her scary, sexy stuff on Halloween, and we wandered into the Time Tunnel, a psycho-delic maze, complete with David Crosby almost cutting his hair and Grace Slick begging us to "go ask Alice." I was dumbfounded. "I can't believe it's come to this," I mumbled while Nick laughed his ass off at the slogans: FLOWER POWER, DROP OUT, TUNE IN, and a giant WHY? hot-pinked across a fake brick wall. I had scrawled a huge "WHY?" over my entire poetry book in 1966. It had been the question of the decade. I felt like my eyeballs were spinning one way, then the other on uncontrollable stems, like that time I had smoked way too much pot in Captain Beefheart's backyard. They even spelled Jimi Hendrix wrong—Jimmy Hendrix—a simulated sacrilege. Is this Owsley's purple or Memorex? The experience left me gasping for air. Nick ran off to get a glow necklace and a funnel cake while I stood there in a stupor remembering the real thing. Peace and love, brother, sister.

The whole sixties culture has been chewed up, eaten, and assimilated into the nineties, where it assumes mythical proportions. Almost like it never happened at all, like maybe George Orwell or Aldous Huxley wrote the entire decade into a blockbuster best-seller that has stayed on the list for twenty-five years. So many of the heroes are dead, the music is considered "classic," and my friends from the love-ins have gone the way of the saber-toothed tiger. 'Scuse me while I kiss the sky. Have the hippies merged into the society they spurned and spat upon? A whole lot of them have. I see them peering out of tinted office building windows, mutilated mouths stretched wide. The silent screamers. But that night at English Acid a sixties rehash was very much alive and flowering. It's fascinating to see the rock boys and girls attempting to resemble me and mine when we were peaking and freaking out on the Sunset Strip. I don't know whether to feel proud, haughty, or petrified. At least I never became a silent screamer.

Lynn and I squished into a booth next to a throwback couple who probably live in their VW van and gaze daily at a Peter Max calendar from 1969. When I apologized for the tight fit, the bearded guy with the beaded headband said, "Cool, man." I can dig it. I ordered a seabreeze from a pissed-off, chunky frizz-pot when two young girls bathed in black giggled up to the table to tell me that I had validated their existence. I've looked at people the way those girls looked at me that night—sort of through the eyelashes, head down, breathless, and ecstatic. Gee, thanks, dolls!

I had been sweating next to the mellow couple for about forty-five minutes when through the smoky haze I saw Jimmy Thrill walking toward me. The lust-adrenaline snapped right out of hibernation and did a little dance of joy up and down my spine. He was wearing a black fedora, a jacket full of studs, skin-super-tight flared black jeans, and a lazy, totally unself-conscious, shining bright smile. His walk was a cross between a slink, a strut, and a swagger. I saw stars. I saw the rings around Saturn. That God-sent sensation is always unexpected and profound, shattering the serenity like a starry-stellar hacksaw. When matchmaker Lynn jumped up so Jimmy could sidle in next to me, I didn't know what to expect. He looked at me from under his hat through streaky, shiny blond hair. "I had a dream about you last night," he said, which was an age-old yet bewitching line.

"You were leading a meeting, telling a whole crowd of people that all the answers they were looking for were inside themselves."

Wow. Did he have my number, or what? Then a booming voice announced Rattlesnake Shake, and he was writhing around onstage—sweating, dripping, wailing—stripping off most of his clothes within minutes and swan-leaping into the audience with no caution, no fear, no shame. Unabashed, unapologetic, and *totally* uninhibited, he was so refreshing in this uptight, sheathed, just-so George-Michael (no offense) MTV world. We *need* more wild boys and girls. During the encore I tore out a check stub with my number on it, handed it to Jimmy's friend, Spidey, and left without good-byes.

II

The next day, after Nick had been dreadful all morning and had gone grumpily off to school, I was sitting around with Ariana, having one of our soul-to-soul digathons, when she very casually said, "I think I'll stay an extra day so I can go with you to see what that ASAP program is all about." Oh no. Everything stopped. All I could hear was somebody's lawn mower whirring in the distance. Ariana must have had a flash. She had previously agreed with me that Nick needed to be home, so what was up? I had been attending "Tough Love" meetings like she suggested—but she had seen a lot in the few days surrounding the barbecue. She had witnessed the frantic outburst with his friends, and the evening before I had asked Nick to do something and he said a simple "No." Without any excuses, whining, conniving, he just refused me. I told him there would be a consequence, and he said, "I don't care." He was nonplussed, unmoved, his face a blank mask—and it had sent a dark squiggle of fear through me.

But I still couldn't face what needed to be looked at until Ariana took the moo-cow by the udders. "How about calling ASAP today?" she asked sweetly. Grasping at straws, I decided to call Nick's teacher first, to see if she thought he might need a live-in program. Please say no. Very quickly she conceded that it was a good idea. "Someone has to get through to Nick, and I can't seem to do it. He's begging for help." I put down the phone and stared across the room, feeling my face droop. I had been living with Nick's behavior for so long I didn't realize—I didn't *want* to realize—that his troubles had surpassed my ability to make them all better. Could he really need to get away from me for awhile? No. Please. I felt like running into the ocean, jumping off the highest mountain. I couldn't look at it, didn't want to see. Wasn't love enough?

Instead of running anywhere, I called the ASAP program and brought Nick's Aunt Ariana along to scope the joint. It looked like a little boardinghouse—not at all foreboding or medical, but sort of homey, kooky, comfortable. Since it was a twelve-step program, drugs were used as a last resort, and a lot of emphasis was placed on staying clean and sober. Of course, Nick had never been near drink or drugs, but an AA concept certainly couldn't hurt, considering Nick's obsessive-compulsive tendencies and possible genetic overload. Nutty-looking teenagers with Led Zeppelin T-shirts ate lunch in the cafeteria or played Ping-Pong on the patio. I saw a stream of pubescents troop off to group therapy behind a giant white-haired man with several earrings in each ear. There was a well-stocked arts-and-crafts room where, hopefully, Nick would create a few masterpieces. Some of the kids were actually laughing.

One of the counselors, Betty, empathized with my indecision, and told me to call her husband, Dallas Taylor, for more information. Dallas Taylor. He used to play drums with Crosby, Stills and Nash, and I remembered him as a massive drugged-out mess. Now he was serving his fellow freaks by counseling kids in trouble. What a small world! For once I didn't feel so much like an alien adrift among the tight-assed, white-frocked stern-burns. Maybe these were cool people who might really understand.

On the way back to the car I cried on Ariana's shoulder as she told me how the place felt good to her. "They help people in there. They care, and they're strong. They won't give up," she said, trying to soothe my heavy, thousand-pound heart. Could I be strong enough to send Nick away? Superwoman never had such a ferocious battle to wage. When we got back home, I bent down to pick up some shoes that Nick had kept neglecting to take to his room and pulled my back out. Pain screeched up my spine and I fell into a heap. As Ariana helped me to bed, her look implied that I should take this as a sign. The gargantuan problem had manifested in physical form. There was no time to waste.

Michael remembered Dallas from AA meetings, and together we met him at Patrick's Road House, where over uneaten eggs we poured out all our parental woes. Nick would be the youngest patient there, but ASAP had helped kids his age before. There would be one-on-one therapy with a guy called Tony, group therapy, family therapy, twelve-step meetings, and school. As we talked, an unspoken conviction passed between Michael and me like an electric current. Dallas encouraged us to start immediately. "It's such a difficult decision, if you mull it over too much, you'll talk yourselves right out of it." So finally, sorrowfully, we made the plans with Dallas's firm but gentle guidance. "You can't tell Nick he's going until the last minute. He might run, he'll feel betrayed, he'll beg and plead, he'll tear you up with guilt. But be strong," he told us over and over. "You're doing the right thing."

On the chosen day our friend Ron Zimmerman arrived at eight to help Michael take Nick to ASAP. We had no idea how Nick was going to react, but I was certain I wouldn't be in any shape to drive over the hill. I will always be grateful to Ron. He had been through a similar troubled childhood, saw the desperate need for assistance, and gallantly came to our rescue. I had already packed the bag Nick would take to the hospital: jammies, toothpaste, sets of clothes, books, a comb, a brush, shampoo (plastic containers only—no wrist-slitting glass allowed—this concept alone sent panicky pangs shuddering through me), a family photo, a shot of our three cats. I bawled the whole time. I was sifting through his precious possessions, my little boy's things. He was so shy, so emotionally young, so dependent on me. He liked only certain foods, he liked to sleep with the light on. Would he be able to sleep at *all* in strange surroundings? With strange kids? Would he die of starvation? He was so shy he couldn't even order an ice cream cone. How would he deal with the rowdy cafeteria full of problem children? How would he keep the knots out of his hair? I felt like I was in a coma, underwater. Michael and I had spent the night in sleepless misery, huddled together on the couch while the TV droned, the clock ticking unmercifully toward tomorrow.

Eight-thirty came, the designated time to tell him. Bloodshot eyes, acid cups of coffee, Nick unknowingly gathering books, eating Rice Krispies. Lost in agony, I went to the bathroom to wash my face and I heard Nick scream, "No!! NO!!" I came rushing back out to see Nick's horrified, uncomprehending face, "Mom! Mom! Don't send me away! I won't go, I refuse! How could you do this to me, you hate me!!! I'll behave, I'll do everything you ask!! Please, please, *please,* don't send me away!!" He ran to his room, slammed the door—no way to lock it. He would have to be carried out. Michael and I looked at each other, horrified. How could this be happening? Ron and Michael wrestled him, kicking, screaming, pleading to the car. I trembled for Nicky, my sweet unhappy boy, thankful in my pang-ridden state for Michael's stone-solid inner strength, so noble. On the way out the door, Nick shot me a beseeching look of supreme, betrayed outrage, and trying not to break down until he was out the door, I told him I loved him. I'm sure he didn't believe me. I wept from an area of my being that I hadn't even contemplated since September 30, 1978, the day Nick came howling out of my womb. I was moaning like an animal, baying at the moon—my baby taken from me.

June 4, 1990—It was the second hardest day in my life, right next to the day my dad took his last pathetic breath.

Michael called in a monotone shock state to tell me about the miserable ride, the check-in nightmare, and the pain in his heart. We cried, we told each other we were doing the right thing. My mom was equally in torment, almost uncomprehending the need for such an act. Once again she kept her faith in me and in my decision.

I had one more session with Ariana before she went back to Las Vegas.

"I am a young Indian girl tending to a birth in which the mother dies. Care of the newborn falls to me, and I am devoted to the baby, I bond with it, love it totally. When the father of the child returns from a long battle, I am forced to give him the toddler, and I go into a very deep depression." Ariana asked me to see myself at the end of the lifetime, spinning back, spiraling through nontime. "I am a wise woman, soothsayer, story-teller. I never married. I sit in a circle with other Indian women and tell my stories, lessons, teaching them. One story I told and retold was about how I had to give up the baby, and how it taught me to let go of someone I loved for their higher good. Letting go with love."

III

I was stupefied from the decision to take Nick to ASAP. I spent the next few days wandering around Nick's room, perusing his baby photo albums, sitting and stewing about that terrible Monday morning (Monday, Monday—can't trust that day) and the difficult weeks to come. When Jimmy Thrill called, I was mucked up in guilt and depression, my heart light-years away from the carefree promise of romance. But that Friday night one of my favorite off-kilter bands, the Havalinas, were playing. And maybe I was finally learning not to torture myself by dwelling too hard on the pointed-corner facts, because I started putting on my mascara.

I moseyed around the Palace, adrift in my nearsightedness, too vain to strap on my eyewear, squinting into the smoke for a glimpse of my blond date. When you meet someone at a club, is it classified as a actual date, I wonder? After a few minutes of skittering nerves, Jimmy slink-strutted over to me as an unexpected geyser erupted in my center, and we watched the band together. Despite the inner lava, I danced and grooved, attempting flirty nonchalance, feeling his young heat next to me, not wanting to look at him too hard at the same time wanting to stare. How old was he, anyway? And how much did it matter? Upstairs at a small band party, I sat on Jimmy's lap, leaning into him lightly, laughing with Lynn and Dan, feeling pretty and fetching, starlit and warm-blooded, but every so often warding off images of my little boy in chains like they were blows.

I liked the way Jimmy could start up a conversation with anybody, so quick to smile, openhearted, open-minded but slightly secretive, like he knew something wild that nobody else could even fathom. We felt each other out, finding common ground. He was going to Japan next week with his band. Oh, I took my son to Japan. Be sure to see the giant Buddha, the mile of rock-and-roll bands with KISS makeup and two-foot pompadours. I took my son to Japan. My son, my darling son. I thought of him innocently eating Chicken McNuggets with his grandma, thinking he would be going to school on Monday. . . . Oh God, grant me the courage to accept the things I cannot change, to change the things I can . . .

Jimmy kissed me that night—once, leaving me momentarily faint and startled by the depth of the tingle, the echo of his lips. The crazy boiling of my blood just wouldn't stop. Jimmy Thrill was giving me a fever. What do you know? Expect the unexpected—one of my favorite truisms. He walked me to my car, where we stood for a long time. I pushed his platinum locks, shining white in the moonlight, away from questioning hazel eyes. What was in there for me?

IV

We weren't allowed to call Nick for the first few days and had to rely on the counselors to tell us how it was going. We called every hour for the first few days, begging for a crumb of news. The first night he was away I didn't think I would make it.

The first week he sat in on the required sessions without speaking—surly, detached, enraged, determined to prove he had been put in there by mistake. He was "restrained" more than once, strapped to a table, given pills to calm him down. He was so stubborn, given a choice he would opt for the hardest treatment. What was he trying to prove? Should we take him out? Go on like before? Try to cope? Desperate, I called Jaid, and she told me horror stories about Drew at ASAP. "You have to trust them, they know what they're doing." I worried about Nick's spirit being broken, like the taming of a beautiful bucking bronco—a heavy saddle where freedom used to be. I hurt all over like my soul had been fried in crude oil.

Nick called me on the hospital pay phone, but I wasn't allowed to answer. Ten, twenty times a day the phone would ring with a collect call from the operator that I had to refuse. It was unbearable. Dallas told us to keep our answering machines on all the time. We all needed to detach a bit, said Tony, Nick's new therapist with the white crew cut and all the earrings.

Let go with love.

Did a life-affirming turning point really loom around the corner? The first time we could talk to or see Nick was at that first group family meeting. I was gasping for breath, hanging onto a window ledge, but as we filed into the big room with several other sets of beleaguered parents and their angry, confused offspring, as corny as it sounds, I realized I was not alone. As Michael and I nervously sat down in the large circle of chairs, anxiously awaiting Nick's appearance, Betty came up to us. "Nick is refusing to come to group. He doesn't want to see you." As our hopeful faces collapsed into putty muddles, she went on, "It's normal. Most of the kids feel betrayed and are out to make their parents feel guilty, so don't worry about it. He'll come around." Normal. That was encouraging, wasn't it?

Family group meetings followed the twelve-step model: Each of us introduced ourselves and announced our problem of choice. "Eddie, alcoholic, twelve days sober." Applause. "Marie, Eddie's mother, drug addict, four years and three months." Applause. "Sandra, family problems." "I'm Tom, Sandra's step father." Smiles, nods, understanding. We sat through the meeting, blankly observing the agony and healing of others, wrapped up in parental pain like no other. Very famous celebrities and their daughters dressed in black became just like the former jailbird junkie and his adopted, tattooed juvenile delinquent son in ASAP for the third time. An old-time rock hero wept for his thirteen-year-old daughter who smuggled in some acid and went AWOL the night before. The outer-world differences between us dissolved, ceased to exist. We could all learn from the festering of another's open wounds. Take a licking but keep on ticking.

We left without seeing Nick at all that day, dejected, yet slightly encouraged by the compassion and insight of some of the other parents. "Wonderful things are happening for Shannon here. She hadn't looked us in the eye for two and a half years until yesterday." "Peter didn't speak to a soul in this place for three weeks, and now they tell me he's talking too much at group. They can't shut him up!" One counselor told me I would lose the feelings of grief and guilt after about ten days. "And don't feel guilty because you feel some relief!" she warned me. "I'm sure you deserve it."

We, of course, hoped for an easy explanation for Nick's behavior, a psychological name tag to hang on the problem, a diagnosis at last, but it wasn't forthcoming. Nick's uncanny intelligence was hiding some deep-rooted, scary stuff that would take time to discover. We would have to be patient.

At the next meeting, Wednesday night, Nick trudged past us to a chair as far away as he could get and wouldn't look at us, and when it came time for him to say his name, he refused. There was my little blond boy, disheveled, unkempt, miserable, betrayed, and lost on the other side of the room. And I couldn't run to him, shelter him under my mama's wing, take him away from his pain. He had to face it himself, find something inside himself to love, or maybe he never would. This was his chance, our chance, right here and now. Tony told us that Nick had actually started to speak a few tentative mumblings at group and a possible friendship seemed to be forming with one of his roommates. He also admitted that Nick despised and feared him and wished he were dead. Most of the kids did at first. Tony was quite a fearsome-looking dude—heavy-set, about six feet four inches, white crew cut, red face, many, many earrings in each ear—a zero-bullshit, hard-as-nails, in-your-face kind of guy. Sometimes he even scared me, and he pissed Michael off, but I knew Nick wouldn't be able to do what he had done so many times before— he wouldn't be able to wrap Tony around his cute li'l finger. No way.

We soon settled into a routine—two family meetings a week and a private session between Tony, Michael, Nick, and me. Silence at first, discomfort, fidgeting. Tears, accusations, terror, confessions, realizations, apologies. Words never spoken crowded the small room to the stifling point. Gradually—at a snail's pace—we were allowed to take Nicky's calls, talk to him when we felt like it, visit him on Sunday afternoons. He made us fantastic-colored bowls, vases, and cups in ceramics class, and when he made me a lavender heart to hang on the wall, I knew he had forgiven me. I tried not to sob, and

278   *Pamela Des Barres*

it was all I could do to keep from squeezing him in half. From "Please, please, take me out of here" to "When do you think I can come home?" to "Bring me *Led Zeppelin IV,* my Self-Realization altar, some Chicken McNuggets," there was a consistent driblet of progress.

Even though Michael had a hard time admitting certain truths to himself, he was fearless in confronting bullshit during the group family meetings. From being such an active participant in NA and AA, he could point out what other people were avoiding, help them face the hurting facts, and get to the other side. When a session was bogging down, going in circles, Tony called on Michael who could ask, "Wait a minute, wait a minute. Do you love your son? Why don't you cut the crap and tell him so?" Tony even had Michael play the acting dad with kids whose parents didn't show up, giving him a chance to use his agile, stinging brain for the greater good. The kids loved him. After all, he had been one of them, on the floor with his nose bleeding from too much coke, singing rock and roll, blind stoned and out of control, and now he was a bad-guy actor on *MacGyver* and had ten years' sobriety. Nick started to admire his dad for a whole new reason and see him in a new light. So did I.

The air was being cleared, making way for truth that had been disguised in a various array of costumes. When it came my turn to identify my problem, I announced myself as a codependent. I wasn't quite convinced that I really fit into the category, but I wasn't an alcoholic or a drug addict, and *something* had brought me and mine into this room. When my darlings were bored, angry, unhappy, I thought it was all my fault—a peculiar kind of reverse egomania. I listened to all types of moms tell their stories of doting and devotion in the name of love, letting their over-loved ones trample down any and all personal boundaries, getting their respect squashed in the process, and I recognized myself in them. Some of the examples were extreme, so it took me awhile to realize that by trying to be a good wife and mom, I had gone over the top and hit bottom. "Hi, I'm Pamela, Nick's mom, codependent." Nick, who had recently accepted us fully back into his life, looked over at me with big questioning eyes. Michael smiled. So did Tony. He actually barked out a big laugh. A couple people congratulated me after the meeting like I had just flushed my stash down the toilet.

Progress! Nick seemed to be letting his guardwall down, smiling for real. But sometimes after a visit with my little boy in the sterile sitting room, munching junk food, babbling about silly things, doing squiggles, I missed him so much—tucking him in at night, cuddling with him, laughing at things only we thought were funny, watching dumb shows on TV, I wanted him back home with me so bad. I wondered how much longer I could stand it.

V

With Nick gone, I was on my own for the first time in many years. Time was not of the essence; I didn't have to wake up to a shrilling alarm or worry about filling Nick's after-school hours. Except for the meetings at ASAP, I had zero responsibilities, a holiday from the grinding give-give-giving that almost killed me—and everyone else. When the guilt over my newfound freedom finally ebbed, I started feeling like a kid again. The knot between my shoulder blades went away, the pain in my solar plexus disappeared. I didn't have to sleep with my dental "nightguard" anymore, because I stopped gritting my poor teeth into dust particles. I had been living with the stress for so long that when it let up I felt like I had grown a true set of wings.

Jimmy Thrill came back from Japan and called me that very day. His band had driven the girls wild, they had made little Jimmy Thrill dolls with lots of yellow yarn and followed him down the street to lick his armpits. Interesting custom, hmm? He asked about Nick, and I told him I was honestly starting to feel a little relief, just as the counselor had promised me. A tentative trickle of guilt-crossed freedom. A little more freedom than guilt, praise Jesus.

Jimmy and I planned on meeting at the Lingerie, where one of my fave singers, James Intveld, was crooning to his clan of be-bopping bobby-soxers. If James Dean had ever cut a record, it would have sounded like James Intveld. Certain music still created havoc inside me, and I wanted to share that feeling with everybody else—and I always will.

I slithered into my tightest black ensemble, lacy stockings, highest heels, frothed the red hair as far as it would go, red lips for days. I immersed myself in the music, feeling it through every inch of my body, dancing alone, high on it. When I came to, Jimmy was two feet in front of me, no mistaking the look of lazy longing in his eyes and the secure grin of someone real comfortable in his own sweet skin. One of those involuntary shudders streaked through me. How long had he been watching me dance? He exuded a bright, careless joy of life, of optimism, of excitement. How old was he, anyway, and how much did it matter?

He was twenty-four. When I had been painting graphic pictures of Mick Jagger's balls for my high school art class, bobbing my head up and down at Mother Neptune's jazz club with Victor Hayden, Jimmy Thrill was busy being born. If I had been walking past a pretty blond lady pushing a stroller back in 1966, and somebody pointed to the cherub baby boy in Pampers and said, "There's your future lover-doll, circa 1990," I would have split my lace tablecloth frock laughing—then asked the pretty lady the tot's name so I could keep an eye out. Ha!

He came back home with me, where we lounged on the couch, listening to soul music, and spent several hours in each other's wide open mouths. Otis Redding begged for some tenderness way off in the distance, and I was being held like something precious. Aah . . . swept up in the beats of his heart. It was so hot in there the fire department should have been called. After rolling around in hormonal haze, reeking of wicked perfume, Jimmy stood up in front of me and pulled his shirt over his head, and I caught a glimpse of a tattoo dragon peeking over his pale shoulder. I touched so-soft skintight skin, my fingers melting, as the candles burned down to liquid, the first early bird twittered. "You'd better go," I whispered. "What?" Sincere surprise in his voice. But I stuck with the idea, even as my girl-spot quivered, until he was out the door. I wanted to wait just a tiny bit longer, not rush into it, but glide slowly, anticipate the lovely inevitable.

After seeing Jimmy a few more times, I thought the time was ripe. We went to a Japanese karaoke bar to watch a few people make asses out of themselves. We were just pushing back the threat of sizzling temptation, our hands touching—an electric shock—thigh pressing thigh, sultry eyes. Some aging flubber-pot full of sake got up to sing "Like a Virgin," and we both knew what was going to happen. I was so high on the expectation, I was reeling, bombed on the certainty of fully requited lust. We took off in separate cars—I was planning to get there first so I could deck the place out with low lights and dangerous music. Stuck in a horny reverie, I turned onto La Brea— red lights flashed behind me. Oops, at that last stop sign I hadn't come to a complete stop. What do you expect? I was about to commit a delicious carnal act. To my outrage, the sturdy wax-figure cop shone his flashlight in my bespectacled eyes and announced they were bloodshot. He asked me to get out of the car and walk a straight line in front of a neon used-Jeep joint. "You've got to be kidding," I yawped, "I'm not drunk!!" Trying to stay calm, I unstrapped my high heels and walked toe to toe down La Brea, saying the alphabet, perfectly, I thought. "You forgot a few letters," he said officiously, "I'm sorry," and he yanked my hands behind my back, handcuffing me roughly, doing his duty. I pleaded with the wax dummy, telling him all about the candles I had to light, the sweet music I had to put on the CD player, how tonight was the Big Night, couldn't he show some mercy to a fellow human being??

"If you blow below the limit, I'll bring you right back to your car," he promised. At the station I blew big breaths into this scary-looking contraption, praying hard, and when I came in under the limit, Mr. Wax Man seemed dejected. "Book her anyway!" his big, graying copper-boss boomed, "Teach her a lesson," and I broke down. "How can you do this to me?? I'm not drunk!! He's waiting in my drive-way!!" On and on, shrieking, sobbing into deaf cop ears. I was put into a smelly gray cell with two hookers who talked all night about the policeman who set them up. "Who would think that a dick could have a dick that bii-iiiig?" one of them marveled repeatedly, while I agonized. What did Jimmy think of me? How long had he waited? They let me out at six-thirty gray dawn, and as I filled out papers, my arresting officer said to me, "You're the one who wrote that book, aren't you? My second cousin used to play with the Eagles." Isn't that terribly interesting, you big jackass? When the court date came up, the case was thrown out because I had no previous DUI and had blown under the limit. Who can I sue?

Jimmy had waited so long in my driveway that he had fallen asleep. He told me this when he called at nine to see if I was all right. Even though I was a double wretch, I invited him over to dinner that night, buying something ultra-fancy at the French take-out and fobbing it off as my own. Could that be considered lying? I couldn't eat. My heart had invaded my stomach, stretching it to capacity. I put on the Ink Spots, doo be doo be doo be doo be doo be doo be do, and we went at each other like starving beasts. As pieces of my naughty Victoria's Secret love-garments were yanked off, an X-rated halo appeared over his head. He tied my garter-belt over my eyes and went to the kitchen looking for some ripe, juicy fruit. We were definitely compatible in that area, which was no surprise to me. His scent ate me up, his skin felt like my own, and he had, uh-oh, kisses sweeter than wine. Sweeter than the wine Jesus created with the flick of His holy wrist.

July 4—All over Jimmy, him all over me—everybody thinks we're a far-out match. The age difference is thrilling to me, titillating, and he makes me feel totally youthful and glowing. He's caring and intuitive, acts directly on his intuition. We have a beautiful spiritual link—and he's horny for me! The feeling that seems to erupt so softly out of the ethers is so life-affirming. The Gods placed him in my life right now, and he's really helping me in this difficult time. Is it not growth to still feel like a girl? What the fuck is maturity, anyhow? Live each moment as it comes.

August 1—*Jimmy and I are gradually interlocking. Almost every night we talk, talk, talk, make love endlessly, listen to mutually loved music, laugh, and grow. He is full of light, and I connect with him there. It feels magical. He's so wise for his years, has his own original way of putting things, so clean-spirited and un-fucked up. He thinks Science of Mind without ever having been there. Two nights ago he told me I was god-given, "the ultimate woman." One of his lyrics is, "I'm not just the boy next door, I'm the man you can't ignore." He's a man-child, so sweet I ache. He says he's going to take me higher than love.*

September 1—*Days go by with Jimmy in their own time. It's been so revelatory—I'm opening up to him, and he to me—petals wide. I crave him when he's away, or just across the room. He says the greatest things onstage: "We're all one big soul, but I'm an older soul than the rest of you mother-fuckers." Ha ha. It's like God has said, "Okay, doll. One more time—the perfect rockboy/man on a silver platter, only this time he comes complete with a soul connection, spiritually evolved, unaddicted, self-confident, and totally tuned in." He's so fucking gorgeous it drives me wild. He ripped my panty-hose to shreds the other night and pulled my earrings out with his teeth. He doesn't even realize what a trigger and catalyst he is for me and mine. He's truly a being of light; we're linked in a higher realm. I have to remember that when I'm feeling like doing too much for him—the way I did with Michael and Nick, and all the other men in my life. I have wind chimes in my heart, Disneyland fireworks going off nonstop."*

I'll never let go of Walt and his mouse. And why should I?

Jimmy wrote songs about me and left love notes all over the house, and every day was like finding buried treasure: "You're a sweet scent that I wear internally . . . I feel your skin under mine—and your smile is the sign—to go even further—for you are the angel—and I am the wing—you are the song I began to sing. . . . I feel your soul flow inside my veins, a vision of pure love that purifies my mind. . . . you are a divine religion that I believe in and that shrine of purity you release in my heart will never go away. . . . I am a junkie, strung out, waiting for a fix of you. . . . You are the source of my power, the smell of my flower, you're my cigarette, I'm ad-dicted. . . ."

I don't know why they call it "falling" in love, it's more like "swooping" in love, and it was happening to me.

Chunks of life crept into my romance dance and the miracles going on at ASAP. I started working on a concept for a magazine called *Twist* with a guy called Quay Hays—a go-getter entrepreneur type who thought I had panache. I actually got Annette Funicello and Ozzy Osbourne together to interview each other, and the stuff Ozzy confessed to apple-pie, peanut-butter, mouse-ears Annette was mind-boggling. She dared to ask him uncool questions about his addictions that hip journalists avoided. He asked if Walt had really been frozen, and tears sprang to her eyes. It was starting to look like a thrilling printed-page enterprise, but right about that time the world fell out from underneath the magazine industry, but Quay and I are still open to assistance from ballsy investors.

I was asked to appear on the game show *To Tell The Truth* and couldn't resist seeing two other girls say, "Hi, I'm Pamela Des Barres . . ." I had to coach them, and it was so bizarre to hear them answer questions about my life and come out with all kinds of cock-eyed answers. The two girls I did the show with were at least ten years younger than me, so that made me feel good. You're so vain, you probably think this song is about you.

When Jimmy and I weren't wrapped tight in our amorous cocoon, we went out to see the Indigo Girls, Was Not Was, and the divine Al Green, where we spun into loveland, tight together, tied together by the music. I went to all of his Rattlesnake Shake shows, finding myself back at the Whisky a Go Go over two decades later, surging around with people two decades younger than myself, watching Jimmy enter another world onstage, his eyes rolling back, sweat streaming down his half-naked body, girls reaching for him, wanting to enter that unreachable place only he could see, feel, hear, touch. He doesn't hold back; he doesn't know how.

VI

The fact of Jimmy hit Michael hard at first. He went through some of what I had to endure during those miserable few months when he futzed around with the cosmic home wrecker three years earlier. But I was honest about my feelings for Jimmy, so there was no crap for him to wade through. I had come to respect Michael for who he *really* was; we had come so far together, and there was no need to conceal the truth from each other anymore. "I'm happy for you, Pammie, I'll just have to deal with it."

Nick had gotten established at ASAP, decorating his room with Japanese animation posters and rehashed Led Zeppelin paraphernalia. His roommate Frank was a Zep devotee, which inspired Nick to request *Houses of the Holy* and a portable CD player, and Daddy complied. It was some sort of warped karma for me—my own son thought Jimmy Page was a guitar god—a definite case of "whodathunkit?" Nick was pissed because they made him chop the wires on the speakers down to three inches long so they couldn't be used as a noose. Thank glory Nick had never pondered suicide. Whenever he regressed to rebellion and stubbornness, his CD player was taken away. Once it was locked in storage for three weeks. Many times he had to sit in his room while everybody else went to the Friday movie. They just weren't taking his shit, and it was working.

In therapy with Tony, Nick was putting names on his black fears, turning them into something he could work through and discard. Previously he had tried to stay invisible, cowering, keeping his vulnerable artistic innards well hidden. But at ASAP Nick had to deal with his peers constantly within an enclosed space—meetings, group sessions, breakfast, lunch, dinner, school, free time—with no escape. He was forced to communicate, and before long, his far-flung humor and unique perspective emerged and gained him adoring attention. I think it surprised him initially, then gave him some true self-appreciation. The change in him was a joy to behold. Being different and special began to seem positive, not like deathly torment. And when Robert Plant came to town Michael made arrangements to take Nick and his Zep-adoring roommate Frank to the concert and to meet Robert backstage. Talk about feeling cool.

As for me, twice a week for over four months I sat in a circle as boxes of tissues were passed around to wipe up copious tears, while people dredged up their long-buried newly faced truths. Often I felt a stunned flash of self-recognition dawn on my own face. I used to feel put-upon and taken advantage of, and I now saw the whiny-pants behavior as a form of manipulation, an attempt to make the loved one dependent upon me so I didn't feel so powerless. I caught myself still tending to Michael, giving him tender bits of advice like a cooling salve, making it *all* better, and he reminded me—sometimes very loudly—that he could handle whatever it was himself. I was faced with retraining my entire being—a chance that most people never take, preferring the comfy haven of what they already know. Change is frightening, leading straight to the big unknown, but what I already knew wasn't working—it was failing. I had always thought of myself as a freewheeling, freaky chick, ready for anything, willing to take all kinds of chances. Okay, so let's see how we can handle this one, doll.

At first I watched everything I did and said, like an eyewitness, judge, and jury. Eventually the new point of view took hold and folded into my life like whipped honey, the glitches standing out like a HALT! sign. It's a constant process, and I still catch myself with a codependent Kahlua and cream in my hand and have to dump it down the drain before it reaches my lips.

We started working with Tony on Nick's "home contract"—the laws that would govern our relationship after he left the hospital. A lot of emphasis was put on choice. If he chose not to follow the rules, he had to pay the price of having a privilege revoked. We started out simple to make sure the contract wasn't too daunting: Take out the trash, make your bed, only two hours of video games per day, etc. Nick was relieved that the rules and punishments weren't too harsh, but we knew he had mixed feelings about leaving ASAP. It had become a safe place.

Finally the day came. I pulled up at ASAP and was bowled over backwards to see Michael behind the wheel of a flashy new sports car, suntanned and wearing shades! Michael, the non-driver, who had always called a cab or relied on others (ME!) to get him from A to B. He smiled. "It's about time, don't you think?" Through the ASAP program he had thrown out the worn and torn concept that he didn't have the temperament to drive a car. And here he was, on Nick's big day, to drive his son home! I was awash in drippy tears, so touched and heartswollen proud of him!

During the inevitably tense and sad/happy good-byes—though Nick was so excited to ride in the new car with his daddy driving— he hugged Dallas, Laurie, Betty, and even the once-formidable Tony for a long time, a physical expression of friendship he couldn't bring himself to make before he went to ASAP. And when we pulled into the driveway at home, Nick was startled and overjoyed to see T.J. and his friend Dan waiting on the porch with a messy cake they had made for him themselves. A banner was draped across the front door. It said, WELCOME HOME, NICK.

Welcome home, Nick—and amen.

VII

With Nick finally back home, my days as a post-pubescent, sleeping-'til-noon, free-bird wildcat had come to a close, and the timing, as usual, was just right. I had to get back to work, regain a semblance of order. As Nick rubbed his beloved purring cats, I got such an aching mom-urge to bundle him up in his tattered blue baby blanket and rock him to sleep with a lullabye, but I knew I had to back off and let him grow up. I was supposed to expect more of him, let him do things for himself. I would have to tie my hands and heart behind my back for awhile.

Jimmy and I had painted his room white, gotten rid of the baby bunks, packed his dusty robots and kiddie books into boxes, redecorated Japanese style, and it had a less cluttered, preteen feeling. Nick loved it. After the initial tippy-toeing around, and being overly good and careful about what he did and said, which only lasted a day or two, Nick got back into the swing of his life, but now it seemed he was really right in the middle of himself, living his life for real. I realized he had been hiding in his own shadow, afraid of who he was, and he had now started to understand how special he was in the real sense of that defamed word. He became *more* of who he was. He began to truly accept himself. We followed the home contract as best we could, and we still do, most of the time. Nobody's perfect, right? (Actually we are *all* perfect, but we do imperfect things on occasion. Ha!) All of us—Nicky, Michael, and I—were changing, bobbing souls in motion, striving for a higher level of consciousness, more aware, more fully ALIVE.

Who knew how Nick and Jimmy would hit it off? I had told Nick that someone new was in my life, and he seemed okay about it, but he was used to having me all to himself, kowtowing, placating, serving, doting. Jimmy gave us a few days to settle back in together, then came over for dinner, eager, full of smiles, curious, ready to interact with the unique kid he had been hearing so much about. He just expected the two of them to get along, and they did. From instant one, he spoke to him like an equal. At twenty-four, Jimmy had no interest in becoming parental in any way, which was perfect because Nick already had the best dad in the world. Shy, slightly intimidated at first by this constant sunny presence, Nick gradually loosened up, tolerating, accepting, and finally enjoying. Jimmy got him a Japanese fighting fish for his birthday, and it clinched their friendship. One day as we were driving over the hill to school, Nick asked, "Mom, how old is Jimmy?" When I told him, he said, "Isn't he a little young for you, Mom? He's closer to my age than he is yours." His math was accurate, but I launched into a beauteous rap about souls colliding and how the age range is irrelevant. He laughed at me, but I was sure he knew what I was talking about. He always does.

Now that Michael was driving, he spent more time with Nick, and their relationship got thick and mighty, rich and real. Nick tested us hard, and still does—he's a flesh-and-blood teenager, after all—but with less frequency and much less hysteria. He's a lot more comfortable within his boundaries. Michael started taking Nick on weekend trips, bringing him to the set of his TV shows and movies, and Nick's self-confidence quotient kept rising. And Michael and I had reached a new understanding. Not exactly a clean slate, but at least we were holding tight to the erasers, surrounded by chalk dust.

VIII

I suppose this is where I'm supposed to wind up my life into a few clever closing paragraphs—summing up all I've written, all I've lived, narrowing it down to put a nice, neat capper on the whole thing. All I can say is that every day is fraught and overspilling with jack-in-the-box surprises, and I intend to keep it that way. The right music can still find a place inside me that has never been opened, lifting the top off an unborn feeling, creating a new space to be filled up with more living. I've definitely got the music in me.

I'm finally crazy about myself. We have to adore ourselves—above all others, as stingy and ego-bloated as that might sound. All my life I've heard "Love thy neighbor as *thyself*," and never comprehended the meaning. What's not to love? You don't know what love is until you can latch onto a glowing chunk of God inside yourself and match it up with the glistening chunks lurking in everybody else.

I certainly see the radiance of His Nibs in my imaginative, unconventional (to put it mildly) son. I'm so delighted he landed in my life. I'm completely thankful to be his mom, to know that blessed and pure, whole love that can only come shimmering through an umbilical cord.

The love I feel for Michael is more real and true. Nothing in between, no more fibs, no more fiction. I'm so grateful we didn't toss our relationship to the winds like so many other busted-up couples. As I've said over and over, why give up, cover up, and stomp on so many years, so many feelings, so much pain, ecstasy, agony, love? We know each other better and have so much to give each other that no one else can. Years of life history—and our son, Nick.

Jimmy continues to wrap me tight in his fine joy of life. We've been living together for quite some time now, and I am one half of a true-blue couple. The seemingly gargantuan age difference is not even something we consider anymore. Jimmy never really paid much notice to the seventeen-year gap, anyway. When you find something that feels so right, so bright—plant a bed of flowers around it and dance. I know what love is on the deepest physical level and how it feels to reach the highest, brightest place within my being—no fear, total forgiveness, adoration of life, locked within the body—at the same time escaping it. No words can come close to describing that deep and thundrous unity with the universe. I have entered other lifetimes having sex with Jimmy—brown, hot bodies tossing around in gigantic green jungle leaves—another time, just past children, bathing in sunken marble, furtive, stealing each other—locked together at the groin. Still, we live day to day, moment to moment. I have learned the fine art of reveling in the second with Jimmy. You just can't pin down the future, it'll wriggle away from you.

Life is so grand—even the most difficult storm-wracked days are full of suspense. Hour to hour, you can't predict it. It's always "anything can happen day," and I know we create it. I often wonder—I actually daydream sometimes—when I get a spare instant to reflect—about living a calm and gentle life in a place where I could count on each day being just like the one before. I could un-create my whirlwind existence, move way out to the West Valley, or up into what's left of the California mountains, meditate in a cross-legged position until serenity claimed me—or spend my days at a straight, predictable job, ignoring the silent scream, just so I could count on some comforting consistency. Everydayness. I could even go back down to the shimmering hills of Kentucky, cook delicious turnip greens with my auntie, and drop out entirely like Victor once did, but I know I'd miss the adrenaline-rush action, all shapes and sizes—here, there, and anywhere, hair-raising glory of my everyday life. I'll have to tap into that calm and gentle, serene state within myself more often, so I can stop wasting my time wondering and daydreaming, kicking the empty can down a dried-up stream. You know that old saying, "the suspense is killing me"? Well, dolls, the suspense is what keeps me alive.

Epilogue

Poor Nick had a chilling experience at the local high school we attempted to enroll him in after ASAP. During nutrition on his second day, a pack of kids surrounded him and asked if he was a boy or a girl. His hair streamed down his back and he wore, as usual, very colorful and highly inventive clothing. After ignoring the taunts, he finally announced, "I'm both," just to confuse and piss them off. At that point they started to chase him through the school, out of the school grounds and down the street, where he ran into a handy-dandy police station for protection. Two hundred kids chased Nick down the street. Wow. Luckily—or, as fate would have it—Ariana was here on a visit, and went down to the school to pick him up. The teacher was shaken and chagrined as he explained the situation, "Nothing like this has ever happened here, I'm at a loss to explain it, I'm sorry. So sorry." Aunt Ariana brought Nick home and listened to his story of terror and said, "Nick, do you see how much power you have?" and he didn't flip out. Later, when I asked how the experience had made him feel, he stated, "Mom, I had an O.B.E." An O.B.E? "An out-of-body experience." He told me he watched his body running faster than it ever had from a safe distance, way up above. So *that's* how he got through it.

Eventually, he was happily placed at Linden Center, a progressive school in Beverly Hills, the very same site where Michael went to his first AA meeting. He's been there for a year and a half and he's doing well. He's finally reaching the age and stage when he can enjoy his individuality. He's developing a social network of his own. Just last week I dropped him off on Melrose with his girlfriend, Carina, and watched him walk into the crowd of trippy-hippy, trendoid types, laughing and amused with his life, and I felt so damn choked up and happy. He's a teenager, he walks around on Melrose, he goes to concerts, he speaks Japanese, he still has his spiritual altar, he comes home from school smiling (most of the time).

There isn't anything Nick and I can't talk about and crack up over. Just a few days ago we laughed so hard about a goofy expression on the face of a ceramic poodle that we collapsed in a heap of spasms in front of several concerned swap-meet sellers. He calls me into his room to enjoy the cock-eyed commercials running through his Japanese videos, and we roll on the floor, hysterical with glee. When he was asked to bring a sample of his favorite music to share at school, he listened to all the rap bands and Marky Mark stuff before slapping Captain Beefheart in the cassette machine. "Fast and bulbous, the mascara snake, fast and bulbous." Jimmy bought me the complete set of Jack Kerouac's recordings, and Nick has been on a nonstop listening binge, astonished and laughing, then writing zany stacks of his own poetry. My fave is entitled "The Red SlipSlide of Old Bones." The Linden Center just brought in a teacher to work on a screenplay with the kids. He asked them to suggest their favorite character to be incorporated into the plot, and Nick wanted the baby from the early David Lynch film, *Eraserhead*. What can I say? Nick is a true artist, a step ahead, a step apart. He's the kind of guy who would have inspired me to scrawl his name all over my notebook in junior high, but he's my son and a friend for life.

Nick's dad spends more time with him than ever, and he remains a sweet soulmate for me. When Michael reached ten years sobriety, he invited me to the AA meeting to give him a cake. From the podium, where he usually makes everyone laugh, he brought people to tears by "making amends" to me in front of the sober bunch. "I put her through Hell and I'm truly sorry." Apology accepted, Mikie.

He has been working his butt off on TV and in the movies. At one point he was appearing in *Roseanne, MacGyver,* and *The New WKRP in Cincinnati* all at once. He just stared down Tommy Lee Jones on the Big Screen, and has just landed another humding role in a MMP (major motion picture)! He sees Ariana on a regular basis, and has done so much work on himself that honesty is starting to dribble out of his sun-tanned pores. He pumps a lot of iron and has a pretty actress girlfriend, verging on serious fame, who hugs me whenever she sees me. Very sweet. She bought a jacket from Jimmy at one of our yard sales—one of those fabulous patchwork sixties numbers. It looked really cute on her.

Still, Michael and I go to lunch and dinner, he buys me little gifts, and sometimes big ones. We talk on the phone three times a day, we seek advice from each other, we continue our meetings with Tony, Nick's therapist—the guy Nick feared and now adores. Michael took Nick and me to Roseanne and Tom Arnold's wedding, and it was so sweet and perfect—buckets of love being dumped on everyone. We go to swap meets, The Renaissance Faire, I go to his wrap parties, he comes to my dinner parties. We will always be there for each other, and it's a relief and a reward.

I appreciate my friends more every day. There's a lot of hand-holding and intense phone-consulting in my life. It's so great to know I can count on my precious pals to pull me out of a stuck and sputtering state of mind with just a few words. Patti lives in a big house on Long Island now and I miss her so much. We sat together chomping pasta in an old New York eatery recently, and we both burst into drizzling tears in the middle of our girl-chat. She and her almost-hubby just had their second child, Liam, a brother for year-old Emmelyn, the cutest kid since Nick was a toddler. Melanie and Donnie are always away. The last time I saw them was on TV. Sad but true. I miss them madly. My dear Catherine married a divine Englishman, Stephen Blacknell, and I was the maid/matron of honor once again. Dee Dee and Tony Kaye broke up, and she just moved to Santa Monica, yay! A girlfriend neighbor! I'm working on my next book with my oldest friend, Iva. We went through grade school, junior high, high school, and the Sunset Strip school of learning together—and now we're writing partners! Ariana visits us many times a year and all of her clients troop through the house in varying degrees of spiritual evolvement. Some have to sit on the couch for awhile after a reading and all kinds of other worldly conversation takes place. Fascinating chit-chat. Ariana always reminds me about important stuff. "The sure way not to heal and grow," she says sweetly, "is not to forgive." "Get out of that reactive swamp," she smiles, "You're reacting instead of living." Ariana is here right now, and Moon Zappa just left, feeling a whole lot better. She tells me her daddy, Frank, is doing okay. He's been very ill and I pray for him daily.

I've lost some friends. Miss Lucy died of AIDS last year, leaving behind a young son who is HIV positive and a teenager who lives in Reno. She was so full of her giant love for life, I can't imagine her not cavorting somewhere on the planet. Miss Sandra died of cancer a few months ago, and I'm sure her four kids are full of sorrow. When she was pregnant with her first daughter, Raven, she painted a big star on her bare tummy and went out dancing—so proud of her impending earth-motherhood. That leaves four GTO's. Sparkie is still a big exec at Disney. She and I just went to our twenty-fifth high-school reunion (so scary) where we twisted the night away with guys who wouldn't look at us in those blasted Cleveland halls. Everyone had read my book and looked at me like I was Pamela Des Barres from another planet and not Pam Miller from Reseda, California. I finally spoke to Cynderella after many, many years and found that she is now Cynderella Sincere, having been married to a fellow named Alphonse for four years. She's taking writing courses in college, working on a novel, and tending a vegetable garden. Thank God she's alive. Mercy got married a few months ago to a guy named Leonard who looks just like Ike Turner. I had the wedding party at my house, and Mercy was all dolled up, gold and silver tinsel sprouting from her head in abundance, and when Jimmy told her how fetching she looked, she announced, "All the Mexicans love me." The newlyweds fed each other cake, they accepted the congratulations and gifts, then slipped out into the night. God, I hope they're happy.

My dear Victor had his first "aboveground" art show here in Santa Monica at the Robert Berman Gallery, and many delightful people came to pay him homage and buy his bright and mysterious "acid primitive" paintings. I have two on my wall and they mesmerize all of my visitors and change the patterns in their brains if they gaze at them for just a little too long. He recently snagged an Absolut Vodka campaign, and pretty soon the rest of the world will glom onto his way-over-on-the-other-side alternative viewpoint. Vic always chooses the scenic route over the ugly mainstream, and reminds me to do the same.

But I'm still plowing through that blasted mainstream, hoping to meet up with the movie company brave enough to take on *I'm with the Band* and get it on the big screen. I've had so many handshake almosts with hotshots verging (but not quite) on hipness. "Yeah, baby, I'll make your movie," then I never hear from them again. I finally got a cool manager, Eric Gardner, who manages my pal Cassandra "Elvira" Peterson, that edged-out Todd Rundgren, the Stone who stands alone, Bill Wyman, Dr. Timothy Leary, and Paul Shaffer, among other eclectic standouts. We'll see. I'm optimistic as usual. Drew Barrymore has reached the nubile age of seventeen and wants to play me. Christina Applegate has expressed interest. We even got a few calls from the cream-crop agent of that baby-doll Oscar nominee, Juliet Lewis. I've always wanted Moon Zappa to play one of the GTO's.

I am now managing Jimmy Thrill Quill's band, Big Rig Jackknife, a hopalong, fever-pitch, country-raunch band thrashing with soul. They've been in the studio doing demos with Niko Bolas, a swell guy who thinks he's just discovered an entire troop of Elvises, circa 1957. Several sniffing-around A and R guys (no gals, unfortunately) have been in and out of the studio trying to remain cool. I've booked gigs for the band, I rounded up a tour, I've called out the music biz dogs on a few occasions, and the whole thing is always fraught with sky-hopes and an any-minute overnight success story. We went down to Nashville to play a club, and when Jimmy took off his shirt, the proper ladies gasped and the string-tied industry shook to the core.

So dolls, I'm still hanging tight to the rock and roll lifeline, merging it with country-love like good old Gram Parsons tried to do many moons ago. God, I'm so happy to be alive. Jimmy's drummer, Josh, played a one-off gig with the Rock Bottom Remainders at the gigantic book convention in the glory city of Anaheim, and guess who played guitar and sang some old fifties tunes with demented newly written lyrics? An incredibly prolific inspiration of mine, one of the people I've always wanted to meet—Stephen King. And I shook his hand. He even dragged his look-alike wife, Tabitha, over to meet me. He called me Pam Des Barres, but there were layers of people all around and I didn't get the chance to correct him. Fun things continue to happen at a rapid pace. Hooray Hoorah! In fact, one of my top-ten experiences took place just the other night. I was interviewing the fabulous Helena for my first piece in *Premiere* magazine—we had just settled down in front of some giant bowls of Greek garlic pasta, and I was ready to click on the recorder when she said, "Oh, wasn't that the gate?" A moment later I looked up and Marlon Brando was standing in front of me. "Who's this, Helena, she's very pretty." I realized I was actually growing up when I extended my hand and said, "Nice to meet you," pretty as you please, instead of mewling like an out-of-control nutbag. I wondered briefly if I should mention those many pleading messages I left on his machine twenty years earlier, or how he gave me that astute advice, "Look to yourself for the answers," instead of complying with my wishes and inviting me over in the middle of the night. I decided not to. He sat down and gabbed away with us for almost an hour. I was wearing a Jack Kerouac T-shirt which led into a conversation about all types of literature. We discovered we had a mutual favorite, Toni Morrison, and raved back and forth about *Beloved,* one of my all-time A-1 books. Friendly, warm, whip-sharp, hysterically perceptive, and extremely curious, he made me feel relaxed and jazzed-up all at once.

So, when I say life continues to be grand, *grand,* GRAND, I can't even begin to tell you what an understatement that is. Being a late bloomer isn't so bad after all.

Now that I'm finished with this book, I'm sitting here wondering why I felt I had to dip deep down, shred and expose myself, like a gutted doe strapped across somebody's headlights. And I recall that beautiful cosmic movie, *Starman,* the one in which Jeff Bridges (oh well, perhaps someday) plays that sweet, innocent soul from another planet. Remember, when he saw the dead deer strapped to a hunter's car and, with otherwordly compassion, raised it from the dead and watched it trot back into the forest? The reborn doe, recapturing her life. That's sort of the way I feel.

INDEX